LAST OPERAS AND PLAYS

LAST OPERAS AND PLAYS

BY GERTRUDE STEIN

EDITED AND WITH AN INTRODUCTION BY

CARL VAN VECHTEN

VINTAGE BOOKS
A DIVISION OF RANDOM HOUSE
NEW YORK

FIRST VINTAGE BOOKS EDITION, October 1975

Library of Congress Cataloging in Publication Data

Stein, Gertrude, 1874–1946.
    Last operas and plays.

    Reprint of the ed. published by Rinehart, New York.
    CONTENTS: Introd.: "How many acts are there in it?" —Yes is for a very young man.—The mother of us all.— Doctor Faustus lights the lights. [etc.]
    I. Van Vechten, Carl, 1880–1964. II. Title.
PS3537.T323A19   1975   812'.5'2   75–11618
ISBN 0–394–71695–7

Manufactured in the United States of America

CONTENTS

"HOW MANY ACTS ARE THERE IN IT?"

I

"IT WAS DURING this winter," writes Gertrude Stein in *The Autobiography of Alice B. Toklas*, "that Gertrude Stein began to write plays. They began with the one entitled, *It Happened a Play*. This was written about a dinner party given by Harry and Bridget Gibb. She then wrote *Ladies Voices*. Her interest in writing plays continues. She says a landscape is such a natural arrangement for a battlefield or a play that one must write plays."

The Yale *Catalogue* gives 1913 as the date for the writing of *It Happened a Play*. From that day until a short time before the Greater War began Miss Stein continued to write, and to publish, plays. The first of these appeared in *Geography and Plays*, 1922. *A Village*, "a play in four acts," was published separately in wrappers in 1928 and *Lend a Hand or Four Religions*[1] was included in *Useful Knowledge* the same year. More of these unconventional dramas came out in *Operas and Plays*, in the Plain Edition, 1932. *A Play Without Roses: Portrait of Eugene Jolas* (1932) and *A Play a Lion for Max Jacob* (1932) are to be found in *Portraits and Prayers*, 1936. A series of plays begins on page 63 of *The Geographical History of America*, 1936. They are called to the attention of the reader by Thornton Wilder in his preface to that volume. *Daniel Webster: Eighteen in America: a Play* was printed in *New Directions 1937* and in the posthumous *First Reader*, 1947, there are three more plays.

The present volume, I believe, contains all of the remaining unpublished plays, the manuscripts of which exist in the vast collection of Steiniana in the Yale University Library, and further the librettos of the operas and ballet and the play which have been performed on the stage. It was Miss Toklas's expressed wish that this volume should carry a title such as *More Operas and Plays*, perpetuating Miss Stein's original title, *Operas and Plays*. The actual title was suggested by Donald Gallup, curator of the Collection of American Literature in the Yale University Library, who is also responsible for the colla-

[1] *The Autobiography of Alice B. Toklas*, p. 257: "This play has always interested her immensely, it was the first attempt that later made her *Operas and Plays*, the first conception of landscape as a play."

tion of the typed copies of these plays with the original manuscripts. He has been furthermore of every possible assistance in the preparation of the text for this volume and his advice, frequently sought, has never been denied. Both Miss Toklas and I are exceedingly grateful to him.

Gertrude Stein's conception of playwriting differs from that of any other dramatist whose work has reached the theatre or the printed page. Her frequent use of the word "landscape" in connection with the drama indicates that she conceives a play as static in form. She has said that anything that could not be a story could be a play and again that "When I see a thing it is not a play for me, but when I write something that somebody else can see then it is a play for me." In *The Making of Americans,* she confessed, "I write for myself and strangers," and later, in conversation, withdrew the strangers. She frequently remarked that what an author conceived and what the public would make of this conception were two distinct phenomena. In addition, it may be stated that her plays abound in the use of compression, repetition, mystification, and a casual employment of whatever was going on around her at the moment of writing; qualities inherent in her books as well. Thornton Wilder[2] believes that her sprinkling of the text arbitrarily with "Act I, Act III, etc." is her satirical jab at pedantry and formalism in general, her way of saying, "Don't fence *me* in!"

It is obvious that the ways in which one of Miss Stein's plays, even the more easily understandable of them, can be produced are countless. She has said that Maurice Grosser seemed to understand how her plays could be performed and it is true that Maurice supplied extremely skillful scenarios for *Four Saints* and *The Mother of Us All,* but he himself has told me that any number of other plots or arrangements of the characters would be equally valid.

Reading recently in a book by Igor Stravinsky in which he has collected lectures he had delivered to young undergraduates at Harvard University, I discovered a passage which seemed to me to describe the work of Gertrude Stein, speaking basically, quite as well as it explains the intentions of this Russian composer. He begins by stating that music based on ontological time is generally dominated

---

[2] In his brilliant Introduction to *Four In America,* he further comments on Miss Stein's discovery that there are two kinds of writing: the kind in which the words mean what they say and the kind in which "the meaning has to be meant as something (that) has been learned."

by the principle of similarity and he continues: "The music that adheres to psychological time likes to proceed by contrast. To these two principles which dominate the creative process correspond the fundamental concepts of variety and unity. All the arts have recourse to this principle. The methods of polychromatics and monochromatics in the plastic arts correspond respectively to variety and unity. For myself, I have always considered it is more satisfactory to proceed by similarity rather than by contrast. Music thus gains strength in the measure that it does not succumb to the seductions of variety. What it loses in questionable riches it gains in true solidarity.

"Contrast produces an immediate effect. Similarity satisfies us only in the long run. Contrast is an element of variety, but it divides our attention. Similarity is a striving for unity. The need to seek variety is perfectly legitimate but we must not forget that the One precedes the Many. Variety surrounds me on every hand. So I need not fear I shall be lacking in it, since I am constantly confronted by it. Contrast is everywhere. Similarity is hidden; it must be sought out, and it is found only after the most exhaustive efforts. When variety tempts me, I am uneasy about the facile solutions it offers me. Similarity, on the other hand, poses more difficult problems but also offers results that are more solid and hence more valuable to me."

This, it seems to me, is another, and perhaps even better way of expressing Gertrude Stein's statement that she followed Cezanne's procedure of filling in every inch of space on the canvas with details, each of which is of equal importance. At any rate if it succeeds in explaining Stravinsky's own work, it is even better as exegesis for writing by the author of *Three Lives*.

II

Four Saints in Three Acts, with a musical score by Virgil Thomson, was originally produced in the Avery Memorial of the Hartford Athenaeum, at Hartford, Connecticut, February 8, 1934 and subsequently has been performed in New York and Chicago. It has been sung in concert, over the radio, and it has been recorded. This opera was first published in America in 1934 and this text inadvertently was reproduced in *Selected Writings of Gertrude Stein* which I edited in 1946. Most texts when set to music suffer changes and omissions and the alterations in this instance are elaborate and extensive. Of course, the complete original text may be examined in *transition*, No. 16 (June 17, 1929) or in *Operas and Plays*, published in Paris in 1932, but these are no longer generally available. In any case, this is the first instance the complete text has been published in America.

Miss Stein has said of this: "And so it was natural that when I wanted saints that they should be Spanish saints. There are saints everywhere. There have been saints in Italy and in France and even in Germany and I suppose in Austria, I do not know anything about them, but the important saints have been Spanish and Italian and that is natural enough, there must be really weather in which to wander in order to be a saint . . . A saint a real saint never does anything, a martyr does something but a really good saint does nothing and so I wanted to have Four Saints that did nothing and I wrote the *Four Saints in Three Acts* and they did nothing and that was everything. Generally speaking anybody is more interesting doing nothing than doing anything."

In spite of which admonition Maurice Grosser found many agreeable things for the saints in Gertrude's play to do.[3]

Similarly, it is an abridged text of *The Mother of Us All* which is printed by the Music Press with Virgil Thomson's score. In this instance the composer not only cut the text, but also shifted the order of at least one of the scenes. When this play was finished Gertrude Stein sent it to me with instructions to read it and to pass it on to Virgil. I pored over the pages with mounting enthusiasm and it was a pleasure to telephone Virgil that Gertrude had given him something very special indeed to set to music. When he read the text his opinion completely confirmed mine. So, indeed, did that of the subsequent audiences after the opera was eventually composed and produced.

A letter Jo Barry wrote me on April 10, 1946 gives an interesting insight into Gertrude Stein's method of work and is direct evidence of her manner of introducing topical material into her writing; sufficient excuse for reproducing it here: "Yes, in a way, in a sort of Ernest Dowson way, I'm being faithful to an Irish girl

---

[3] On page 108 of *Everybody's Autobiography*, Miss Stein says, "In the meantime they had played *Four Saints* in America and that was exciting. And now I should write Spain a play and it would begin, Act I First Spaniard. There is no second Spaniard. Second Spaniard. There is no first Spaniard." So far as I know this promising drama was never written.

who will eventually come over to Paris. It's our forthcoming marriage (she is pratiquante—and I, of course, am non-Catholic) that
formed the background of Jo the Loiterer's marriage with Indiana
Elliott—'was it civil or was it religious?' You might be interested
in the origin of the title for Jo the Loiterer: G. S. was putting
in some of the people she knew [4]—Gallup, Virgil, Atlan (he's the
painter you asked about but more later) and asked me what I
wanted. I said I would want to wander on the stage and talk to
myself, as Susan B. and Daniel W. orate at each other. So the
character was Jo the Wanderer for awhile. Then I told her about
the time I was arrested in Ann Arbor at the University for picket-
ing. But the charge was loitering! There was no law against picket-
ing. I was found guilty and went to jail for one night. That's when
I said 'Any one can be called a loiterer!' I like the opera—I like the
orientalism of Jo.

"As for Atlan (in the opera he is Herman—in life he is Jean)
his career is summed up thusly: 'Before the flowers of friendship
faded friendship faded'—an abstract painter, Gertrude was asked
to write an introduction for him for his catalogue at an exhibition.
She did. She mentioned surrealists as pornographs. Atlan's friends
are surrealists. He rejected the introduction. They are very cool
to each other now. Especially G. S. And I am rather cool to Atlan's
paintings now . . ."

The opera, commissioned by the Alice M. Ditson Fund of
Columbia University, was produced in Brander Matthews Hall
May 7, 1947, and was presented there for several performances.
Notable interpretations were given by Dorothy Dow as Susan B.
Anthony, Belva Kibbler as Anne, Alice Howland as Constance
Fletcher, and William B. Horne as Jo the Loiterer.

A great many persons present at these performances almost
automatically began to identify the leading character with Gertrude Stein herself and the character of Anne with that of Alice
B. Toklas. The parallels between the careers of Miss Stein and
Miss Anthony are fairly obvious; at any rate they are by no means
esoteric. In the moving finale in which the statue of Susan B.,
unveiled in the Halls of Congress reflects upon "My long life, my

---

[4] Several other plays in this volume employ the names of actual persons and
actual dogs. A few of these are Mildred Aldrich, Maud Crutwell, Mabel Sterne,
Basket, Pépé, Louis de Kerstradt, Sir Francis Cyril Rose, Carley Mills, Barbette,
Neith Boyce, Meraud Guevara, Jane Heap, May Sinclair, and Henry Fuller.

long long life," which at last she is aware is a martyrdom "not to what was won but what was done," it becomes only too evident that much that Gertrude Stein wrote for the role of Susan B. in this piece, finished shortly before her death, might equally well apply to the author herself.[5] The end of the opera, as performed, actually seemed to be a farewell to Gertrude Stein. Both the internal and external evidence is strongly in support of the analogy theory. Of course, Miss Stein may have created this condition unconsciously. However, it will be noted that the real characters who are living were all friends of Miss Stein and the others either wore invented names or, like Daniel Webster,[6] were figures on which she had reflected extensively. With the single exception of Dr. Anna Howard Shaw, who is not identified in the play, none of these characters seems to have had the slightest connection with the real Susan B. The final touch seems to be when Susan B. sings, "Daniel was my father's name," as Daniel was Gertrude Stein's father's name as well.

Yes is for a Very Young Man is the first play without music by Gertrude Stein to see production. A young actor with extraordinary intuition, Lamont Johnson, touring Europe with a U.S.O.

[5] On May 14, 1947 Alice B. Toklas wrote me: "Baby didn't at all feel it was she herself (i.e. Susan B.) haven't I told you how heroic Baby felt her to be and that was explained by her having one Quaker parent and Anne was not I but the Reverend Anna Shaw—who had such a handsome head (a cumbersome body) and who was capitonée as Susan B. never was." I should explain, perhaps, that "Baby" was part of my own special name for Gertrude Stein.

The Dictionary of American Biography says in part regarding Dr. Anna Howard Shaw: "After 1888, when she and Susan B. Anthony first met they were intimate friends; for eighteen years they campaigned together for woman's rights, attended conventions, appeared before committees of Congress, and went to conventions in Europe . . . Her personal life was centered upon her home, her friends, and members of her family; with her lived Lucy E. Anthony, a niece of Susan B. Anthony, who was her private secretary, friend, and companion for over thirty years. As a lecturer she had no equal among women, a distinction that was acknowledged not only in the United States but abroad. Her voice was rich and musical and she could speak for several hours without any apparent strain. . . . She was only five feet tall and rather stout. Her hair, worn in a pompadour, grew white at an early age, but her black eyes sparkled and her smile won an audience immediately."

[6] Donald Gallup informs me that Gertrude Stein was from the beginning impressed with the ease with which sections of Daniel Webster's speeches could be incorporated in the opera. I am unfamiliar with this orator's speeches, but this would be an interesting field for investigation.

company, acting in *Kind Lady,* secured the rights to *Yes* from
Miss Stein and took it back to America with him where it was
produced for the first time at the Pasadena Playhouse, March 13,
1946. Toni Merrill (Mrs. Johnson) Jane and Robert Claborne, all
members of the touring U.S.O. company appeared in the Pasadena
production, along, of course, with Lamont Johnson himself.[7] An
earlier projected production by GIs in Biarritz was abandoned.

There was an extended correspondence, all of which is at
Yale, between Lamont Johnson and Miss Stein about suggested
alterations, before the play was produced. This correspondence is
of the deepest interest, but much too involved for selective quota-
tion. Miss Stein felt that Lamont Johnson had a sympathetic understanding of the play and, accepting his suggestions, made extensive
changes and additions to the original text, which did not get incorporated in the English edition of the play, published in 1948.
The following is a list of the principal alterations:

Act I, Scene III in its entirety.

Act I, Scene II, from the exit of Ferdinand to the end of the
scene.

Act I, Scene II, from the end of Ferdinand's long speech
("Oh, hell, I guess, oh hell") to the spot where Ferdinand says,
"Yes, Constance, [8] I am going away."

Act I, Scene II, a page, until Constance says, "Denise is right,
I don't understand."

[7] One of Miss Stein's added scenes arrived too late for incorporation in
this production. The second production of this play was given by the Forty-
eight Theatre in London on four consecutive Sundays, beginning May 16,
1948, with Robert Marsden as Ferdinand, Marion Jennings as Constance,
Willoughby Gray as Henry, and Pauline Wynn as Denise. These performances
followed the incomplete English text. The first complete production of the
play was given at Princeton by the University Players the week of July 26,
1948, so successfully, indeed, that the run was continued the following week.
In these performances Karl Light appeared as Ferdinand, Morris E. Kinnan,
jr., as Henry, Rayna Sue Klatzkin as Constance, and Patience Hartman as
Denise. John Capsis was the director. On and after October 29, 1948, the
Théâtre Intime at Princeton gave eight more performances of the play, again
under the direction of John Capsis and with Karl Light and Morris E.
Kinnan, jr., in their original rôles. The women and the settings were new. In
the text of the play which follows, the stage directions added by the Pasadena
director are printed in Roman type.

[8] In one of her letters to Lamont Johnson, it is interesting to note that
Gertrude Stein asserts that the role of Constance was suggested by Clare Boothe
Luce.

The final addition, sent to Lamont Johnson, February 5, 1946, is in Act I, Scene II, from the beginning to the point where the servants leave the stage.

Donald Gallup writes me about these changes: "None of the above passages is in the mimeographed script prepared for the abortive Biarritz production and I am pretty sure they are all more or less the result of requests for clarification and expansion made from the Pasadena group, and therefore all written after the first of December, 1945."

Donald Gallup, a one-time Major of the U. S. Army, stationed in Paris, continues: "The play in its original form was either already complete when Gertrude and Alice returned to Paris on December 15, 1944, or finished very shortly afterwards, for I remember that Gertrude mentioned it when I first went to see her on January 5, 1945, and I know that I read it in its then complete form in manuscript in the notebook which is now at Yale when I went to 5 rue Christine for the second time on January 12, 1945. It was not long after that there began to be projects for its presentation (Alice had already copied it hurriedly for Katharine Cornell to take back to New York with her) and everybody was asked for suggestions for filling it out to full evening's length. (Jo) Barry and (Alan) Campbell were in on this and a good many others including a Russian GI whom I never met. I remember that both Gertrude and Alice suspected that the Russian interest in putting on the play in a Paris theatre was part of a plot of the Russians for getting control of all the theatres in Paris. At about this time there was a very active effort to have the play presented in French and Gertrude made a translation of it into French for this purpose. This manuscript, titled *En Savoie* (the original English title was *In Savoy*) is also at Yale.

"The scheme for the production of the play at the American Army University at Biarritz constitutes another phase of this rather extraordinary history. A group of drama people at Biarritz, including among others, Richard Whorf, passed an evening at 5 rue Christine reading the play with Gertrude, and everything was set for the production, and for Gertrude and Alice to go down to Biarritz to supervise it, when there was some mixup. . . . There ensued several Paris-Biarritz telephone conversations and the outcome was that all plans for the performance were cancelled. Incidentally, Riba-Rovira had already done at least some designs for the sets." Further designs for the decor, one of which appeared in *Theatre Arts* for July 1946, were made by Technical Sergeant James Buckley.

Alice Toklas's account of the abandonment of the Biarritz production gives the details of this mixup: "It was Gertrude's objection to a workshop production," she wrote me on November 12, 1946," . . . that is a production without scenery and to a specially invited audience—that caused her to ask for an immediate return of her manuscript from Biarritz. We did have such a time when Biarritz proposed this—precious Baby blew a fuse—we stayed up till the next morning getting the people at Biarritz on the phone. She wished her play to be produced in an ordinary way, simply, realistically, before ordinary theatre-goers. She considered it a play like any other—except perhaps for its quality—that the characters were portraits and of ordinary people, that there was nothing mystical or symbolical about them or their actions." I might add to the above reports the fact that Robert Lewis who has long held a profound respect for this play and hopes eventually to produce it, has always insisted that it is not a war play, not a play about the resistance, but a dramatization of the way different people behave in any crisis.[9]

[9] Gertrude Stein's own account of her intention in creating this play, written for the program of the Pasadena production, is worth examination: "My mother when I was little used to tell me stories of her girlhood in Baltimore during the Civil War and the divided families with northern and southern sympathies. Then there were a whole series of plays, *Secret Service, Alabama, Shenandoah,* and then there was Winston Churchill's *Crisis,* a story of St. Louis, with the same theme. I loved these stories and then when I was in France during the occupation, knowing intimately all the people around me, I was struck with the resemblance to the stories my mother used to tell me, the divided families, the bitterness, the quarrels and sometimes the denunciations, and yet the natural necessity of their all continuing to live their daily life together, because after all that was all the life they had, besides they were after all the same family or their neighbors, and in the country neighbors are neighbors.

"And so this play formed itself in my mind and all the time I was writing it I felt that I was writing in the spirit of the plays I had loved as a child, the plays of the Civil War.

"Then there came the four young ones from the Pasadena Community Playhouse and I told them about it and they felt as I did about it and we all were very much excited and now I want the audience to realize that French families were divided as our American families were divided in our Civil War and even in our Revolutionary War, and it is complicated and simple, and I hope it will make you feel the French as they really were during the long years of the occupation."

Donald Gallup goes on to say that there are several changes of names in the scripts: "Claude in the early manuscript becomes Denise and the Olympe-Clothilde speeches are often reversed. The stage directions (in the prompt-book and published copies) are usually elaborations of hints given by G. S. It is impossible to be sure about certain minor alterations between manuscript and typed copy in the case of *Yes*, because we do not have (in the Yale Library) all the intermediate scripts in which G. S. made corrections."

It should be stated categorically that Norma Chambers [10] suggested the change of title, originally *In Savoy*, to *Yes is for a Very Young Man*, although, of course, the revised title occurs in the script.

As much of Gertrude Stein's text as was employed by Lord Berners for his ballet, *A Wedding Bouquet*, performed for the first time at Sadler's Wells, London, April 27, 1937, by Ninette de Valois, Harold Turner, Robert Helpmann, Margot Fonteyn, and others, is printed with the score of this ballet, published in 1938 by J. and W. Chester. This text was derived from the play titled, *They Must. Be Wedded. To Their Wife*, to be found in *Operas and Plays*, 1932, a volume, as I have indicated earlier, no longer readily available. Never before published in America in any form, the complete text is offered to readers of this volume.

Gertrude Stein and Alice B. Toklas visited London for the opening of this ballet. She writes about the event in *Everybody's Autobiography*: "And so I do write a lot of plays and they are things for somebody to see and somebody does see them, sometimes there will be lots more of them given. They are doing one in London Lord Berners has put music to it and Pépé the little Mexican dog is going to be on the stage not in person of course but a little girl (Joyce Farron) to play him but even the littlest little girl is going to be a very large little Mexican. Alice Toklas wanted them to put a little one on wires little like the real Pépé but they said it had to be a little girl. Basket did not mind he might perhaps if he saw him. As yet they have not done any of mine without music to help them.[11] They could though and it

---

[10] Norma Chambers: American actress, recently seen in New York in the musical version of *Street Scene*.

[11] Written, naturally, before the production of *Yes* in Pasadena.

would be interesting but no one has yet. I always had a feeling that Maurice Grosser might but then he wants to be a painter . . . and besides anyway probably no one would let him."

This ballet has not yet been produced in America, but when the Sadler's Wells company eventually visits New York, it may well be in their repertory.

On May 10, 1938, Gertrude Stein wrote me on a postcard: "I have just finished the first act of *Faust*, I think you will like it, when I get some more done I will send it along." On another postcard, dated June 20, 1938, she says: "The opera is finished and Alice will be typing it now and sending, the theology and the drama I hope will be to your liking." . . . In a letter postmarked July 26, 1938, she has this to say: "I am so glad that you liked *Faust*. I have been struggling with this problem of dramatic narrative and in that I think I got it and I am so pleased that you like it. . . . I wrote to Bennett suggesting that they print the *Faust* in a little book, I think it might be popular, what do you think and it might be illustrated by some very clever drawings that a young Turk Abidin Dina made for it just before we left, he only illustrated the first act, if you think this is a good idea and I have referred Bennett to you well we will . . . Gerald Berners is to do the music . . ."

Gerald Berners, indeed, had commissioned the work, Gertrude Stein's contribution to the long line of operas and plays on the subject of the Faust legend, and he had expected to set it to music. The following letter to Gertrude Stein dated December 3, 1939, from the Yale Collection, explains why he did not do so:

"My dear Gertrude, I was delighted to get your letter and to hear that things are not too bad with you. What I want to say is, and it makes me very sad to say it—that all inspirational sources seem to have dried up: I can't write a note of music or do any kind of creative work whatever and it's not for want of trying and I don't believe I shall be able to as long as this war lasts. I feel confronted with the breakdown of all the things that meant anything to me and the thought of it has got into my subconscious and filled it to the exclusion of anything else. Not being able to find a note of music is driving me mad. I don't know when I shall be able to go on with *Faust*. That is why I very reluctantly suggest that you give it to some one else. Virgil Thomson [12] perhaps. It makes me miserable to think of any one else doing it but it is unfair to you if I keep hold of it when I can't do it and I really feel at the present moment that I shall never be able to write music again.

"Love from Gerald."

Before he had abandoned the idea, Lord Berners had suggested several alterations, suggestions which were adopted by Gertrude Stein. For instance, he requested that she supply a solo for Faust at the beginning of the opera. On February 8, 1939, she wrote me: "This is an additional bit of *Faust*," and she enclosed this aria. Early in the fall of 1938, Bennett Cerf informed me that he had written Gertrude that he would not publish the text of the opera. This is the first time then that it has seen the light of print.

In *Everybody's Autobiography*, Gertrude Stein writes: "I have wanted to write a whole book about words of one syllable. In a play I have just written called *Listen to Me* I keep thinking of words of one syllable. It is natural to write poems of words of one syllable and some live with words of three letters and some live with words of four letters. In the play *Madame Recamier* [13] I did it and it makes a very good poem." On another page of *Everybody's Autobiography*, there is more about *Listen to Me*: "In English novels a baronet is always villainous or peculiar, and sometimes both, I have in my life known two baronets and they are not at all villainous, they are gentle and sweet but they are peculiar, Berty Abdy [14] is one and Francis Rose the other one . . . Francis Rose is a painter . . . Berty Abdy is not a painter I have made him in my play *Listen to Me*, he is the Sweet William who had his genius and who looked for his Lillian. He has his genius, his genius is in being that thing, in having his genius and looking for his Lillian, he dislikes with a violence that is disconcerting all modern art and all Americans, and to prove that the exception proves the rule he is very fond of me . . . Later when we were in Cornwall together his wife Diana kneeled upon the eye of the big chalk horse there to wish what there is to wish for and so I have told in the play *Listen to Me*."

Byron seems to be more of a discussion of playwriting rather than an actual play and *A Play of Not and Now* obviously was in-

---

[12] A fine suggestion!

[13] 1930. Published in *Operas and Plays*, 1932.

[14] Lord Robert Abdy.

spired by Mrs. Ehrman's famous dinner to Gertrude Stein [15] in her house in Beverly Hills, which is described in *Everybody's Autobiography*.

About the other plays in this volume very little is known and there is nothing I can say on this occasion.

CARL VAN VECHTEN

November 7, 1948
New York

[15] In the Saturday Review of Literature, May 24, 1947, James Thrall Soby remarks sapiently: "One of the good points about commonsense, so conspicuously, her (Gertrude Stein's) quality, is that it does not need to be true so long as it is usually."

YES IS FOR A VERY YOUNG MAN

1944 ⋅ 1945

ACT ONE

ACT TWO

ACT ONE ⸱ Scene 1

June 1940. The garden outside DENISE's chateau. A tree
with circular bench at center. Garden furniture at left.
Stage Right is dimly lighted. FERDINAND sprawls on a
bench. DENISE *is sitting and shelling peas.*

DENISE. Oh dear I am so tired of working I wish I could be rich
again, oh dear. I want to be rich, anyway I never want to shell a pea
or dig a potato or wash a dress. I want all vegetables to grow in cans
not in the ground. I want all clothes washed in a laundry and I want
all stockings bought new and thrown away. That is what I want, oh
dear. Ferdinand, when Henry and I were first married and he was
in the army, oh it was wonderful and now he just does nothing, for
Heaven's sake can't you make him earn something and help us.
Ferdinand just don't stand there, take my side, make your brother
Henry do something, I love Henry. You know I love him, he is my
husband but you can influence him. Ferdinand why don't you take
my side, Ferdinand, why don't you take my side?

FERDINAND. Denise, I do take your side, I do, I do take your side,
I take everybody's side. Don't keep at me, you make me cry, I know
you're miserable. I take everybody's side, that is the way I am, I do
take everybody's side.

DENISE. Don't cry, Ferdinand, no Ferdinand don't cry, no don't cry,
but I am not everybody. I am just me, why don't you take my side.

FERDINAND. (FERDINAND crosses away angrily) My God, Denise,
everybody's side, no you are right, Denise, I don't take anybody's
side, of course I don't take anybody's side, of course I don't take anybody's side. My God look at us, here we are, can you take sides when
you are in prison. Denise, we are all in prison, every Frenchman is in

3

prison, no you are right, Denise, I do not take anybody's side, how I want, how I do want to take everybody's side, but you can't take sides in prison, every Frenchman in France is in prison, but you can't take sides in prison, that is what prison is. Go away, Denise, I can't take anybody's side.

(FERDINAND sits hopelessly on bench at the tree)

DENISE. (Following FERDINAND pleading) Don't cry, Ferdinand, you said you don't cry but you do cry, Ferdinand, why do you cry like that? It's silly to say we are in prison, just take my side, talk to Henry. You know I love Henry. You just be sensible and talk sense. I know what is the matter with you, it's that American Constance, she likes you to talk like that, but you frighten me when you talk like that about prison, don't talk like that. Constance likes you to talk like that, it makes her feel, well you know what I mean.

(Goes back to shelling peas)

I like you to cry, Ferdinand, but I like you to take my side, and remember you belong to me. You are Henry's brother and you belong to me, and you should talk to him about earning money and making me comfortable, Ferdinand. You will always take my side, tell me you will.

FERDINAND. Denise, can't you see, can't you feel, this is no time to talk about anything but what has happened to France. Denise, can't you see.

DENISE. Oh Ferdinand, you just talk and talk, Constance, she is American and she likes you to talk, but if Henry does not work and earn money, he will sulk, he won't talk to me for days, he'll just sulk, Ferdinand, you just have to make him earn money, you just have to. I won't have him sulking and sulking and not talking to me for days. I just won't.

FERDINAND. (Crosses to DENISE solemnly) Denise, as surely as France will be free, as surely as France will come back, as surely as someday we will be Free, so surely will Henry do what he has to do, he will not do what you want him to do.

DENISE. You are nothing but a boy, Ferdinand, why should I listen to you, just a boy. What does Henry talk to Constance about, they talk all the time. Oh dear, I wish Henry would not sulk. I wish he would be like my brother Achille. Oh, how I wish he would be handsome the way he is and not sulk, he is handsome but how he sulks. Ferdinand, be on my side, make him work, he never sulked when he was in the army, he used to come home with Achille, and we were all so happy. Ferdinand, be on my side.

FERDINAND. Denise, Denise, it is going to be so long. Denise, every day is going to be so long, in a defeat, the days are short and the weeks are long and the year, oh the year, once it is over, but is a year over really over, a whole year, a whole year of defeat, it is all so long.
(*He crosses away*)

DENISE. Henry is just going back to his old ordinary life.

FERDINAND. (*Dropping down on the bench*) He is not, nobody is going back to his old ordinary life.

DENISE. He is.

FERDINAND. He is not.
(HENRY *comes in, he throws himself down under the trees, he turns toward* FERDINAND)

HENRY. Have you seen the Armistice notice?

FERDINAND. No, I couldn't look.

HENRY. I looked, there it was, on the barn, all day yesterday. The rain was coming down, a group of farmers were standing there reading the notice, they didn't say anything, it rained, they read, they went away, and then there it was, it was raining nobody was reading it, nobody, and it was raining and then I saw two of them standing there, and they said, France needs discipline, and then two others stood and read it, and the old one said he couldn't believe it, I heard one old one say, No I don't believe it, no I don't, I don't believe it, and I heard his son say, come along old man, of course you can believe it. Well, said the young one, for my generation there is nothing to believe, but your generation, of course you can believe it.

And it just kept on raining and the notice of the Armistice was there on the barn. Oh my God, and it got darker and it rained and it was there, and then I heard Achille, yes your brother, Denise, say that there was going to be an army. My God an army, my

God, Marshal Petain's Army. One hundred and twenty-five thousand men. My God, not a French army, Marshal Petain's Army.
My God.

DENISE.   (*Still shelling peas*) Achille said that. You listen to me,
Henry. Oh dear I am so tired of working, I wish I could be rich.
Listen to me, Henry, why don't you join the army like Achille, why
don't you? Oh dear, oh dear, why won't you? For Heaven's sake,
don't lie there sulking. Well I want to be comfortable even if you
don't, and the only way for you to earn something is to go back
to the army. Look at Achille, he has gone back to the army and
my brother knows best about everything. Why don't you do what
he does, join Marshal Petain's army.

HENRY.   Marshal Petain's army, Marshal Petain's army, I would just
as leave vomit as join Marshal Petain's army. You make me sick
with your Achille, Achille, Achille. Don't you know, can't you remember, you make me sick, can't you remember that while Marshal
Petain is forming that miserable little army of one hundred and
twenty-five thousand men, that miserable little toy army, my two
brothers are rotting in prison in Germany with two million of your
fellow countrymen, if you can't remember my brothers you can
remember them. Achille, Achille, Achille, you make me sick.
        (*Lifts himself up to sitting position*)

DENISE.   Don't you dare, don't you dare say anything against
Achille, didn't he bring down six of the enemy's airplanes, didn't
he, and you never did, he did.

HENRY.   Yes and now he has forgotten who those enemies are, yes
he has, and he licks their boots and he wants them to win. Pah,
you all make me sick.
        (*He lies back and looks up at the trees*)

DENISE.   If I were not married to you Henry, I would never forgive
you.
        (*And her tears drop down on the peas*)
        (*Silence. A Young Woman in white comes on the terrace*)

DENISE.   Oh Constance. Come I am so miserable.

CONSTANCE.   (*Joining* DENISE) What is it, is it the peas?

DENISE.   Yes, it is always peas, it is always peas, but now there is the only way I could get away from peas and Henry won't, he won't, he won't.

CONSTANCE. Henry won't what?

DENISE. He won't join the army and if he did he would earn enough and I would only have to shell his peas and my peas, not everybody's peas. Oh it is just too miserable of him. Ferdinand, you always take my part, shouldn't he join the army, shouldn't he. Achille has.

CONSTANCE. (Sitting beside DENISE) Oh Achille.

DENISE. Oh you are an American and you do not understand, Achille knows—

CONSTANCE. My dear, American or not, I do know that Achille, he is nice, he is sweet, he is not much of a worker.

DENISE. He brought down five airplanes all by himself.

HENRY. Six!

DENISE. Six.

CONSTANCE. Yes I know, of course and he is so modest he never mentions it and he does not wear his decorations, but everybody does know about those six planes.

DENISE. You are horrid and American, American and horrid. Ferdinand, say something, you always understand, say something.

FERDINAND. Yes, sure I understand you and Achille too, but I understand Henry too. Oh nonsense, there is no sense to it, I am not like some, I do think the Marshal has helped France by making his armistice, but an armistice is not peace, it is a truce and as long as there is no peace we are at war with Germany even if we are not fighting and an army is just silly, an army that is not supposed at any time to fight against Germany. It is just silly. No, Henry is right, he should not join a silly army like that.

HENRY. (*Looking up*) And you might add, Ferdinand, to be an army under the Marshal who lets our two brothers rot in prison in Germany while he makes a toy army that can never fight for them. Oh, let everybody shut up, let everybody shut up, shut up, shut up.

DENISE. (Going to HENRY) I won't shut up, I won't, Achille—

CONSTANCE. Oh for Heaven's sake, quote your mother or your uncle or your father, if it has to be in the family but not always Achille, besides he is too modest to speak, of course he is.

DENISE. Don't you dare talk like that, Constance. Well if you want that I quote my mother, she says well she does not say she wants Germany to win but she says Germany will win, and when they do a noble family like ours that has always owned land in France will once more rule over France and teach everybody what discipline is.

HENRY. Yes, discipline, you can't do a day's work without making a fuss, always making a fuss, and all your ground gets less and less productive. Bah, aristocrats make me sick, everything makes me sick, everything.

> (HENRY *and* DENISE *go off quarreling into the house.* FERDINAND *lying at her feet and looking up at* CONSTANCE *who is seated in a chair*)

CONSTANCE. Denise is very lovely.

FERDINAND. Yes.

CONSTANCE. And Henry really loves her.

FERDINAND. Yes.

CONSTANCE. And she loves Henry.

FERDINAND. Yes.

CONSTANCE. And you, Ferdinand?

FERDINAND. Yes.

CONSTANCE. Yes can be said too often.

FERDINAND. Yes.

CONSTANCE. (Walking away from him) It is all just commencing, everything is just commencing.

FERDINAND. Yes.

CONSTANCE. Oh Ferdinand, don't be stupid and annoying.

FERDINAND. (Following her) Constance, Constance, what can I say, what is there to say but yes, no does not mean anything, no not now, but yes, yes means something. Oh my God, yes means you, it means you, yes it does, you do not want it to mean you but it does, yes, yes, yes.

CONSTANCE. (Very slowly) Yes, yes is for a very young man, and you Ferdinand, you are a very young boy, yes you are, yes is for a very young one, a very young man, but I am not so young, no I am not, and so I say no. I always say no. You know, Ferdinand, yes you know that I always say no.

FERDINAND. Yes.
     (Silence)

CONSTANCE. And life now, Ferdinand, is it yes.

FERDINAND. It is yes to me.

CONSTANCE. Yes and it is no to me. I love to think of you as yes, Ferdinand. You should love to think of me as no.

FERDINAND. Don't be like an enemy, Constance, don't be like a cruel enemy, a cruel enemy who always says no, cruelly no, until at last he says yes and that is death. Do not, Constance, do not say no, if you must say no, say it afterwards, say yes first, say yes, Constance, you must say yes.

CONSTANCE. My poor Ferdinand, even if I said yes, it would be no, it must be no, my poor Ferdinand, it is all just commencing and you know, how well you must know that it must commence with no, and go on with no and end with no, my poor Ferdinand, it must be so.

FERDINAND. Yes.

CONSTANCE. Yes, Ferdinand, it must be no.

FERDINAND. There is no difference between defeat and victory then.

CONSTANCE. There is none now certainly not now. Ferdinand, Ferdinand, no there is no difference between defeat and victory, not yet, wait, Ferdinand, it will always be no, but wait, Ferdinand, wait.

FERDINAND.   Yes.

CONSTANCE.   Henry does love Denise.

FERDINAND.   Yes.

CONSTANCE.   Denise does love Henry.

FERDINAND.   Does she?

CONSTANCE.   (Turning from him) Yes, Ferdinand, she does.

FERDINAND.   And you, Constance, whom do you love?

CONSTANCE.   Love, whom do I love?

FERDINAND.   (Goes to her) You love me.

CONSTANCE.   Do I love you?

FERDINAND.   Yes.

CONSTANCE.   No Ferdinand, it is easy to say no, Ferdinand, we must, we must, there is no love, Ferdinand. There is no love, we must, there is no love, you know it, and never, never forget it, there is no love, no, no, no, never forget it, there is no love, there is so much, there is no love, Ferdinand.

     (He takes her in his arms)

No, no, no, there is no love. Ferdinand, you do know it, you know there is no love.

FERDINAND.   Yes.

     (As DENISE *comes down the stairs with sewing basket,* FERDINAND *goes out of the gate.* DENISE *comes over to* CONSTANCE, *seated*)

DENISE.   Oh are you all alone, Constance?

CONSTANCE.   Yes, one has to be alone sometime.

DENISE.   All right, I'll stay with you so that we can be alone together, that is the nicest way of being alone, you know it is, being alone together.

CONSTANCE.   Yes, of course you silly, come and let us be alone together. Come and sit down and let's talk.

DENISE.   (Sits, mending sock) Oh I am so tired, all this fuss and trouble, and oh dear, I ought to be taking potato bugs off the potato plants. My mother has taken my father off to do that. Well, I suppose my mother was wise, she, well, they started rich and after the last war they became poor, so poor they have to take their own potato bugs off their potato plants. I often wonder (*Giggling*) whether mother did it just to keep father being always with her. You know, Constance, in their society, father would not have been faithful but, dear me,

　　　(*Giggling*)

if they have to work on the farm together, and mother is always there, what can he do, poor father.

CONSTANCE. Do you think that your mother is really poor?

DENISE. What do you mean, Constance?

CONSTANCE. Well, I do often think that your mother has hidden away enough, largely enough, it would be like her to do it, so your father would have to search for potato bugs with her, and

　　　(*Dreamily*)

nobody would know but Achille and he would forget and in all that disorder, perhaps it is all lost forever, but anyway, anyway, what does it matter.

DENISE. Of course you are crazy, Constance, you always are crazy, of course it would matter. Someday I am going to have a little girl, Ferdinand would so love to have me have a little girl, and Henry would so love to have me have a little girl, a baby girl, Henry and Ferdinand, Ferdinand and Henry, they would so love to have me have a little girl. Whom do you think it would look like when I had my little girl, Constance. Would it look more like Henry or would it look more like Ferdinand.

CONSTANCE. (*Nastily*) Perhaps it would look like Achille and your mother. You never can tell.

　　　(Moves away laughing)

But are you going to have a baby, Denise?

DENISE. Perhaps yes, perhaps no, how can I have anything with a husband like Henry who won't join the army. Tell me, Constance, what are American men like, you never talk about them, what are they like, tell me, Constance.

CONSTANCE. What are they like, well I suppose men are always alike.

DENISE. No they are not, you know they are not, no. Why won't you tell what American men are like. I can't marry one because I am married to Henry, but I have cousins, perhaps they might like to marry one. Tell me, Constance, do they take good care of their women.

CONSTANCE. Do they, they certainly do, they take care of them magnificently, they give them everything they want.

DENISE. Oh do they, really do they, how nice, not like Henry. Oh how nice, and Constance, are they attractive and passionate like our men. Tell me, Constance, are they?

CONSTANCE. (*Dreamily*) Are they, no perhaps not, perhaps they ask less and they give more, perhaps they do, why do you want to know about American men, why do you ask, you are not interested, why do you ask?

DENISE. (Following CONSTANCE) Not because I want to surprise all your secrets, Constance, all or any. Have you any secrets, Constance? Tell me about American men, I want to know so that my cousin can marry one of them. Oh dear, perhaps Ferdinand is right. Perhaps we are in prison. Oh dear, we used to have so many people come visiting, so many coming and going and now could one come or could she go to him? Oh dear, perhaps Ferdinand is right, but no, Ferdinand is not right. One stranger is like another stranger, one stranger is like another stranger Constance, and strangers do not trouble a Frenchwoman or a Frenchman, not any stranger, do you think they do, Constance? Tell me about American men. Do you like them better than Frenchmen, than my Frenchman, tell me Constance?
(*And then interrupting herself*)
Listen, an airplane, listen.
(*She screams*)
Oh Henry, listen, an airplane, I am sure it is Achille.

HENRY. (*At upper window*) Stop your screaming, stop it, it's a Boche airplane, stop it, even Achille would not drive a Boche airplane, shut up.

DENISE. Come down, Henry, come down. Constance is telling me all about American men, come down Henry.

HENRY. (*Closing the window with a bang*) Oh, shut up.

DENISE. You see, Constance, you see, I am right, we French people are not interested in strangers. But tell me, tell me about American men, if Henry was an American man would he not work to make me comfortable. Is that what you and he talk about so much, tell me Constance.

> (FERDINAND *coming up behind silently, stands a moment and then says*)

FERDINAND. Are there any American men, Constance, were there any American men and did you love them?

> (*Silence. The roar of German tanks passing the road below, they listen*)

DENISE. Did you see the Godets, Ferdinand?

FERDINAND. No they are gone.

DENISE. Gone where?

FERDINAND. Gone where, gone when, when, where, that is what one asks, where can anybody go, go where, My God, go where, all France is on the way, they don't know where they are going and are they on their way. My God, go where.

CONSTANCE. Yes I too was about to go, to go not somewhere but anywhere and one of my neighbors, a farmer said to me, Mademoiselle, go where, I am an old man and I tell you in time of danger stay where you are, there if you are killed, you know where you are and you are there, if you live through it you are still there, there where you are. Mademoiselle in time of danger stay where you are, trying to go away from danger is useless, stay where you are, mademoiselle, in time of danger stay where you are. I stayed.

DENISE. (*Bitterly*) Yes you stayed.

FERDINAND. (*Softly*) You stayed.

CONSTANCE. Yes, I stayed.

> (*Silence. Once more on the road below the German tanks are passing*)

DENISE.   American men do everything for their women, they earn a lot of money and their wives spend it, that is what Constance says. Oh Henry
    (*She calls out*)
come down quickly, listen to what Constance says.

HENRY.   (*Coming in quickly* carrying one shoe) What is it, Constance.

DENISE.   She says that American men earn lots of money and that their wives spend it, that is what she says. Listen to what she says, Henry, you love to listen to what she says, listen to what she says, listen.

HENRY.   (Putting on sock, DENISE has been mending) Oh hell, you make me tired.

DENISE.   But listen, Henry, listen. All you would have to do would be to join the army like Achille and you would earn enough, not like those American men Constance admires so much but enough, listen, Henry, listen.

HENRY.   Yes, listen, listen.
    (*They listen as the tanks pass on below*)
(*Bitterly*) Yes, listen, you make me sick, yes listen, listen, listen.
    (*He turns away and* DENISE follows him still talking. FERDINAND *and* CONSTANCE *are left alone*)

FERDINAND.   (Listening to the tanks) Yes listen, it is all so unreal, Constance, is it unreal to you, it seems less unreal to you than it is to me, to us, is it because you are more practical. After all you are American, is it all more real to you than to us, to us it is horrible but not real. Is it all more real to you, Constance and therefore not so horrible. Is it, Constance? And American men, Constance, are there American men, Constance, are there, is Denise right, are there?

CONSTANCE.   (Goes to him) Tell me about Frenchmen, Ferdinand, tell me about France.

FERDINAND.   (Turning from her) You won't let me tell you about myself and yourself but you want me to tell you about Frenchmen and France.

CONSTANCE. Yes.

FERDINAND. There I have made you say yes.

CONSTANCE. Did you think that you had deprived me of that pleasant word forever?

FERDINAND. Sometimes I almost had hoped so.

CONSTANCE. What do you mean, Ferdinand.

FERDINAND. I mean that if I was strong enough to stop your saying yes completely and forever then I was strong enough to eventually make you say yes completely and forever.
(FERDINAND embraces her)

CONSTANCE. (Breaking away) Silly boy, tell me, yes, tell me about France and Frenchmen, tell me what Frenchmen are, what France is.

FERDINAND. France is a country that can be beaten but not conquered, that can be a phoenix and rise from the ashes. Yes, that is France, it always has it always will, it likes to change, it has had so many governments, sometimes it is bitter fun to count them, but what are governments, a government should leave civilians alone, protect them from their enemies and not cost too much, when they can't protect them from their enemies, then there has to be another government, and oh dear, were we not protected or were our enemies too strong, Constance. I think so much, Constance, do say yes, protect me from my enemies, that is the enemies within, those without, I will do all I can, believe me.

CONSTANCE. (Sits on bench drawing him down beside her) Yes I believe you but tell me tell me what are Frenchmen like, you are only a boy but tell me what are Frenchmen like.

FERDINAND. Frenchmen, what are Frenchmen like, what are they like? Well, one thing they are not, they are lovers and they are not obedient.

CONSTANCE. But I like men to be obedient.

FERDINAND. Obedience is a curse. That is what makes Germans and you wait, Constance, your country will find out, obedience makes people predatory. The Germans are obedient and obedient people must sooner or later follow a bad leader, that is what the Germans do but we French, we are not obedient. We love but we are not obedient. Constance, say yes, say you do love me.

CONSTANCE. Silly boy, tell me some more about what Frenchmen are. You are only a boy but do tell me some more what Frenchmen are.

FERDINAND. (Gets up angrily) Frenchmen are Frenchmen and France is full of Frenchmen. Just wait it may be a long wait, defeat is long, so long, but France is full of Frenchmen say yes and wait.
    (*Just then* DENISE *and* HENRY *come down.* DENISE *calls out*)

DENISE. Henry is coming with me to get potato bugs off the potato plants, do you want to come too, Ferdinand. Constance is too daintily dressed, but come along, do come along, see Henry help me get potato bugs off the potato plants.

HENRY. (*Sticking out his foot*) These shoes will never crush to death a potato bug upon a potato plant so long as one Boche remains uncrushed on the soil of France.

DENISE. Don't be silly, Henry, we have to eat potatoes whether the Germans are here or are not here. You are just being silly, earning a living and killing potato bugs just has to go on. You are just being silly, Henry, come along.
    (*They go off*)

CONSTANCE. Is this a beginning, Ferdinand?

FERDINAND. Don't be silly, Constance, Henry loves Denise, he is a Frenchman, he is not obedient. Don't be silly, Constance. You pay attention to me, don't be silly, Constance. I am your lover, don't you know what I am, I am your lover, I am a Frenchman. I love you, I am not obedient, I am your lover.

CONSTANCE. Yes, Ferdinand, how old are you, why Ferdinand, you are at that stage when your food card gives you the right to have cigarettes and chocolate. Just think, if you are not twenty-one, you can eat chocolate, and if you are over eighteen you can smoke cigarettes, and you are just those silly years when you can smoke cigarettes and eat chocolate at the same time, but you can't smoke cigarettes and eat chocolate and love at the same time and be a man at the same time and have me say no and yes at the same time, you want too much, Ferdinand, you want too much. Be a boy, Ferdinand, be a boy, I want you to be a boy.

> (*Silence. Below the tanks are rumbling.* HENRY *comes bursting in*)

HENRY. My hat, that woman, potato bugs, that woman.

CONSTANCE. What woman, Henry.

HENRY. Denise's mother, my sainted mother-in-law. Potato bugs, potato bugs. She'll drive me crazy.

CONSTANCE. What has she done?

HENRY. (Pacing furiously) Done, nothing but talk, but how she talks and what she says. In between potato bugs she talks about how now that France is organized very soon the working people will have to work for what their employers agree to give them. And what will they agree to give them? Well, I can tell you if my cherished mother-in-law has anything to say about it they won't give them anything. I told her what she calls work is just amateurish make-believe, that she never finished anything, that nothing grew, that the potato bugs flourished and she said that I knew nothing about discipline but when I did—

> (DENISE *comes charging in*)

DENISE. Henry, how dare you talk like that to my mother?

HENRY. I tell you all here and now, now and here, solemnly I tell you, if I ever again hear a Frenchman or a Frenchwoman pronounce that word discipline I'll punch their head, and that goes for your mother, Denise, your poor father and Achille have never heard the word. Discipline, how I hate that word, that is the word that all retired government employees use, all retired officers use, discipline, they who never had to fight the battle of life, they who have a sure job and then a pension, they who never had to struggle, discipline, pah, discipline.

DENISE. Well, where is the struggle you're making, where is the money you are earning. Discipline that is what you need, go back to the army and get discipline, like Achille, my mother is right.

HENRY. Bah, it is the unsuccessful people in the world who want to discipline everybody.

DENISE.   Well are you so successful, would you eat any potatoes if they were not yours, would you?

HENRY.   Perhaps yes, perhaps no, who can tell, who can tell, come along. Denise, come along.
(*They go into the house*)

FERDINAND.   Well.

CONSTANCE.   Yes, well, very well.

FERDINAND.   And you, Constance, what are you going to do?
(Sound of tanks below)

CONSTANCE.   What am I going to do, what can I do, I am going to stay.
(She sits, listening)

FERDINAND.   Stay here?

CONSTANCE.   Yes, stay here.

FERDINAND.   Stay here in France?

CONSTANCE.   Yes stay here in France. Yes Ferdinand stay here in France. Here in France where I have had so many pleasant days.
(Rumble of the tanks grows louder, then fades)
Now when the days will not be so pleasant, what else could I do, I could not not stay in France.

FERDINAND.   (Coming to her) Does that mean more than you say?

CONSTANCE.   That means all that I say, and that means that I stay, stay here, stay in France.

FERDINAND.   (Kneeling beside her) And I will be here too.

CONSTANCE.   My poor boy will you?

FERDINAND.   If you stay I will stay.

CONSTANCE.   My poor boy, I hope so, but what can anybody say, perhaps neither of us will stay. Well, anyway, I will begin and stay and you will stay too. Be quiet, Ferdinand—
(FERDINAND buries his head in her lap)
always quiet, until there is no more quiet, no more quiet, no, no more quiet, Ferdinand.

Curtain

ACT ONE ⟩ Scene 2

CONSTANCE's park two years later. Lights come up on stage right. A rustic bench, tree stumps, etc. CONSTANCE is alone, as OLYMPE enters.

OLYMPE. (*Covering her face with her apron*) Mademoiselle, mademoiselle.

CONSTANCE. What is it, Olympe, what is it?

OLYMPE. Oh, Mademoiselle, there I was sitting quietly in my kitchen and cleaning the vegetables, poor Mademoiselle, I cannot cook much but vegetables but I had the sauce left over from the rabbit and that would make the spinach tasty, and I have not told Mademoiselle, it was to be a surprise but Clothilde found an egg.

CONSTANCE. An egg!

OLYMPE. A real egg, a fresh egg and I was cutting it up to garnish the spinach indeed I was cutting it up very fine to make it look more than one egg, the poor Mademoiselle, and there I saw passing the window a Boche, a Boche. Oh, Mademoiselle, oh, Mademoiselle, I never thought to see one of them in my kitchen again, after they went two years ago, after the armistice, and we were the free zone, not so free but still no Boche in my kitchen, but I should have known, Mademoiselle, I should have known. Never once without twice, I should have known, Mademoiselle.
   (She sits on tree stump)

CONSTANCE. Olympe, what does he want?

OLYMPE. What does he want, Mademoiselle, he wants to steal murder burn, but above all steal, Mademoiselle, he wanted to have some keys.

CONSTANCE. What keys?

OLYMPE. What keys, Mademoiselle, I was very dignified, I never showed anything of all I felt, I said, Monsieur le Capitan, must of course have any keys he wishes, but what keys. And just then my sister Clothilde came in, and I came out to warn Mademoiselle. No,

Mademoiselle, I should have known never once without twice and Mademoiselle, Mademoiselle, never twice without thrice, we will have them once again, once again, after this and then if we are not all dead it will be all over. Oh, Mademoiselle, Mademoiselle.

CONSTANCE. But Olympe.

CLOTHILDE. (Enters calling) Mademoiselle, Mademoiselle, they are gone, this time they are gone.

CONSTANCE. For Heaven's sake, Clothilde, for Heaven's sake, what's happened.

CLOTHILDE. You see, Mademoiselle, I said to the Boche capitain, what does Monsieur le Capitain desire, and he said he wanted the keys of the gate of the park, and I said certainly, Monsieur, certainly, and he said who lives here, and I said Madame lives here, she is a relation of the old gentleman, Monsieur de Thuys, who died recently. He said he wished to see Mademoiselle, I replied that unfortunately, and Madame would most certainly regret it exceedingly, but Madame was occupied at the moment and would therefore be unable to see Monsieur le Capitaine, but if Monsieur le Capitain would have the kindness to return in an hour Madame would undoubtedly then be able to receive him.

CONSTANCE. My gracious and what did he say?

CLOTHILDE. He said it was of no importance, he only wished to have the key of the park gate, so that the soldiers could camp there in case of bombardment by the English and Americans while they were passing through the village.

CONSTANCE. My gracious and what did you say Clothilde.

CLOTHILDE. I said that Madame would undoubtedly accede to his request and that indeed I could take it upon myself to give him the keys without disturbing Madame, which indeed I was quite certain he would not desire.

CONSTANCE. My gracious, Clothilde, when you are at your best it is magnificent.

CLOTHILDE. Yes, Mademoiselle, yes it is not for nothing that I as a young woman was trained by the very severe Mme. la Comtesse de Genes. I have never ceased to be thankful for that training.

CONSTANCE. My gracious, and there is nobody here, no Boches.

CLOTHILDE. No, Mademoiselle, no, of course not, of course not, Mademoiselle need never be uneasy, I will always be here, always, Mademoiselle.

OLYMPE. Not once without twice, not twice without thrice, you hear me, not once without twice not twice without thrice.

CONSTANCE. Well, cheer up, Olympe, the twice was not so bad.

OLYMPE. You never can tell about the third, Mademoiselle, you never can tell.

(FERDINAND enters)

FERDINAND. How do you do everybody, what's the matter.

CONSTANCE. The Germans.

FERDINAND. Yes I know they were up at the house too.

CONSTANCE. And what did they do.

FERDINAND. Just wanted to look around and they looked.

OLYMPE. (As she and CLOTHILDE exit) Never once without twice, never twice without thrice.

FERDINAND. Constance!

CONSTANCE. Ferdinand, what are you going to do? Have you made up your mind, have you decided?

FERDINAND. Almost, not altogether, but almost, yes, almost. Yes I guess I will go.

CONSTANCE. Where?

FERDINAND. (Dropping down on a tree stump) To Germany. You see Christian, you know Denise's young brother, he too is twenty and our class is called and perhaps, yes I better go. You see—
(He continues meditatively)
No you don't know. I did not tell you but Christian and I went up the mountain to have a look at the maquis. Well, I don't know, it is pretty bad, they are a pretty lawless lot, gutter snipes you know. Oh yes, not all of them, but anything awful they order you to do you got to do. I don't blame them but could I do it if they ordered

me to do something dreadful. Could I, I am not sure I could. And then anyway, I have two brothers, officers, prisoners in Germany and then there are my father and my mother, if I did not go what would happen to them. Oh hell, yes I guess, Oh hell.

(*He crosses away*)

CONSTANCE.   But Ferdinand.

FERDINAND.   I know Constance, I know, but you know I always say yes.

CONSTANCE.   Yes, of course, but not this yes.

FERDINAND.   Yes this yes. Constance, do I love you as I did, yes and no Constance. Yes and no, you are cool you are refreshing you are like water cool and fresh, but blood is hot, that is it is hot when it is not cold in death.

CONSTANCE.   But Ferdinand, I do not understand.

FERDINAND.   Yes, Constance you do understand, you understand being cool like water, fresh and cool, and all right Constance, what can I say, I can only say Yes Constance, I can only say that today, today is not tomorrow, today is today, and I am going away today. Yes Constance, I am going away today.

CONSTANCE.   But Ferdinand, there will be a tomorrow, yes I can say yes to you, Ferdinand. Ferdinand there will be a tomorrow.

FERDINAND.   Whose tomorrow, no Constance you do understand but you will not understand, you like water remain still and if there is a ripple you still remain still, no Constance no, see Constance, see how our rôles are reversed you used to say no, and I used to say yes, and now I say No and you, you say yes, Oh Constance, will it never be that we say yes, both yes, or no, both no, and that it will be So. Yes and No, such little words such little words to say and no, no, oh Constance, yes I am going away. Yes Constance, I am going away.

(DENISE *enters like a whirlwind*)

DENISE.   Hello Constance, Oh you are there Ferdinand, well I can't help it if it is your family but I have to tell you anyway how awful they are. You know Constance, Henry and I have just come back from staying with Lis family and imagine just imagine it, one day they said that the Marshal was a cretin, one of those awful imbecile things that have a goitre, they said he was a cretin, it was a priest, a cousin of theirs who said he the Marshal, Marshal Petain is a cretin, if it had not been for his sacred office, the priest, I would have struck him, imagine it.

CONSTANCE.   But Denise you knew what their opinions were before you went.

DENISE.   Yes, of course I did, but opinions, well one has to be patient and they are Henry's family but to call, a priest to call Marshal Petain a cretin.

(HENRY *enters bursting with laughter*)

HENRY.   Hel-o-o-o everybody. Oh there you are Denise, there you are. Your pig is dead.

(He sits on a stump)

DENISE.   Pig, our Pig is dead.

HENRY.   Yes, your pig is dead. Now that the miserable little French army is demobilized, Achille is a farmer, and one of your rabbits died of some kind of rabbit disease and Achille thought that the pig would like it, rabbit disease and all, and he fed it to the pig and the pig is dead, that's all the pig is dead.

DENISE.   You beast, if you were not my husband and going to be the father of my child, I would kill you. You beast. Poor mother, and the pig cost so much and now what will we eat, poor poor mother, Oh, you beast.

(DENISE exit)

CONSTANCE.   Is the pig really dead?

HENRY.   You bet he is dead, dead and rotting and even, well even Achille knows you can't eat him. Come along, Denise, come along and console your mother. Achille just takes it modestly, he doesn't mind. Six planes, one pig, what the hell.

(HENRY exit)

CONSTANCE.   Really and truly Ferdinand, you are going to Germany, what does Henry say.

FERDINAND.   (Seated by tree) Henry says that if the war was going to finish in six months then I should stay here but as it is not going to finish in six months but will go on for years yet I had better go.

CONSTANCE.   Henry says that?

FERDINAND.   Yes, Henry says that.

CONSTANCE.   Oh dear, that does make me feel funny.

FERDINAND.   Constance, my poor Constance. Yes Denise keeps on saying it but there is something in it, my poor Constance. You don't understand. How can you understand, no Constance, you do not understand.
(Coming down to her)
There are so many points of view in a Frenchman, of course he cannot agree with any other Frenchman but he cannot even agree with himself inside him that is to say with the other Frenchman which is him. No my poor Constance you do not understand.

CONSTANCE.   But Henry. Henry to tell you to go, to tell *you* so, to tell *you* to go, to go to Germany, you are right Ferdinand, I do not understand. To tell you to go to Germany to help make weapons, which will kill your friends, no Ferdinand, I do not understand.

FERDINAND.   Poor Constance no you do not understand, but after all you are not of a French family no you do not understand. Listen, you always have to choose and struggle to persist, we are not a large population, you have to keep making up your mind, you wait it will all come out right but Henry is right I had better go, he says so, I had better go.

CONSTANCE.   (*Bitterly.*) (Crossing away) You are as bad as Denise and Achille.

FERDINAND.   Perhaps, but I had better go.

CONSTANCE.   (*To herself*) How can I go on with Henry, how can I, how can I go on.

FERDINAND.   Don't be silly, you just make up your mind that you don't understand and you just go on working with Henry. No don't get it into your head that I am going to Germany to do something over there for the resistance. I am just going to Germany because all of my age have to go and there is nothing else to do.

CONSTANCE. (Sits desperately on bench) No, I don't understand, Denise is right, I don't understand.

FERDINAND. When our class is called we go, all men are like that, you Americans never did that, but from the time we are born we Frenchmen know the day and the hour that we have to go to be a soldier, we call ourselves a class and when we are babies we know we belong to a class that is called by the date of the year when we come to be twenty. And then we must go.

CONSTANCE. But Ferdinand you are not going to fight, you say you are not going to fight.

FERDINAND. No not to fight, to persist to exist, but not to fight, no, not to fight.

CONSTANCE. Well then why do you go?

FERDINAND. Well, Marshal Petain, Denise's Marshal Petain, our Marshal Petain he says the class of forty-two must go, he has made excuses he has done what he could to delay but we must go.

CONSTANCE. No, I don't understand. No I don't understand. Denise is right I don't understand. But Ferdinand you did come here to live in this little village so you would not have to go and now you go, Denise is right, I do not understand, no I do not understand.

FERDINAND. My poor Constance, Yes I came to this little village to live and you were here, Constance, yes, you were here, yes, when they were making excuses and helping to save time and Frenchmen, yes we all scattered and hid.
          (He sits beside her)
But now if we do not go worse will happen to everyone, and we must go, yes Constance we must go.

CONSTANCE. But your father and mother could not want you to go you are only a boy Ferdinand, boys cannot endure what you will have to endure if you go. Why not let men go, not boys, surely your father and your mother would not want you to go.

FERDINAND. My dear, my dear, I am not a boy, at most I am a very young man, and a very young man is not a boy, perhaps a very young man is old enough to love and live, to go away and to come

back again, perhaps Constance perhaps, yes Constance yes I must
go and not stay.

    (He starts to go)

Yes Constance, you will stay and not I, I will go away.

CONSTANCE. No I don't understand. I don't understand. Denise is
right I don't understand.

FERDINAND. Denise, well I think she and Henry will find it easier
after I am gone, besides there will be their baby and Denise will
think that it looks like me.

CONSTANCE. Ferdinand.

FERDINAND. (Moving away) Yes she will you'll see she will. I'll
see you again Constance, oh, how do you think I will stand the long
years of exile, how can I, what will I be homesick for, I wonder,
they say you are homesick for such funny things.

    (He turns back)

CONSTANCE. I know what I am homesick for, I am homesick for
a roast chicken and I am homesick for the quays of Paris, often
and often I am homesick for the quays of Paris and a roast chicken.

FERDINAND. Well, I will be homesick for something, perhaps for
everything. Goodbye, Constance, goodbye.

    (CONSTANCE runs to him as he exits)

DENISE. (On the other side of the wall) Henry Henry Henry,
Ferdinand will come back tell me he will.

HENRY. Why not, anybody can come back, the funny thing is to
go, yes that is the funny thing anybody can come back.

DENISE. Oh Henry and when he comes back will he, when he
comes back, but Henry will he come back.

HENRY. I tell you why not, why not come back. He's gone at least
I guess he's gone.

DENISE. (Shouting) Henry you don't mean that he hasn't gone,
that he is gone to join the terrorists, oh Henry, tell me he's gone,
he has gone.

HENRY. Of course he's gone and if he hasn't gone whose business
is it anyway, whose business is it.

DENISE. But Henry he has gone where.

HENRY. To Hell, he has gone to Hell, everywhere is Hell, of course he has gone to Hell.

DENISE. Oh Henry, you are sure he has not joined the terrorists.

HENRY. Hell what are terrorists, who are terrorists, which are terrorists, where in hell, you make me sick, which is hell, where is hell.

DENISE. Well anyway he has not gone to join the terrorists.

HENRY. No.

DENISE. (*Screaming*) No I say he has not gone to join the terrorists.

HENRY. Well if you say so it has to be so.

DENISE. (*Reflectively*) He might have changed his mind, he might have joined the terrorists, Henry do you know that he has gone to say goodbye to Constance so as to change his mind and join the terrorists.

HENRY. Oh shut up.

DENISE. Tell me Henry is Constance in with the terrorists, tell me Henry.

HENRY. Have you ever seen a terrorist.

DENISE. (*Shouting*) Not unless you are one Henry.

HENRY. Well and if I am one.

DENISE. Henry Henry no no no, no sometimes, but no, Constance, no, she likes to, you know, she likes to.

HENRY. She likes to what.

DENISE. She likes to feel as if she was, oh you know Henry, Americans are like that, you know they are, yes she might want Ferdinand to be a terrorist, but she would not want you to be a terrorist, don't think you excite her like that, Henry don't think it.

HENRY. Well if I was a terrorist how would it show.

DENISE. (*Screaming*) You are not a terrorist Henry you could not be the father of my child and be a terrorist, you could not be, Henry.

CONSTANCE. (*Looking over the wall*) Ferdinand has gone.

DENISE. Yes and has he, listen to me, Constance, listen to me, he has gone to Germany.

CONSTANCE. Of course he has gone to Germany, at least I suppose he has gone to Germany.

DENISE. You have no heart Constance, you have no love Constance, you have no life Constance, you have no child Constance. Has Ferdinand gone to Germany.

CONSTANCE. (*Startled*) Of course he has gone to Germany.
     (*Dreamily*)
He was going to be homesick for us all, us all, of course he has gone to Germany.

DENISE. I look at you Constance and I don't know, has he gone to Germany. Henry he won't say, and you, you say, has he gone to Germany.

CONSTANCE. Well of course he has gone to Germany, if he has not gone to Germany where could he go.

DENISE. The terrorists.

CONSTANCE. But he said.

DENISE. Yes I believe him but I don't believe Henry and I don't believe you, what do I know what you know about terrorists what do I know. I believe him but what is the use of believing him when
     (*She screams*)
Henry, he has gone to Germany he is not with the terrorists.

HENRY. Oh shut up.

DENISE. I know you have been crying Constance so he has not gone to the terrorists, you would not cry if he had gone to the terrorists.

HENRY. (*Jumping over the wall*) Go to hell.

CONSTANCE. Ferdinand has gone.

DENISE. Yes he has gone, he has gone to Germany.

CONSTANCE. Yes he has gone, he has gone to Germany.

Curtain

ACT ONE ⸕ Scene 3

Winter evening 1943. A village railroad station. CON-
STANCE stands watching the track as sound of train
fades in distance. A German soldier walks slowly
across the platform and exits. GEORGES POUPET, a workman, enters quietly.

GEORGES.   Bonjour, Mademoiselle.

CONSTANCE.   Oh Georges, there you are, I do like the way a
Frenchman is a workman and a farmer, you don't know which,
most anywhere a workman is a workman and a farmer is a farmer
but you, how can I tell are you a workman today or a farmer?

GEORGES.   I guess Mademoiselle, I am just a Frenchman.

CONSTANCE.   Listen, Georges, what was that funny kind of a train
I just saw passing?

GEORGES.   Funny, well yes, it looks like a small boy's idea of a
train.

CONSTANCE.   It looks like a teapot with that funny cover on it.

GEORGES.   Well I guess it can bust almost as easily as a teapot if
it comes to a try.

CONSTANCE.   But is it it, Georges?

GEORGES.   Yes it is, Mademoiselle, it is it, it is.

CONSTANCE.   And Monsieur Henry has he told you to tell me anything?

GEORGES.   Don't you ever be in a hurry, Mademoiselle. Just you be
natural, you will do your part, just you be natural.

CONSTANCE.   But the train.

GEORGES.   It will pull out and then you just be natural and let
somebody who wants to know know that it has pulled out, any
minute now. You just be natural Mademoiselle, remember just be
natural. Yes a Frenchman is a workman and a farmer, he is just

naturally a Frenchman, you just be natural Mademoiselle, you always do your part. Goodbye Mademoiselle.

(GEORGES *moves away along the track.* DENISE *comes in*)

DENISE.   Constance.

CONSTANCE.   (*Turning*) Hello Denise, what are you doing here, your father and mother and Achille took the last train. Where were you?

DENISE.   Oh Constance I was so busy I had to find someone to take care of little Christine, oh she is so sweet the baby is such a darling, and she does, yes she does, she looks exactly like Ferdinand. I am always telling Henry so, and he says yes she does, she does look just like Ferdinand.

CONSTANCE.   But Denise, how are you going to get to the funeral, the next train won't get there till evening.

DENISE.   Oh that is all right, you know there is no regular funeral.

CONSTANCE.   No regular funeral.

DENISE.   No of course not, poor cousin William, they did not know which bones were which and it would have been awful to bury the bones of one of those terrorists instead of poor dear young cousin William's.

CONSTANCE.   What do you mean Denise?

DENISE.   Well you know that cousin Etienne was killed, that is almost six months ago and he had a proper funeral, he was killed at home.

CONSTANCE.   Yes of course, you all went to the funeral.

DENISE.   Yes poor dear cousin Etienne, he was killed because his brother William was doing his duty as a militian.

CONSTANCE.   But if Etienne was not a militian.

DENISE.   Yes but they were looking for him for William, two men who had quarreled, with him, about some black market, I don't know just what and poor dear cousin Etienne was standing at the window of their chateau and he told the terrorists what he thought of them and they killed him. Oh yes he had a beautiful funeral. They found among his papers one that said that he knew he was the least intelligent of his brothers and he could only be of use staying home and farming and perhaps being killed for one of them and he was, and his mother was so sure now that dear cousin Etienne was in heaven, he could intercede for his brothers and they would none of them be killed, and now poor cousin William who was burning a farm where those wicked terrorists were defending themselves was killed and fell into the flames and was burned up with them, and now poor dear William he can only have a mass he cannot have a funeral. Poor dear young cousin William.

CONSTANCE. A Frenchman killing Frenchmen, how can you Denise, how can you talk like that, how can you?

DENISE. But Constance you do not understand, they are not Frenchmen, they are terrorists and it is the duty of real Frenchmen like my cousin. It is their duty, their duty, their duty, it is their duty.

CONSTANCE. Well I hope every Frenchman who feels it is his duty to kill Frenchmen will end like your cousin William.

DENISE. Oh you and Henry and Henry's family who call Marshal Petain a cretin, you don't know what it is to do your duty, you don't you don't, you don't.
        (A train whistle is heard)
Oh there is my train, goodbye Constance, go up and look at baby Christine, do look at baby Christine, the darling, I am going.
        (*And she crosses the tracks to the train*)

CONSTANCE. My goodness.
        (HENRY *enters*)

HENRY. Hello Constance.

CONSTANCE. Just too late Henry, Denise has just gone, you have missed her.

HENRY. I aimed to miss her.

CONSTANCE. Yes she was all full of how the militias do their duty.

HENRY. Yes I know, but this time it is not Achille, no Achille is Achille, and I went to school with him and he was always Achille, but even he knows better, not even Achille talks like that, it's the

mother, you know she is the direct descendant of the family of
Joan of Arc.

CONSTANCE.   Joan of Arc?

HENRY.   Well, yes I think it was Joan of Arc, it was somebody like
that, yes I think it was Joan of Arc, and as Joan of Arc put the
French King back on his throne and saved France so Denise's
mother thinks she is going to put the king back on his throne and
save France and incidentally her chateau and her property. You
ought to hear them, my God you ought to hear her, just hear her,
yes it's all true enough she is a descendant of the family of Joan
of Arc, she has all the papers, yes it is true, my God it is true, they
make me sick.

CONSTANCE.   Henry have you heard about the armored train? I saw
it pull out in the direction of Bourg. Is everybody warned?

HENRY.   You bet everybody is warned, did you send the message
when it left?

CONSTANCE.   Yes just as I saw it pull out of the station I sent word,
by Georges Poupet.

HENRY.   Don't worry it will be in a ditch, perhaps it is in a ditch
now, probably.
          (*Behind* HENRY *a man with knapsack begins to walk rap-
          idly up and down*)

CONSTANCE.   Don't turn Henry keep on talking to me. Oh about the
baby, anything, keep on talking to me.

HENRY.   All right. Whose baby did you see, anybody's baby you
know?

CONSTANCE.   Yes, an American—Yes my cousin's baby, not your
cousin's baby, my cousin's baby.

HENRY.   Oh Hell.

CONSTANCE.   What shall we do?

HENRY.   First thing to do is to do nothing. How did you recognize
him?

CONSTANCE.   By the way he wears his hat, it's a family matter that, only blood cousins wear their hats like that, none of your cousins wear their hats just like that, and it's hard to copy, just the way it sits on the head. I tell you I know, he is a blood cousin.

HENRY. All right, pay no attention, and if he gets on a train, let him alone, always let everybody alone, let everybody alone.

CONSTANCE. Just a minute, just a minute, yes there is the train, don't turn, Henry. Yes he is on, the train is moving out. God bless him.

HENRY. Perhaps you were mistaken.

CONSTANCE. Don't you believe it. I know a cousin when I see him, you cannot fool me, he was a cousin.

HENRY. Say, you better shut up, here comes somebody who is nobody's cousin, at least I hope to God he is nobody's cousin.

CONSTANCE. What.

HENRY. Oh for Heaven's sake shut up.
(A GERMAN SOLDIER *approaches them*)

GERMAN. How do you do?

CONSTANCE AND HENRY. How do you do?

GERMAN. (*To* HENRY) Isn't the factory working today?

HENRY. Sure it is, I came down to see my wife off, she is going to the funeral of her cousin a militian who was killed by the terrorists. I just had time to come down to see her off but not to go with her and after all I was too late, she was gone.

GERMAN. Yes, yes.
(*And then looking at* HENRY *suddenly*)
How many maquis are there in this town?

HENRY. Maquis, Maquis, there are no maquis in this town.

GERMAN. What is the use of saying there are no maquis in this town? I know how many maquis there are in this town, I know their names, I know where they live, I know what they do and I admire them, they are defending their country. I admire them.

HENRY. I tell you there are not any maquis in this town, I know this town, I know everybody in this town, I know perfectly well that there are no maquis in this town, it is not a kind of a town to have maquis in it, they are not the kind of people to be maquis, you ought to know that I tell you there are no maquis in this town.

GERMAN. Of course there are maquis in this town, I can tell you the exact number of maquis, there are seven maquis in this town, there are three militians and there are seven maquis, but you just tell the maquis that they need not be afraid. I admire them and I would never let anybody do them any harm, not anybody, I admire them, they are good citizens, I admire them.

HENRY. I tell you there are no maquis in this town, how can there be any maquis in this town? Look at that mountain, have you ever been up that mountain, have you ever gone hunting up that mountain with a dog, well you would know you would have to take along a bottle of water for the dog to drink, and how can there be maquis on a mountain that has no springs on it, don't be silly, all this talk about maquis makes me sick, there are no maquis in this town, the town has not guts enough in it to have maquis in it, I tell you there are no maquis in this town.

GERMAN. Don't get excited, yes, it's all right, I know just who are the maquis in this town. I can tell you that nobody will ever touch any of the seven maquis in this town. They are good citizens, I admire them.

(*And the* GERMAN *walks away*)

CONSTANCE. Who is he really, Henry?

HENRY. I don't know who he is, they call him the interpreter, I don't know who he is, they say he is a degraded officer, I don't know who he is, nobody knows who he is or what he is, he just talks like that, he talks like that every now and then he talks like that, and nothing happens, he always talks like that and nothing happens.

CONSTANCE. But Henry, what does he mean?

HENRY. I don't know what he means, I don't know whether he knows what he means, I don't know what he means, I don't know whether God knows what he means, I don't know, I don't know what he means.

Curtain

ACT TWO , Scene 1

CONSTANCE'S *salon three days later.* CONSTANCE *is standing at the French doors watching,* HENRY *comes in.*

HENRY. (Hurrying to the fireplace) Oh I am cold, I am just chilled to death, three days up in those mountains all night waiting for the parachute to come down and of course it didn't come.

CONSTANCE. But it did come.

HENRY. Of course it came, would I be here if it had not come? My gracious I am cold, I am frozen. Give me a drink. My gracious it was cold.
          (CONSTANCE *giving him a drink*)

CONSTANCE. (*Timidly*) And Henry, did you hear anything about that man I said was my blood cousin, did you hear anything about him?

HENRY. What should I hear about him, you don't suppose he would be so foolish as to be sitting on top of a mountain waiting for dynamite to fall from Heaven, the way we do, anyway perhaps he wasn't an American.

CONSTANCE. But he was, Henry, he was I can always tell, it was the way he walked, but mostly it was the way he wore his hat. An American man wears his hat differently from a Frenchman or an Englishman. Yes he does.

HENRY. Well, all right, all right, perhaps he does wear his hat differently, yes I told the boys if they know anything to let us know, but how can they know which one we saw. It might have been a Canadian.

CONSTANCE. (*Doubtfully*) It might.

HENRY. Well anyway there was one thing, the TNT is here and it's hid and now to move it, your American can't help with that, so forget him. He seemed to know where he was going. Now you know where the stuff is hid, will you get it moved and I'll go back to the factory. Oh it's cold my feet are cold and my head is cold and my fingers are cold but it's all hid and there won't be any more for ten days now so get it moved, get it moved.

(*As he goes out he turns and says*)

The armored train is in the water in a ditch. I saw it.

CONSTANCE. (*Calling* OLYMPE *and* CLOTHILDE) Olympe, Clothilde, go and tell the neighbor that I want to see Georges Poupet, I want him to cut some wood up for me, if he has the time.

DISTANT VOICES. Very well, Mademoiselle.

(CONSTANCE turns on radio, during a German news broadcast, GEORGES POUPET *comes in*)

CONSTANCE. Georges, the stuff has come, it is in the usual place, can you get it and leave it somewhere for it to be taken away?

GEORGES. Well, Mademoiselle, you see I can't put it in my house, that is where I usually keep it for them to take away, but the last time I had some there I did not tell you, while I was at my work at the railroad and my wife was out on an errand, three Germans came to the house and said they wanted to look around. My little girl was there and she said I was at work and her mother was out and she did not have the key, so they said they would wait and my wife came along and they asked where I was and my wife said that of course I was at the railroad yard working and what did they want. Well they said they wanted to look around, certainly she said come in and she took them in and she opened a bottle of wine and they said they wanted to look around, and she said certainly, you must do what pleases you, and they said well they guessed there was nothing particular to look for, and my wife said not that she knew of and they drank some more wine and then they went away. When I got home I was more worried than my wife because in the attic there was a lot of stuff. So now what shall I do? I could put it in my wine cellar but how to let them know.

CONSTANCE. Don't worry about that, they can be let know.

GEORGES. All right, Mademoiselle, you can count on me. They never notice me. I put the pack on my back and I carry a hoe on the front of my bicycle and they think I have just dug up my potatoes.

CONSTANCE. But can there always be potatoes.

GEORGES. Ah, in this country Mademoiselle, there are always potatoes young potatoes or old potatoes and if there are not potatoes there are turnips, don't you worry Mademoiselle, just you let them know where my wine cellar is and I will leave the key in a hole in the wall. There is no wine there so they can come. Goodbye Mademoiselle, I'll come in and tell you if everything is all right.

CONSTANCE. Goodbye Georges. I won't wish you good luck because that does sometimes bring bad. Do you know when I used to see you men with a pack on your back I used to be jealous, I thought you were getting more to eat out of the country than I was.

GEORGES. Well it is getting something to eat all right because the sooner we get these birds out of the country the sooner we will have more to eat. Goodbye Mademoiselle.
(GEORGES *leaves.* CONSTANCE *watches him go.* DENISE *comes running in, breathless*)

DENISE. Constance, Constance, oh Constance, Constance.

CONSTANCE. What is it Denise, what's the matter?

DENISE. Oh Constance, this morning I was not feeling very well, I was tired and so I did not get up but decided that I and my little daughter, the tiny little baby Christine and I would have our breakfast in bed together. I always dreamed when I was a little girl that someday I would be grown up and having a baby girl and we would have breakfast in bed together. Well we were having breakfast in bed together and I thought I heard Henry's voice outside and I payed no attention and we went on having breakfast together, Baby Christine and I and then I thought I heard another voice and then suddenly I knew, it was Ferdinand and then I sat up in bed and I cried and I cried and I cried and Baby Christine cried and I cried and I cried and there was Ferdinand standing in the doorway and I cried and I cried.

CONSTANCE. And what did Ferdinand say?

DENISE. Say, what did he say, why he did not say anything, he was just there and as I cried I said, look Baby Christine is just the image of you. I always tell Henry so and he says so, Oh

Ferdinand she is just the image of you and there I sat in the bed and I cried and cried.

CONSTANCE.   And what is he going to do?

DENISE.   I don't know, Constance, I don't know what he is going to do, he is going to see his family, I suppose he is going to see his mother and his father, oh Constance. And I must go back to Baby Christine, Oh Constance.
    (*And she dashes away*)
    (*Suddenly* FERDINAND *appears* at the French doors)

CONSTANCE.   (*Running to him*) Oh, Ferdinand.

FERDINAND.   Yes, I am here.

CONSTANCE.   Are you really here?

FERDINAND.   Yes, I am really here.

CONSTANCE.   Stand in the light, let me look at you, you don't look thin, you look rather fatter than you did but your color is not good and your lips are pale.

FERDINAND.   Yes, that German food is bloating, it does not suit French stomachs.

CONSTANCE.   But did you have enough?

FERDINAND.   Enough, whatever you have is enough, but we helped out by buying black.

CONSTANCE.   But I thought they said there was no black market in Germany.
    (FERDINAND *goes to fireplace*)

FERDINAND.   (*Laughing*) No there is no black market in Germany for Germans but there is lots of black market in Germany for foreign workers. You see foreign workers work everywhere, on farms, in bakeries, in butcher shops, in grocery shops and they carry the stuff around as truck drivers and of course everybody steals a little and they trade it and they sell it among themselves, the Germans have nothing to do with it and then others go out and steal a little of the stacks of vegetables that are covered with earth. In one way and another there is a lively traffic among foreign workers.

CONSTANCE. But isn't it dangerous, do not the Germans punish it dreadfully?

FERDINAND. Germans, what can they do, it takes all their police to keep their own people under, they have none to spare for the foreign workers, there are almost ten million of them, what can the paltry police do with that, no, we have no arms, we cannot resist or fight but we can steal and we all do and I tell you that the black market for foreign workers is a mighty lively affair.

CONSTANCE. (Sitting down near fire) It is all so strange, tell me more. Did you suffer?

FERDINAND. Suffer for myself, no. I was very well off as I was about the most educated one in my factory they made me what they call the confidence man, that is the man who acts between the French workman and the Germans, to settle quarrels and difficulties of all sorts. That is the reason I am here, as a man of confidence I was given ten days leave.

CONSTANCE. And then, Ferdinand?

FERDINAND. And then I disappear.

CONSTANCE. Into Germany?

FERDINAND. No Constance, not into Germany, no not into Germany, in a way there my life was not hard but in a way, you know I went to see my brothers. I did not see both, I only saw one.
        (He sits beside her)
Oh it was pretty bad. Because of my position in the factory they gave me permission to go and see my brother. I travelled a good many miles and then at last I saw him, well up in the north. I went by railroad, and when I arrived they took me in to see him, it was in a room and I was told to sit down and then he came in accompanied by two guards and one of them sat down at a table and there were two chairs opposite for us. When I saw my brother come in, three years of prison, three years, more than three years, tears came to my eyes and I almost broke down. My brother gave me one stern look and I pulled myself together, I understood, a Frenchman should not shed tears before a German. We sat next to each other and I showed him the photographs I had brought from home and he showed me those he had on him all that time

and we each one put his back in his pocket. And the German adjutant said, you have exchanged photographs which you were told not to do. Silence, said my brother, you have a list of the photographs I had, examine them, see if they are changed, and he placed his package on the table, the man mumbled something. Examine them, said my brother, and apologize, and the man half opened the package and mumbled an excuse. My brother and I parted, he was still a French officer with the pride of a French officer.

CONSTANCE. You poor boy.

FERDINAND. Yes, while we were in the factory, it is funny you know there are so many funny sides to a Frenchman. You know I hate to say it but it is true the French were the only ones in the factory that did any work and not because they wanted to help the Boches, goodness knows not that. Not any of them that, not even Denise's brother Christian, not that, but Frenchmen can't see work before them and not do it, they are funny that way, they are. If they see work before them they do it, they just can't help themselves, they just can't so they were the only ones who did any work, most of them, the Greeks and the Italians and Poles, etc., did not work just because they were lazy but the Russians, oh the Russians they were wonderful. They could work but they wouldn't they wouldn't. How horribly they were treated, beaten and starved and then not until they were almost dead did they give in and work for a month until they had built a little strength and then they would again refuse.

CONSTANCE. And did you get to know any but the French?

FERDINAND. Only the Russians. You couldn't trust the Poles, the Belgians, the Dutch, they might betray you and the Italians and the Greeks were not interesting, but the Russians you could trust as you would a Frenchman. One I got to know very well. One day he said quite calmly, some day we will beat the Germans, that I believe and when we have beaten them we will make them miserable. The quiet tone in which he said it, well you know we Frenchmen, we forget and forgive and forgive and forget. You know they say of us we have no rancor and we haven't. Well perhaps this time, perhaps.

CONSTANCE. And now Ferdinand?

FERDINAND. (Rising to go) As I told you Constance, I will disappear, nobody will know where I am not even Henry. I will disappear, I might be dead, I will disappear.

CONSTANCE. (Rising) Yes, Ferdinand.

FERDINAND. Goodbye Constance.

CONSTANCE. Goodbye Ferdinand.
(FERDINAND *leaves. A long pause then voices from below*)

VOICES. Mademoiselle, Mademoiselle, Georges Poupet wants to see you, he wants to see you.

CONSTANCE. Tell him to come in.
(GEORGES POUPET *comes in*)

GEORGES. It's all right Mademoiselle, it's all right, everything is all right. It's carried and it's put away in my wine cellar on the mountain and the key is there, it's all right.

CONSTANCE. And nothing happened, Georges?

GEORGES. No nothing, you know those stupid Germans, they would never suspect a man of fifty, a trusted railroad employee would be carrying explosives for the maquis in a sack on his back, not they, they are stupid, they think young men would be doing that, so they always examine the things young men carry but they never stop us old ones, and that is the reason we old ones do all the carrying. We don't let any young ones do what we can do. They go up into the mountains, into the snow to receive it, we old ones can't do that and beside the Germans are scared to go up into the mountains, but the carrying, no we old ones do that.
(HENRY'S *voice outside calling harshly*)

HENRY. Constance, are you there?

CONSTANCE. Yes and Georges too, come in.
(HENRY *comes in, his face is filled with fury and grief*)

CONSTANCE. What is it Henry, what is it, Georges is here, everything is all right.

GEORGES. What is it?

HENRY. What is it, what is it, those dirty beasts, those dirty Boches, those loathly birds, they have killed my father.

CONSTANCE. Killed your father, Henry?

HENRY. Yes, killed my father.

GEORGES. Killed your father, Mister Henry?

HENRY. (Pacing) Yes, killed my father, he was a retired surgeon but he went around as there are so few doctors to do what he could, went around, old as he was, on his bicycle, and those dirty Boches said that he had taken care of some maquis and they caught him on the road and they shot him and they left him there. Oh my God, they shot him and they left him there, and my poor mother, all alone there. She telegraphed and she said the Germans killed him. She put it in, the Germans killed him so Denise and her damned family could not say that it was terrorists and maquis who shot him. Oh my God, oh my God. I love my wife, I adore my baby.

 (Drops down on sofa sobbing)
Oh my God, oh my God. Where is Ferdinand?

GEORGES. Mister Henry, Mister Henry, we will avenge him, Mister Henry, we will and soon.

HENRY. You bet your life, Georges, and mine and everybody's, we will avenge him, every one of us will avenge him. Where is Ferdinand?

CONSTANCE. Ferdinand is gone.

HENRY. Gone home to our family?

CONSTANCE. No, Henry, no. He said he would not go home, he thought it best not to go home. He said he would disappear, and not even you would know where he was, he would disappear.

HENRY. (Rising) My God.

GEORGES. Mister Henry.

Curtain

ACT TWO ⁊ Scene 2

CONSTANCE's salon, August 25th, 1944. Intermittent gunfire in background. CONSTANCE is at radio, the gunfire draws her to window, then she rushes back to radio as HENRY enters.

CONSTANCE.   Henry. What's happened Henry?

HENRY.   My father is avenged. My knuckles are broken but my father is avenged.

CONSTANCE.   Henry what happened?

HENRY.   We fought, we killed, we made prisoners and I beat the prisoners up. I did not shoot them, I beat them up, my knuckles are broken and my father is avenged.

CONSTANCE.   Oh Henry, now everything is going so well, every-thing is terrible. Henry, Henry.

HENRY.   There you are Constance, yes, how can you hate, how can you when you have never suffered, that is to say when your country has never suffered. France has suffered, how many times she has suffered, how many times she has been avenged. How often have sons avenged their fathers. I have avenged my father, and pretty soon now we will avenge our country, pretty soon.

CONSTANCE.   Will it be very soon, Henry?

HENRY.   It will be soon.
          (CONSTANCE sits slowly at sofa)
I have not told you but Ferdinand knew about my father being killed.

CONSTANCE.   Oh Henry, have you seen him?

HENRY.   Yes I saw him but he knew about it before I saw him. He hunted me up when he heard and after he too had avenged my father.

CONSTANCE.   Did he?

HENRY.   Yes, Constance, he did, he did avenge my father. It is queer how he heard about it. He had been sent on a mission to find out something that was happening and he had to go into a government office and there he heard two men talking and they told that my father had been killed. Ferdinand was there at the door and he heard them tell that my father had been killed.

CONSTANCE.   Poor, poor Ferdinand.

HENRY.   Don't worry, my father is avenged, don't you worry about that. Ferdinand did and I did it, they have paid, those dirty beasts have paid.

CONSTANCE.   Henry, it is not true that I do not understand. I do understand but oh, dear.

HENRY.   I know, it is all right, but you see, feeling the way you do, well it makes me sick. You don't want the reward of your work. You've worked well, but you don't want the reward of your vengeance and so you don't want the reward of your work, what work, the reward of your work is vengeance, and you don't want is the use of working if you do not want the reward of your work. What's the use? Well, I do and I'll have it. I have avenged my father, so has Ferdinand and now I will avenge France and so will Ferdinand. That is the reward for our work. You have worked well Constance, but you don't want the reward of your work. You wait, not you but perhaps, well no use talking, no use, you're nice, you're courageous but you have no guts, Constance. You don't want the reward of your work.

>   (HENRY *storms out of the room.* CONSTANCE *begins to play with the radio, suddenly the announcer announces*)

ANNOUNCER.   Attention, attention, attention, Paris is free. Attention, attention, Paris is free.

CONSTANCE.   I don't care what Henry says, that is the reward of my work.

>   (OLYMPE *and* CLOTHILDE *enter the room*)

CLOTHILDE.   Oh Mademoiselle, is it true, is it, is it true that Paris is free.

OLYMPE.   Georges Poupet just called out that Paris is free.

CONSTANCE.   (*Kissing them on both cheeks*) Yes, my dears, it is true, where is Georges, I want to kiss him, Georges.

GEORGES. (*Coming in*) Yes, Mademoiselle, it is true, Paris is free and we are free, we have just shot fifty Boches that were left in the marshes, shot them like rabbits, they are like rabbits, when they do not win they run like rabbits and we shoot them like rabbits. I shot five. Shot them dead, all five of them.

CLOTHILDE. Of course you did, you good brave Georges.

OLYMPE. We heard you shoot them.

CLOTHILDE. When we remember how they occupied this house in forty and how they slept in the house.

OLYMPE. And took sunbaths all naked on the lawn.

CLOTHILDE. And then the day of the Armistice, the beasts.

OLYMPE. We were just two sad lonely old women.

CLOTHILDE. And they put their phonograph in front of our kitchen door and it blared out all their horrible German songs.

OLYMPE. And each one would come into the kitchen and call out—

CLOTHILDE. France Kaput. And we just wouldn't cry in front of them.

OLYMPE. No we just wouldn't.

CLOTHILDE. And they broke open our trunks and they stole all our shoes and stockings.

OLYMPE. All we had.

CLOTHILDE. Oh the dirty beasts, Germany Kaput.

OLYMPE. Germany Kaput.

CLOTHILDE. Oh Georges.

OLYMPE. Oh Mademoiselle.
(*They both fall weeping*)
Yes, now we can cry, now they are gone, gone forever.

CLOTHILDE. Yes, now we can cry, now we can.

CONSTANCE. (*Patting them both*) Now pull yourselves together, we have to make flags, French flags and American flags and English flags and Russian flags.

GEORGES. No use in making them, Mademoiselle, you can buy them, and American and French flag ribbon.

CONSTANCE. From whom?

GEORGES. (*Laughing*) From the bazaar, the biggest collabo in this town, the one who said everybody should send their sons to Germany to help the Germans and he was consistent enough, he sent his. He has his store full of flags. French flags, English flags and ribbons, no, no Russian flags. Everybody is in there buying them, he is just coining money.

CONSTANCE. Will I ever understand? But Georges, where did he get them?

GEORGES. Get them, he always had them, he was sure the Germans were going to win but he kept them all, well he always keeps everything. I suppose some of them were left over from the last war and now he is as pleased as anything to have them and to sell them and everybody is as pleased as anything to buy them.

CONSTANCE. But Georges, how is it that the Germans did not find them?

GEORGES. Because he had them put away, hid them if you like, but what difference would it make. The Germans, bah, the Germans, they never found anything.

CONSTANCE. Well, all of you go to that collabo and buy a lot of them and we will cover the house with them and lots of ribbon for the children.
(*They all go out.* DENISE *comes rushing in*)

DENISE. Hello Constance.

CONSTANCE. Are you pleased, Denise, pleased that Paris is free?

DENISE. Of course, of course, well yes, of course, although, well yes, of course, do you know Constance, Achille is joining the army, he says that he will help the Americans beat Japan.

CONSTANCE. He does say that does he. Well you can tell him from me, that the Americans don't want him, they won't have him. You can tell him that from me.

DENISE. What do you mean, won't have him? They have to have him, the French army wants him, of course they want him, he has written to his old captain to tell him he is ready to join him. My gracious not want an aviator who has brought down six enemy planes. Of course they will want him.

CONSTANCE. (*Angrily*) I tell you they don't want him and they won't have him. The French army can take him if they want him, we don't. But anyway Denise, what does he want to fight for now, why doesn't he stick to his opinions?

DENISE. Of course you don't understand, you never understand. As long as the Marshal was at the head of the government, he obeyed the Marshal, any good soldier would and now that the Marshal is not any longer at the head of the government, why naturally Achille obeys the man who is at present at the head of the government and so he joins the army. Anybody ought to be able to understand that.

CONSTANCE. So Achille is just like a dog, when you tell him to come to heel he comes to heel and when you tell him to fight, he fights. What's the use of being a man if you are going to be like that, what is the use? Well I can tell you the American army does not want anybody like that fighting with them. I don't much think the French army does either.

DENISE. You are just jealous, you don't know anybody who has ever brought down six airplanes.

CONSTANCE. And did not wear his decorations because he was so modest although everybody knew about it.

DENISE. You are horrible, I always hated you but when America was not successful I did not care so much but now that America is successful, that she has gotten rid of the dear Marshal, that she has opened the door to Bolshevism, that she hates the aristocracy, I tell you Constance, I just hate you, hate you and all Americans, I hate you.

CONSTANCE. And still Achille wants to fight side by side with them.

DENISE.   Well, if he does it is because he does because as a soldier he does.

CONSTANCE.   There is no use talking, Denise, they won't have him. Nothing could make me believe the French army would have him. No I don't believe they would have him in spite of his six airplanes. No, all this time, well we did not say much, but now France is free we tell each other what we really think. No the French army does not want Achille.

DENISE.   You beast, if they don't take him I know it will be your fault, the fault of those awful Americans, and it will break my mother's heart and it will disappoint Achille, and never, never, never, no never will I speak to you again, no never.
         (*She rushes out.* CONSTANCE *sits down heavily*)

CONSTANCE.   Oh, my gracious.
         (OLYMPE *and* CLOTHILDE *come in with arms full of flags*)

CLOTHILDE.   Oh, Mademoiselle, just think there are lots of little children in this town who have never seen any flag.

OLYMPE.   Not any kind of a flag, not even a Boche flag.

CLOTHILDE.   You know they never carried flags, we don't know why but they never did and little children who are now five and six years old have never seen a flag.

OLYMPE.   And certainly never seen a French flag. You should have seen, they touched the flags so timidly.

CLOTHILDE.   And one little one wanted to know what it was.

OLYMPE.   And we knew you would like it and we pinned pieces of American ribbon on each one and then we made them stand up in front of the French flag and say, "Vive la France."

CLOTHILDE.   "Honor to the Maquis."

OLYMPE.   And the darlings, they all said it.

CLOTHILDE.   And we were so happy and they are so happy and it is all so wonderful.

OLYMPE.   We are free and everybody's eyes are all smiling.

CLOTHILDE. Oh dear me.
(*They both begin to cry*)

OLYMPE. Yes.
(*They both begin to laugh*)

CLOTHILDE. We can cry now all we want.

OLYMPE. Yes, Mademoiselle, we can.
(HENRY *enters*)

HENRY. Hello you old dears, my gracious, you have gotten flags, has the old collabo any left now that you have bought out the collection. Well, hang them out, hang them out.
(OLYMPE and CLOTHILDE exit with flags)

CONSTANCE. Henry, I have just had a dreadful quarrel with Denise, a really dreadful quarrel.

HENRY. (Pouring himself a drink) Did you? Well one does and one does not but one mostly does, did you?

CONSTANCE. Yes, Henry and this time really this time we probably will never speak to each other again.

HENRY. Well, perhaps not and then perhaps you will. You never can tell.

CONSTANCE. Henry, don't be so unfeeling.

HENRY. Unfeeling and I have just come from a wonderful family scene, Denise was not there, she was busy quarreling with you but all the rest of them were there.

CONSTANCE. And Achille.

HENRY. Achille, my gracious, poor Achille, he is holding his head and surrounded with papers he must sign to get back into the army. But in every one there is the question, what did you do for the resistance. No, they don't say, what did you do in the great war, daddy, but what did you do for the resistance. And, oh my goodness, Achille, what did he.

CONSTANCE. Well then he won't be taken into the army.

HENRY. Not unless he finds out that he did do something for the resistance. You never can tell perhaps he will find out that he did something for the resistance, perhaps he will.

CONSTANCE.   Oh Henry, it is so awful now we are all so happy and we are all quarreling. Oh Henry it is awful.

HENRY.   Why not, if not why not. Oh you ought to see them. You see now of course, now there is going to be communism, anyway that is the way they feel about it and they think, the old mother thinks, of course the old father never thinks anything, the old mother thinks she better divide up the property among the children so the communists won't notice as they might if it was all together, but she hates to let go. How she hates to let go.

CONSTANCE.   And what do you get, Henry?

HENRY.   Well, as the most unpopular son-in-law I only get a duck pond with the meadow around it. My, it's funny. Hello, if there isn't Ferdinand. Come in, Ferdinand, well, well.

CONSTANCE.   Ferdinand.

HENRY.   Yes, there he is.
          (FERDINAND *comes in*)

FERDINAND.   Paris is free.

HENRY.   As if we didn't know it. Yes, Paris is free. Have you said goodbye up at the house, Ferdinand?

FERDINAND.   Yes, I have said goodbye.

HENRY.   Well, so long, old man.

FERDINAND.   So long.
          (HENRY *embraces* FERDINAND *and goes*)

CONSTANCE.   Why are you saying goodbyes up at the house?

FERDINAND.   Because goodbyes have to be said.

CONSTANCE.   Ferdinand, you know I have had a dreadful quarrel with Denise and I do not really think that we will ever speak to each other again.

FERDINAND.   Does that really matter, Constance?

CONSTANCE.   Ferdinand, what do you mean?

FERDINAND. Why should it matter, it's all over. You will never see any of us again, you won't see Henry. Henry loves his wife and adores his little girl and it's all over and that is all there is when it's all over.

CONSTANCE. Is it really all over?

FERDINAND. Yes, really all over. You will go back to the quays of Paris and sooner or later to roasted chickens.

CONSTANCE. And you, Ferdinand?

FERDINAND. Ah, this time I do disappear.

CONSTANCE. Disappear, where to?

FERDINAND. Hush, you did say that yes is for a very young man. You must not ask but I'll tell you just the same, to Germany. No I do not go back there to work, but I am being sent to organize my fellow countrymen.

CONSTANCE. Ferdinand.

FERDINAND. Yes, Constance, this is our war, you have done your share, your countrymen will fight some more, but this is our war, our war, and we will fight it and we will win.

CONSTANCE. Yes, I know, and so it is all over.

FERDINAND. Yes, look facts in the face, Constance, for you it is all over, for Henry it is all over, but for me it is just beginning, yes is for a very young man.

CONSTANCE. Yes, Ferdinand, yes Ferdinand.

FERDINAND. I won't have time to think so I won't think about you and the quays of Paris and the roast chickens and Henry and Denise and the little girl who looks like me, no I won't have time to think. Goodbye, Constance.

CONSTANCE. (Extending her hand) Goodbye Ferdinand.
(FERDINAND shakes her hand, then kisses it and leaves)

Curtain

THE MOTHER OF US ALL

≀ 1946 ≀

ACT I

(Prologue sung by Virgil T.)

Pity the poor persecutor.
    Why,
If money is money isn't money money,
    Why,
Pity the poor persecutor,
    Why,
Is money money or isn't money money.
    Why.
Pity the poor persecutor.
Pity the poor persecutor because the poor persecutor
    always gets to be poor
    Why,
Because the persecutor gets persecuted
Because is money money or isn't money money,
    That's why,
When the poor persecutor is persecuted he has to cry,
    Why,
Because the persecutor always ends by being persecuted,
    That is the reason why.
  (Virgil T. after he has sung his prelude begins to sit)

Virgil T.   Begin to sit.
                    Begins to sit.
                    He begins to sit.
                    That's why.
                    Begins to sit.
                    He begins to sit.
                    And that is the reason why.

ACT I ⸲ Scene 1

Daniel Webster.	He digged a pit, he digged it deep
	    he digged it for his brother.
	Into the pit he did fall in the pit
	    he digged for tother.

All the Characters.	Daniel was my father's name, My father's name was Daniel.
Jo the Loiterer.	Not Daniel.
Chris the Citizen.	Not Daniel in the lion's den.
All the Characters.	My father's name was Daniel.

G. S.	My father's name was Daniel, Daniel
	    and a bear, a bearded Daniel,
	not Daniel in the lion's den not
	    Daniel, yes Daniel my father had
	a beard my father's name was Daniel,

Daniel Webster.	He digged a pit he digged it deep
	    he digged it for his brother,
	Into the pit he did fall in the pit
	    he digged for tother.

Indiana Elliot.	Choose a name.
Susan B. Anthony.	Susan B. Anthony is my name to choose a name is feeble, Susan B. Anthony is my name, a name can only be a name my name can only be my name, I have a name, Susan B. Anthony is my name, to choose a name is feeble.
Indiana Elliot.	Yes that's easy, Susan B. Anthony is that kind of a name but my name Indiana Elliot. What's in a name.
Susan B. Anthony.	Everything.
G. S.	My father's name was Daniel he had a black beard he was not tall not at all tall, he had a black beard his name was Daniel.
All the Characters.	My father had a name his name was Daniel.
Jo the Loiterer.	Not Daniel
Chris a Citizen.	Not Daniel not Daniel in the lion's den not Daniel.

Susan B. Anthony.	I had a father, Daniel was not his name.
Indiana Elliot.	I had no father no father.
Daniel Webster.	He digged a pit he digged it deep he digged it for his brother,
	into the pit he did fall in the pit he digged for tother.

ACT I ⸗ Scene II

Jo the Loiterer.	I want to tell
Chris the Citizen.	Very well
Jo the Loiterer.	I want to tell oh hell.
Chris the Citizen.	Oh very well.
Jo the Loiterer.	I want to tell oh hell I want to tell about my wife.
Chris the Citizen.	And have you got one.
Jo the Loiterer.	No not one.
Chris the Citizen.	Two then
Jo the Loiterer.	No not two.
Chris.	How many then
Jo the Loiterer.	I haven't got one. I want to tell oh hell about my wife I haven't got one.
Chris the Citizen.	Well.
Jo the Loiterer.	My wife, she had a garden.
Chris the Citizen.	Yes
Jo the Loiterer.	And I bought one.
Chris the Citizen.	A wife.

No said Jo I was poor and I bought a garden.
And then said Chris. She said, said Jo, she
said my wife said one tree in my garden was
her tree in her garden. And said Chris, Was
it. Jo, We quarreled about it. And then said
Chris. And then said Jo, we took a train and
we went where we went. And then said
Chris. She gave me a little package said Jo.
And was it a tree said Chris. No it was money
said Jo. And was she your wife said Chris,
yes said Jo when she was funny, How funny
said Chris. Very funny said Jo. Very funny

said Jo. To be funny you have to take everything in the kitchen and put it on the floor,
you have to take all your money and all your
jewels and put them near the door you have
to go to bed then and leave the door ajar.
That is the way you do when you are funny.

Chris the Citizen. Was she funny.

Jo the Loiterer. Yes she was funny.

(Chris and Jo put their arms around each other)

Angel More. Not any more I am not a martyr any more,
not any more.
Be a martyr said Chris.

Angel More. Not any more. I am not a martyr any more.
Surrounded by sweet smelling flowers I
fell asleep three times.
Darn and wash and patch, darn and wash
and patch, darn and wash and patch
darn and wash and patch.

Jo the Loiterer. Anybody can be accused of loitering.

Chris Blake
a Citizen. Any loiterer can be accused of loitering.

Henrietta M. Daniel Webster needs an artichoke.

Angel More. Susan B. is cold in wet weather.

Henry B. She swore an oath she'd quickly come to any
one to any one.

Anthony Comstock. Caution and curiosity, oil and
obligation, wheels and appurtenances,
in the way of means.

Virgil T. What means.

John Adams. I wish to say I also wish to stay,
I also wish to go away, I also wish
I endeavor to also wish.

Angel More. I wept on a wish.

John Adams. Whenever I hear any one say of course,
do I deny it, yes I do deny it whenever
I hear any one say of course I deny it,
I do deny it.

Thaddeus S. Be mean.

Daniel Webster. Be there.

Henrietta M. Be where

Constance Fletcher.	I do and I do not declare that roses and wreaths, wreaths and roses around and around, blind as a bat, curled as a hat and a plume, be mine when I die, farewell to a thought, he left all alone, be firm in despair dear dear never share, dear dear, dear dear, I constance Fletcher dear dear, I am a dear, I am dear dear I am a dear, here there everywhere. I bow myself out.
Indiana Elliot.	Anybody else would be sorry.
Susan B. Anthony.	Hush, I hush, you hush, they hush, we hush. Hush.
Gloster Heming and Isabel Wentworth.	We, hush, dear as we are, we are very dear to us and to you we hush, we hush you say hush, dear hush. Hush dear.
Anna Hope.	I open any door, that is the way that any day is to-day, any day is to-day I open any door every door a door.
Lillian Russell.	Thank you.
Anthony Comstock.	Quilts are not crazy, they are kind.
Jenny Reefer.	My goodness gracious me.
Ulysses S. Grant.	He knew that his name was not Eisenhower. Yes he knew it. He did know it.
Herman Atlan.	He asked me to come he did ask me.
Donald Gallup.	I chose a long time, a very long time, four hours are a very long time, I chose, I took a very long time, I took a very long time. Yes I took a very long time to choose, yes I did.
T. T. and A. A.	They missed the boat yes they did they missed the boat.
Jo a Loiterer.	I came again but not when I was expected, but yes when I was expected because they did expect me.
Chris the Citizen.	I came to dinner.

(They all sit down)

Curtain

ACT I ⨍ Scene III

(Susan B. Anthony and Daniel Webster seated in two straight-
backed chairs not too near each other. Jo the Loiterer
comes in)

Jo the Loiterer.	I don't know where a mouse is I don't know what a mouse is. What is a mouse.
Angel More.	I am a mouse
Jo the Loiterer.	Well
Angel More.	Yes Well
Jo the Loiterer.	All right well. Well what is a mouse
Angel More.	I am a mouse
Jo the Loiterer.	Well if you are what is a mouse
Angel More.	You know what a mouse is, I am a mouse.
Jo the Loiterer.	Yes well, And she.

(Susan B. dressed like a Quakeress turns around)

Susan B.	I hear a sound.
Jo the Loiterer.	Yes well
Daniel Webster.	I do not hear a sound. When I am told.
Susan B. Anthony.	Silence.

(Everybody is silent)

Susan B. Anthony.	Youth is young, I am not old.
Daniel Webster.	When the mariner has been tossed for many days, in thick weather, and on an unknown sea, he naturally avails himself of the first pause in the storm.
Susan B. Anthony.	For instance. They should always fight. They should be martyrs. Some should be martyrs. Will they. They will.
Daniel Webster.	We have thus heard sir what a resolution is.
Susan B. Anthony.	I am resolved.
Daniel Webster.	When this debate sir was to be resumed on Thursday it so happened that it would have been convenient for me to be elsewhere.
Susan B.	I am here, ready to be here. Ready to be where. Ready to be here. It is my habit.
Daniel Webster.	The honorable member complained that I had slept on his speech.
Susan B.	The right to sleep is given to no woman.

Daniel Webster.	I did sleep on the gentleman's speech; and slept soundly.
Susan B.	I too have slept soundly when I have slept, yes when I have slept I too have slept soundly.
Daniel Webster.	Matches and over matches.
Susan B.	I understand you undertake to overthrow my undertaking.
Daniel Webster.	I can tell the honorable member once for all that he is greatly mistaken, and that he is dealing with one of whose temper and character he has yet much to learn.
Susan B.	I have declared that patience is never more than patient. I too have declared, that I who am not patient am patient.
Daniel Webster.	What interest asks he has South Carolina in a canal in Ohio.
Susan B.	What interest have they in me, what interest have I in them, who holds the head of whom, who can bite their lips to avoid a swoon.
Daniel Webster.	The harvest of neutrality had been great, but we had gathered it all.
Susan B.	Near hours are made not by shade not by heat not by joy, I always know that not now rather not now, yes and I do not stamp but I know that now yes now is now. I have never asked any one to forgive me.
Daniel Webster.	On yet another point I was still more unaccountably misunderstood.
Susan B.	Do we do what we have to do or do we have to do what we do. I answer.
Daniel Webster.	Mr. President I shall enter on no encomium upon Massachusetts she need none. There she is behold her and judge for yourselves.
Susan B.	I enter into a tabernacle I was born a believer in peace, I say fight for the right, be a martyr and live, be a coward and die, and why, because they, yes they, sooner or later go away. They leave us here. They come again. Don't forget, they come again.

Daniel Webster.	So sir I understand the gentleman and am happy to find I did not misunderstand him.
Susan B.	I should believe, what they ask, but they know, they know.
Daniel Webster.	It has been to us all a copious fountain of national, social and personal happiness.
Susan B.	Shall I protest, not while I live and breathe, I shall protest, shall I protest, shall I protest while I live and breathe.
Daniel Webster.	When my eyes shall be turned to behold for the last time the sun in heaven.
Susan B.	Yes.
Jo the Loiterer.	I like a mouse
Angel More.	I hate mice.
Jo the Loiterer.	I am not talking about mice, I am talking about a mouse. I like a mouse.
Angel More.	I hate a mouse.
Jo the Loiterer.	Now do you.

Curtain

INTERLUDE

(Susan B. A Short Story)

Yes I was said Susan.

You mean you are, said Anne.

No said Susan no.

When this you see remember me said Susan B.

I do said Anne.

After a while there was education. Who is educated said Anne.

Susan began to follow, she began to follow herself. I am not tired said Susan. No not said Anne. No I am not said Susan. This was the beginning. They began to travel not to travel you know but to go from one place to another place. In each place Susan B. said here I am I am here. Well said Anne. Do not let it trouble you said Susan politely. By the time she was there she was polite. She often thought about politeness. She said politeness was so agreeable. Is it said Anne. Yes said Susan yes I think so that is to say politeness is agreeable that is to say it could be agreeable if everybody were polite but when it is only me, ah me, said Susan B.

Anne was reproachful why do you not speak louder she said to Susan B. I speak as loudly as I can said Susan B. I even speak louder I even speak louder than I can. Do you really said Anne. Yes I really do said Susan B. it was dark and as it was dark it was necessary to speak louder or very softly, very softly. Dear me said Susan B., if it was not so early I would be sleepy. I myself said Anne never like to look at a newspaper. You are entirely right said Susan B. only I disagree with you. You do said Anne. You know very well I do said Susan B.

Men said Susan B. are so conservative, so selfish, so boresome and said Susan B. they are so ugly, and said Susan B. they are gullible, anybody can convince them, listen said Susan B. they listen to me. Well said Anne anybody would. I know said Susan B. I know anybody would I know that.

Once upon a time any day was full of occupation. You were never tired said Anne. No I was never tired said Susan B. And now, said Anne. Now I am never tired said Susan B. Let us said Anne let us think about everything. No said Susan B. no, no no, I know, I know said Susan B. no, said Susan B. No. But said Anne. But me no buts said Susan B. I know, now you like every one, every one and you each one and you they all do, they all listen to me, utterly unnecessary to deny, why deny, they themselves will they deny that they listen to me but let them deny it, all the same they do they do listen to me all the men do, see them said Susan B., do see them, see them, why not, said Susan B., they are men, and men, well of course they know that they cannot either see or hear unless I tell them so, poor things said Susan B. I do not pity them. Poor things. Yes said Anne they are poor things. Yes said Susan B. they are poor things. They are poor things said Susan B. men are poor things. Yes they are said Anne. Yes they are said Susan B. and nobody pities them. No said Anne no, nobody pities them. Very likely said Susan B. More than likely, said Anne. Yes said Susan B. yes.

It was not easy to go away but Susan B. did go away. She kept on going away and every time she went away she went away again. Oh my said Susan B. why do I go away, I go away because if I did not go away I would stay. Yes of course said Anne yes of course, if you did not go away you would stay. Yes of course said Susan B. Now said Susan B., let us not forget that in each place men are the same just the same, they are conservative, they are selfish and they listen to me. Yes they do said Anne. Yes they do said Susan B.

Susan B. was right, she said she was right and she was right. Susan B. was right. She was right because she was right. It is easy to be right, everybody else is wrong so it is easy to be right, and Susan B. was right, of course she was right, it is easy to be right, everybody else is wrong it is easy to be right. And said Susan B., in a way yes in a way yes really in a way, in a way really it is useful to be right. It does what it does, it does do what it does, if you are right, it does do what it does. It is very remarkable said Anne. Not very remarkable said Susan B. not very remarkable, no not very remarkable. It is not very remarkable really not very remarkable said Anne. No said Susan B. no not very remarkable.

And said Susan B. that is what I mean by not very remarkable.

Susan B. said she would not leave home. No said Susan B. I will not leave home. Why not said Anne. Why not said Susan B. all right I will I always have I always will. Yes you always will said Anne. Yes I always will said Susan B. In a little while anything began again and Susan B. said she did not mind. Really and truly said Susan B. really and truly I do not mind. No said Anne you do not mind, no said Susan B. no really and truly truly and really I do not mind. It was very necessary never to be cautious said Susan B. Yes said Anne it is very necessary.

In a little while they found everything very mixed. It is not really mixed said Susan B. How can anything be really mixed when men are conservative, dull, monotonous, deceived, stupid, unchanging and bullies, how said Susan B. how when men are men can they be mixed. Yes said Anne, yes men are men, how can they when men are men how can they be mixed yes how can they. Well said Susan B. let us go on they always listen to me. Yes said Anne yes they always listen to you. Yes said Susan B. yes they always listen to me.

ACT II

Andrew J.	It is cold weather.
Henrietta M.	In winter.
Andrew J.	Wherever I am

(Thaddeus S. comes in singing a song)

Thaddeus S.   I believe in public school education, I do not believe in free masons I believe in public school education, I do not believe that every one can do whatever he likes because (a pause) I have not always done what I liked, but, I would, if I could, and so I will, I will do what I will, I will have my will, and they, when the they, where are they, beside a poll, Gallup the poll. It is remarkable that there could be any nice person by the name of Gallup, but there is, yes there is, that is my decision.

Andrew J.   Bother your decision, I tell you it is cold weather.

Henrietta M.   In winter.

Andrew J.   Wherever I am.

Constance Fletcher.   Antagonises is a pleasant name, antagonises is a pleasant word, antagonises has occurred, bless you all and one.

John Adams.   Dear Miss Constance Fletcher, it is a great pleasure that I kneel at your feet, but I am Adams, I kneel at the feet of none, not any one, dear Miss Constance Fletcher dear dear Miss Constance Fletcher I kneel at your feet, you would have ruined my father if I had had one but I have had one and you had ruined him, dear Miss Constance Fletcher if I had not been an Adams I would have kneeled at your feet.

Constance Fletcher.   And kissed my hand.

J. Adams (shuddering).   And kissed your hand.

Constance Fletcher.   What a pity, no not what a pity it is better so, but what a pity what a pity it is what a pity.

J. Adams.	Do not pity me kind beautiful lovely Miss Constance Fletcher do not pity me, no do not pity me, I am an Adams and not pitiable.
Constance Fletcher.	Dear dear me if he had not been an Adams he would have kneeled at my feet and he would have kissed my hand. Do you mean that you would have kissed my hand or my hands, dear Mr. Adams.
J. Adams.	I mean that I would have first kneeled at your feet and then I would have kissed one of your hands and then I would still kneeling have kissed both of your hands, if I had not been an Adams.
Constance Fletcher.	Dear me Mr. Adams dear me.
All the Characters.	If he had not been an Adams he would have kneeled at her feet and he would have kissed one of her hands, and then still kneeling he would have kissed both of her hands still kneeling if he had not been an Adams.
Andrew J.	It is cold weather.
Henrietta M.	In winter.
Andrew J.	Wherever I am.
Thaddeus S.	When I look at him I fly, I mean when he looks at me he can cry.
Lillian Russell.	It is very naughty for men to quarrel so.
Herman Atlan.	They do quarrel so.
Lillian Russell.	It is very naughty of them very naughty.

(Jenny Reefer begins to waltz with Herman Atlan)

A Slow Chorus.	Naughty men, they quarrel so
	Quarrel about what.
	About how late the moon can rise.
	About how soon the earth can turn.
	About how naked are the stars.
	About how black are blacker men.
	About how pink are pinks in spring.
	About what corn is best to pop.
	About how many feet the ocean has dropped.
	Naughty men naughty men, they are always always quarreling.
Jenny Reefer.	Ulysses S. Grant was not the most earnest

	nor the most noble of men, but he was not always quarreling.
Donald Gallup.	No he was not.
Jo the Loiterer.	Has everybody forgotten Isabel Wentworth. I just want to say has everybody forgotten Isabel Wentworth.
Chris the Citizen.	Why shouldn't everybody forget Isabel Wentworth.
Jo the Loiterer.	Well that is just what I want to know I just want to know if everybody has forgotten Isabel Wentworth. That is all I want to know I just want to know if everybody has forgotten Isabel Wentworth.

ACT II ⸒ Scene II

Susan B.	Shall I regret having been born, will I regret having been born, shall and will, will and shall, I regret having been born.
Anne.	Is Henrietta M. a sister of Angel More.
Susan B.	No, I used to feel that sisters should be sisters, and that sisters prefer sisters, and I.
Anne.	Is Angel More the sister of Henrietta M. It is important that I know important.
Susan B.	Yes important.
Anne.	An Indiana Elliot are there any other Elliots beside Indiana Elliot. It is important that I should know, very important.
Susan B.	Should one work up excitement, or should one turn it low so that it will explode louder, should one work up excitement should one.
Anne.	Are there any other Elliots beside Indiana Elliot, had she sisters or even cousins, it is very important that I should know, very important.
Susan B.	A life is never given for a life, when a life is given a life is gone, if no life is gone

	there is no room for more life, life and strife, I give my life, that is to say, I live my life every day.
Anne.	And Isabel Wentworth, is she older or younger than she was it is very important very important that I should know just how old she is. I must have a list I must of how old every one is, it is very important.
Susan B.	I am ready.
Anne.	We have forgotten we have forgotten Jenny Reefer, I don't know even who she is, it is very important that I know who Jenny Reefer is very important.
Susan B.	And perhaps it is important to know who Lillian Russell is, perhaps it is important.
Anne.	It is not important to know who Lillian Russell is.
Susan B.	Then you do know.
Anne.	It is not important for me to know who Lillian Russell is.
Susan B.	I must choose I do choose, men and women women and men I do choose. I must choose colored or white white or colored I must choose, I must choose, weak or strong, strong or weak I must choose.

(All the men coming forward together)

Susan B.	I must choose
Jo the Loiterer.	Fight fight fight, between the nigger and the white.
Chris the Citizen.	And the women.
Andrew J.	I wish to say that little men are bigger than big men, that they know how to drink and to get drunk. They say I was a little man next to that big man, nobody can say what they do say nobody can.
Chorus of all the Men.	No nobody can, we feel that way too, no nobody can.
Andrew Johnson.	Begin to be drunk when you can so be a bigger man than a big man, you can.
Chorus of Men.	You can.

Andrew J.　　　　I often think, I am a bigger man than a bigger man. I often think I am.

(Andrew J. moves around and as he moves around he sees himself in a mirror)

Nobody can say little as I am I am not bigger than anybody bigger bigger bigger (and then in a low whisper) bigger than him bigger than him.

Jo the Loiterer.　　Fight fight between the big and the big never between the little and the big.

Chris the Citizen.　　They don't fight.

(Virgil T. makes them all gather around him)

Virgil T.　　　　Hear me he says hear me in every way I have satisfaction, I sit I stand I walk around and I am grand, and you all know it.

Chorus of Men.　　Yes we all know it. That's that.

And Said Virgil T.　　I will call you up one by one and then you will know which one is which, I know, then you will be known. Very well, Henry B.

Henry B.
comes forward.—I almost thought that I was Tommy I almost did I almost thought I was Tommy W. but if I were Tommy W. I would never come again, not if I could do better no not if I could do better.

Virgil T.　　　　Useless. John Adams. (John Adams advances) Tell me are you the real John Adams you know I sometimes doubt it not really doubt it you know but doubt it.

John Adams.　　If you were silent I would speak.

Jo the Loiterer.　　Fight fight fight between day and night.

Chris the Citizen.　　Which is day and which is night.

Jo the Loiterer.　　Hush, which.

John Adams.　　I ask you Virgil T. do you love women, I do. I love women but I am never subdued by them never.

Virgil T.　　　　He is no good. Andrew J. and Thaddeus S. better come together.

Jo the Loiterer.　　He wants to fight fight fight between.

Chris.　　　　　　Between what.

Jo the Loiterer.	Between the dead.
Andrew J.	I tell you I am bigger bigger is not biggest is not bigger. I am bigger and just to the last minute, I stick, it's better to stick than to die, it's better to itch than to cry, I have tried them all.
Virgil T.	You bet you have.
Thaddeus S.	I can be carried in dying but I will never quit trying.
Jo the Loiterer.	Oh go to bed when all is said oh go to bed, everybody, let's hear the women.
Chris the Citizen.	Fight fight between the nigger and the white and the women.

(Andrew J. and Thaddeus S. begin to quarrel violently)

Tell me said Virgil T. tell me I am from Missouri.

(Everybody suddenly stricken dumb)

(Daniel advances holding Henrietta M. by the hand)

Daniel.	Ladies and gentlemen let me present you let me present to you Henrietta M. it is rare in this troubled world to find a woman without a last name rare delicious and troubling, ladies and gentlemen let me present Henrietta M.

Curtain

ACT II ⁊ Scene III

Susan B.	I do not know whether I am asleep or awake, awake or asleep, asleep or awake. Do I know.
Jo the Loiterer.	I know, you are awake Susan B.

(A snowy landscape.
a negro man and a negro woman)

Susan B.	Negro man would you vote if you only can and not she.
Negro Man.	You bet.
Susan B.	I fought for you that you could vote would you vote if they would not let me.

Negro Man.   Holy gee.

Susan B. moving down
    in the snow.   If I believe that I am right and I am right if
                    they believe that they are right and they are
                    not in the right, might, might, might there be
                    what might be.

Negro Man and Woman
    following her.   All right Susan B. all right.

Susan B.   How then can we entertain a hope that they
                    will act differently, we may pretend to go in
                    good faith but there will be no faith in us.

Donald Gallup.   Let me help you Susan B.

Susan B.   And if you do and I annoy you what will you
                    do.

Donald Gallup.   But I will help you Susan B.

Susan B.   I tell you if you do and I annoy you what
                    will you do.

Donald Gallup.   I wonder if I can help you Susan B.

Susan B.   I wonder.

(Andrew G., Thaddeus and Daniel Webster come in together)
                    We are the chorus of the V.I.P.
                    Very important persons to every one who can
                    hear and see, we are the chorus of the V.I.P.

Susan B.   Yes, so they are. I am important but not
                    that way, not that way.

The Three V.I.P.'s.   We you see we V.I.P. very important to any
                    one who can hear or you can see, just we
                    three, of course lots of others but just we
                    three, just we three we are the chorus of
                    V.I.P. Very important persons to any one
                    who can hear or can see.

Susan B.   My constantly recurring thought and prayer
                    now are that no word or act of mine may
                    lessen the might of this country in the scale
                    of truth and right.

The Chorus of V.I.P.

Daniel Webster.   When they all listen to me.

Thaddeus S.   When they all listen to me.

Andrew J.   When they all listen to him, by him I mean
                    me.

Daniel Webster.	By him I mean me.
Thaddeus S.	It is not necessary to have any meaning I am he, he is me I am a V.I.P.
The Three.	We are the V.I.P. the very important persons, we have special rights, they ask us first and they wait for us last and wherever we are well there we are everybody knows we are there, we are the V.I.P. Very important persons for everybody to see.
Jo the Loiterer.	I wished that I knew the difference between rich and poor, I used to think I was poor, now I think I am rich and I am rich, quite rich not very rich quite rich, I wish I knew the difference between rich and poor.
Chris the Citizen.	Ask her, ask Susan B. I always ask, I find they like it and I like it, and if I like it, and if they like it, I am not rich and I am not poor, just like that Jo just like that.
Jo the Loiterer.	Susan B. listen to me, what is the difference between rich and poor poor and rich no use to ask the V.I.P., they never answer me but you Susan B. you answer, answer me.
Susan B.	Rich, to be rich, is to be so rich that when they are rich they have it to be that they do not listen and when they do they do not hear, and to be poor to be poor, is to be so poor they listen and listen and what they hear well what do they hear, they hear that they listen, they listen to hear, that is what it is to be poor, but I, I Susan B., there is no wealth nor poverty, there is no wealth, what is wealth, there is no poverty, what is poverty, has a pen ink, has it.
Jo the Loiterer.	I had a pen that was to have ink for a year and it only lasted six weeks.
Susan B.	Yes I know Jo. I know.

Curtain

ACT II ⁊ Scene IV

A Meeting.

Susan B. On the Platform.   Ladies there is no neutral position for us to assume. If we say we love the cause and then sit down at our ease, surely does our action speak the lie.

And now will Daniel Webster take the platform as never before.

Daniel Webster.   Coming and coming alone, no man is alone when he comes, when he comes when he is coming he is not alone and now ladies and gentlemen I have done, remember that remember me remember each one.

Susan B.   And now Virgil T. Virgil T. will bow and speak and when it is necessary they will know that he is he.

Virgil T.   I make what I make, I make a noise, there is a poise in making a noise.

(An interruption at the door)

Jo the Loiterer.   I have behind me a crowd, are we allowed.

Susan B.   A crowd is never allowed but each one of you can come in.

Chris the Citizen.   But if we are allowed then we are a crowd.

Susan B.   No, this is the cause, and a cause is a pause. Pause before you come in.

Jo the Loiterer.   Yes ma'am.

(All the characters crowd in. Constance Fletcher and Indiana Elliot leading)

Daniel Webster.   I resist it to-day and always. Who ever falters or whoever flies I continue the contest.

Constance Fletcher and Indiana Elliot
  bowing low say.   Dear man, he can make us glad that we have had so great so dear a man here with us now and now we bow before him here, this dear this dear great man.

Susan B.   Hush, this is slush. Hush.

John Adams.   I cannot be still when still and until I see

Constance Fletcher dear Constance Fletcher noble Constance Fletcher and I spill I spill over like a thrill and a trill, dear Constance Fletcher there is no cause in her presence, how can there be a cause. Women what are women. There is Constance Fletcher, men what are men, there is Constance Fletcher, Adams, yes, Adams, I am John Adams, there is Constance Fletcher, when this you see listen to me, Constance, no I cannot call her Constance I can only call her Constance Fletcher.

Indiana Elliot. And how about me.

Jo the Loiterer. Whist shut up I have just had an awful letter from home, shut up.

Indiana Elliot. What did they say.

Jo the Loiterer. They said I must come home and not marry you.

Indiana. Who ever said we were going to marry.

Jo the Loiterer. Believe me I never did.

Indiana. Disgrace to the cause of women, out.

And she shoves him out.

Jo the Loiterer. Help Susan B. help me.

Susan B. I know that we suffer, and as we suffer we grow strong, I know that we wait and as we wait we are bold, I know that we are beaten and as we are beaten we win, I know that men know that this is not so but it is so, I know, yes I know.

Jo the Loiterer. There didn't I tell you she knew best, you just give me a kiss and let me alone.

Daniel Webster. I who was once old am now young, I who was once weak am now strong, I who have left every one behind am now overtaken.

Susan B. I undertake to overthrow your undertaking.

Jo the Loiterer. You bet.

Chris the Citizen. I always repeat everything I hear.

Jo the Loiterer. You sure do.

(While all this is going on, all the characters are crowding up on the platform)

They Say.	Now we are all here there is nobody down there to hear, now if it is we're always like that there would be no reason why anybody should cry, because very likely if at all it would be so nice to be the head, we are the head we have all the bread.
Jo the Loiterer.	And the butter too.
Chris the Citizen.	And Kalamazoo.
Susan B. advancing.	I speak to those below who are not there who are not there who are not there. I speak to those below to those below who are not there to those below who are not there.

Curtain

ACT II ⸜ Scene V

| Susan B. | Will they remember that it is true that neither they that neither you, will they marry will they carry, aloud, the right to know that even if they love them so, they are alone to live and die, they are alone to sink and swim they are alone to have what they own, to have no idea but that they are here, to struggle and thirst to do everything first, because until it is done there is no other one. |

(Jo the Loiterer leads in Indiana Elliot in wedding attire, followed by John Adams and Constance Fletcher and followed by Daniel Webster and Angel More. All the other characters follow after. Anne and Jenny Reefer come and stand by Susan B. Ulysses S. Grant sits down in a chair right behind the procession)

Anne.	Marriage.
Jenny Reefer.	Marry marriage.
Susan B.	I know I know and I have told you so, but if no one marries how can there be women to tell men, women to tell men.
Anne.	What

Jenny Reefer.	Women should not tell men.
Susan B.	Men can not count, they do not know that two and two make four if women do not tell them so. There is a devil creeps into men when their hands are strengthened. Men want to be half slave half free. Women want to be all slave or all free, therefore men govern and women know, and yet.
Anne.	Yet.
Jenny Reefer.	There is no yet in paradise.
Susan B.	Let them marry.

(The marrying commences)

Jo the Loiterer.	I tell her if she marries me do I marry her.
Indiana Elliot.	Listen to what he says so you can answer, have you the ring.
Jo the Loiterer.	You did not like the ring and mine is too large.
Indiana Elliot.	Hush.
Jo the Loiterer.	I wish my name was Adams.
Indiana Elliot.	Hush.
John Adams.	I never marry I have been twice divorced but I have never married, fair Constance Fletcher fair Constance Fletcher do you not admire me that I never can married be. I who have been twice divorced. Dear Constance Fletcher dear dear Constance Fletcher do you not admire me.
Constance Fletcher.	So beautiful. It is so beautiful to meet you here, so beautiful, so beautiful to meet you here dear, dear John Adams, so beautiful to meet you here.
Daniel Webster.	When I have joined and not having joined have separated and not having separated have led, and not having led have thundered, when I having thundered have provoked and having provoked have dominated, may I dear Angel More not kneel at your feet because I cannot kneel my knees are not kneeling knees but dear Angel More be my Angel More for ever-more.

Angel More.	I join the choir that is visible, because the choir that is visible is as visible.
Daniel Webster.	As what Angel More.
Angel More.	As visible as visible, do you not hear me, as visible.
Daniel Webster.	You do not and I do not.
Angel More.	What.
Daniel Webster.	Separate marriage from marriage.
Angel More.	And why not.
Daniel Webster.	And.

(Just at this moment Ulysses S. Grant makes his chair
pound on the floor)

Ulysses S. Grant.	As long as I sit I am sitting, silence again as you were, you were all silent, as long as I sit I am sitting.
All Together.	We are silent, as we were.
Susan B.	We are all here to celebrate the civil and religious marriage of Jo the Loiterer and Indiana Elliot.
Jo the Loiterer.	Who is civil and who is religious.
Anne.	Who is, listen to Susan B. She knows.

The Brother of Indiana Elliot rushes in.

Nobody knows who I am but I forbid the marriage, do we know whether Jo the Loiterer is a bigamist or a grandfather or an uncle or a refugee. Do we know, no we do not know and I forbid the marriage, I forbid it, I am Indiana Elliot's brother and I forbid it, I am known as Herman Atlan and I forbid it, I am known as Anthony Comstock and I forbid it, I am Indiana Elliot's brother and I forbid it.

Jo the Loiterer.	Well well well, I knew that ring of mine was too large, It could not fall off on account of my joints but I knew it was too large.
Indiana Elliot.	I renounce my brother.
Jo the Loiterer.	That's right my dear that's all right.
Susan B.	What is marriage, is marriage protection or religion, is marriage renunciation or abundance, is marriage a stepping-stone or an end. What is marriage.

Anne.	I will never marry.
Jenny Reefer.	If I marry I will divorce but I will not marry because if I did marry, I would be married.

(Ulysses S. Grant pounds his chair)

Ulysses S. Grant.	Didn't I say I do not like noise, I do not like cannon balls, I do not like storms, I do not like talking, I do not like noise. I like everything and everybody to be silent and what I like I have. Everybody be silent.
Jo the Loiterer.	I know I was silent, everybody can tell just by listening to me just how silent I am, dear General, dear General Ulysses, dear General Ulysses Simpson dear General Ulysses Simpson Grant, dear dear sir, am I not a perfect example of what you like, am I not silent.

(Ulysses S. Grant's chair pounds and he is silent)

Susan B.	I am not married and the reason why is that I have had to do what I have had to do, I have had to be what I have had to be, I could never be one of two I could never be two in one as married couples do and can, I am but one all one, one and all one, and so I have never been married to any one.
Anne.	But I I have been, I have been married to what you have been to that one.
Susan B.	No no, no, you may be married to the past one, the one that is not the present one, no one can be married to the present one, the one, the one, the present one.
Jenny Reefer.	I understand you undertake to overthrow their undertaking.
Susan B.	I love the sound of these, one over two, two under one, three under four, four over more.
Anne.	Dear Susan B. Anthony thank you.
John Adams.	All this time I have been lost in my thoughts in my thoughts of thee beautiful thee, Constance Fletcher, do you see, I have been lost in my thoughts of thee.
Constance Fletcher.	I am blind and therefore I dream.
Daniel Webster.	Dear Angel More, dear Angel More, there

	have been men who have stammered and stuttered but not, not I.
Angel More.	Speak louder.
Daniel Webster.	Not I.
The Chorus.	Why the hell don't you all get married, why don't you, we want to go home, why don't you.
Jo the Loiterer.	Why don't you.
Indiana Elliot.	Why don't you.
Indiana Elliot's Brother.	Why don't you because I am here.

(The crowd remove him forcibly)

Susan B. Anthony suddenly.	They are married all married and their children women as well as men will have the vote, they will they will, they will have the vote.

Curtain

ACT II ⁊ Scene VI

(Susan B. doing her house-work in her house)

Enter Anne.	Susan B. they want you.
Susan B.	Do they
Anne.	Yes. You must go.
Susan B.	No.
Jenny Reefer comes in.	Oh yes they want to know if you are here.
Susan B.	Yes still alive. Painters paint and writers write and soldiers drink and fight and I I am still alive.
Anne.	They want you.
Susan B.	And when they have me.
Jenny Reefer.	Then they will want you again.
Susan B.	Yes I know, they love me so, they tell me so and they tell me so, but I, I do not tell them so because I know, they will not do what they could do and I I will be left alone to die but

they will not have done what I need to have done to make it right that I live lived my life and fight.

Jo the Loiterer
at the window. Indiana Elliot wants to come in, she will not take my name she says it is not all the same, she says that she is Indiana Elliot and that I am Jo, and that she will not take my name and that she will always tell me so. Oh yes she is right of course she is right it is not all the same Indiana Elliot is her name, she is only married to me, but there is no difference that I can see, but all the same there she is and she will not change her name, yes it is all the same.

Susan B. Let her in.

Indiana Elliot. Oh Susan B. they want you they have to have you, can I tell them you are coming I have not changed my name can I tell them you are coming and that you will do everything.

Susan B. No but there is no use in telling them so, they won't vote my laws, there is always a clause, there is always a pause, they won't vote my laws.

(Andrew Johnson puts his head in at the door)

Andrew Johnson. Will the good lady come right along.

Thaddeus Stevens
behind him. We are waiting, will the good lady not keep us waiting, will the good lady not keep us waiting.

Susan B. You you know so well that you will not vote my laws.

Stevens. Dear lady remember humanity comes first.

Susan B. You mean men come first, women, you will not vote my laws, how can you dare when you do not care, how can you dare, there is no humanity in humans, there is only law, and you will not because you know so well that there is no humanity there are only laws, you

know it so well that you will not you will not
vote my laws.

    (Susan B. goes back to her housework.

       All the characters crowd in)

Chorus.   Do come Susan B. Anthony do come nobody
no nobody can make them come the way you
make them come, do come do come Susan B.
Anthony, it is your duty, Susan B. Anthony,
you know you know your duty, you come, do
come, come.

Susan B. Anthony.   I suppose I will be coming, is it because you
flatter me, is it because if I do not come you
will forget me and never vote my laws, you
will never vote my laws even if I do come but
if I do not come you will never vote my laws,
come or not come it always comes to the
same thing it comes to their not voting my
laws, not voting my laws, tell me all you men
tell me you know you will never vote my laws.

All the Men.   Dear kind lady we count on you, and as we
count on you so can you count on us.

Susan B. Anthony.   Yes but I work for you I do, I say never
again, never again, never never, and yet I
know I do say no but I do not mean no, I
know I always hope that if I go that if I go
and go and go, perhaps then you men will
vote my laws but I know how well I know, a
little this way a little that way you steal away,
you steal a piece away you steal yourselves
away, you do not intend to stay and vote my
laws, and still when you call I go, I go, I go,
I say no, no, no, and I go, but no, this time
no, this time you have to do more than prom-
ise, you must write it down that you will vote
my laws, but no, you will pay no attention to
what is written, well then swear by my hearth,
as you hope to have a home and hearth, swear
after I work for you swear that you will vote
my laws, but no, no oaths, no thoughts, no
decisions, no intentions, no gratitude, no con-

victions, no nothing will make you pass my laws. Tell me can any of you be honest now, and say you will not pass my laws.

Jo the Loiterer. I can I can be honest I can say I will not pass your laws, because you see I have no vote, no loiterer has a vote so it is easy Susan B. Anthony easy for one man among all these men to be honest and to say I will not pass your laws. Anyway Susan B. Anthony what are your laws. Would it really be all right to pass them, if you say so it is all right with me. I have no vote myself but I'll make them as long as I don't have to change my name don't have to don't have to change my name.

T. Stevens. Thanks dear Susan B. Anthony, thanks we all know that whatever happens we all can depend upon you to do your best for any cause which is a cause, and any cause is a cause and because any cause is a cause therefore you will always do your best for any cause, and now you will be doing your best for this cause our cause the cause.

Susan B. Because. Very well is it snowing.

Chorus. Not just now.

Susan B. Anthony. Is it cold.

Chorus. A little.

Susan B. Anthony. I am not well

Chorus. But you look so well and once started it will be all right.

Susan B. Anthony.* All right

Curtain

ACT II ✝ Scene VII

(Susan B. Anthony busy with her housework)

Anne comes in. Oh it was wonderful, wonderful, they listen to nobody the way they listen to you.

Susan B. Yes it is wonderful as the result of my work

for the first time the word male has been written into the constitution of the United States concerning suffrage. Yes it is wonderful. But

Anne.
Susan B.   Yes but, what is man, what are men, what are they. I do not say that they haven't kind hearts, if I fall down in a faint, they will rush to pick me up, if my house is on fire, they will rush in to put the fire out and help me, yes they have kind hearts but they are afraid, afraid, they are afraid, they are afraid. They fear women, they fear each other, they fear their neighbor, they fear other countries and then they hearten themselves in their fear by crowding together and following each other, and when they crowd together and follow each other they are brutes, like animals who stampede, and so they have written in the name male into the United States constitution, because they are afraid of black men because they are afraid of women, because they are afraid afraid. Men are afraid.

Anne timidly.   And women.
Susan B.   Ah women often have not any sense of danger, after all a hen screams pitifully when she sees an eagle but she is only afraid for her children, men are afraid for themselves, that is the real difference between men and women.

Anne.   But Susan B. why do you not say these things out loud.

Susan B.   Why not, because if I did they would not listen they not alone would not listen they would revenge themselves. Men have kind hearts when they are not afraid but they are afraid afraid afraid. I say they are afraid, but if I were to tell them so their kindness would turn to hate. Yes the Quakers are right, they are not afraid because they do not fight, they do not fight.

Anne.	But Susan B. you fight and you are not afraid.
Susan B.	I fight and I am not afraid, I fight but I am not afraid.
Anne.	And you will win.
Susan B.	Win what, win what.
Anne.	Win the vote for women.
Susan B.	Yes some day some day the women will vote and by that time.
Anne.	By that time oh wonderful time.
Susan B.	By that time it will do them no good because having the vote they will become like men, they will be afraid, having the vote will make them afraid, oh I know it, but I will fight for the right, for the right to vote for them even though they become like men, become afraid like men, become like men.

(Anne bursts into tears. Jenny Reefer rushes in)

Jenny Reefer.	I have just converted Lillian Russell to the cause of woman's suffrage, I have converted her, she will give all herself and all she earns oh wonderful day I know you will say, here she comes isn't she beautiful.

(Lillian Russell comes in followed by all the women in the chorus. Women crowding around, Constance Fletcher in the background)

Lillian Russell.	Dear friends, it is so beautiful to meet you all, so beautiful, so beautiful to meet you all.

(John Adams comes in and sees Constance Fletcher)

John Adams.	Dear friend beautiful friend, there is no beauty where you are not.
Constance Fletcher.	Yes dear friend but look look at real beauty look at Lillian Russell look at real beauty.
John Adams.	Real beauty real beauty is all there is of beauty and why should my eye wander where no eye can look without having looked before. Dear friend I kneel to you because dear friend each time I see you I have never looked before, dear friend you are an open door.

(Daniel Webster strides in, the women separate)

Daniel Webster.	What what is it, what is it, what is the false

and the true and I say to you you Susan
B. Anthony, you know the false from the true
and yet you will not wait you will not wait, I
say you will you will wait. When my eyes,
and I have eyes when my eyes, beyond that
I seek not to penetrate the veil, why should
you want what you have chosen, when mine
eyes, why do you want that the curtain may
rise, why when mine eyes, why should the
vision be opened to what lies behind, why,
Susan B. Anthony fight the fight that is the
fight, that any fight may be a fight for the
right. I hear that you say that the word male
should not be written into the constitution
of the United States of America, but I say, I
say, that so long that the gorgeous ensign of
the republic, still full high advanced, its arms
and trophies streaming in their original luster
not a stripe erased or polluted not a single star
obscured.

Jo the Loiterer.   She has decided to change her name.

Indiana Elliot.   Not because it is his name but it is such a
pretty name, Indiana Loiterer is such a pretty
name I think all the same he will have to
change his name, he must be Jo Elliot, yes he
must, it is what he has to do, he has to be
Jo Elliot and I am going to be Indiana
Loiterer, dear friends, all friends is it not a
lovely name, Indiana Loiterer all the same.

Jo the Loiterer.   All right I never fight, nobody will know it's
men, but what can I do, if I am not she and
I am not me, what can I do, if a name is not
true, what can I do but do as she tells me.

All the Chorus.   She is quite right, Indiana Loiterer is so harmonious, so harmonious, Indiana Loiterer is
so harmonious.

All the Men Come In.   What did she say.

Jo.   I was talking not she but nobody no nobody
ever wants to listen to me.

All the Chorus
  Men and Women.   Susan B. Anthony was very successful we are all very grateful to Susan B. Anthony because she was so successful, she worked for the votes for women and she worked for the vote for colored men and she was so successful, they wrote the word male into the constitution of the United States of America, dear Susan B. Anthony. Dear Susan B., whenever she wants to be and she always wants to be she is always so successful so very successful.

Susan B.   So successful.

Curtain

ACT II ⁄ Scene VIII

(The Congressional Hall, the replica of the statue of
Susan B. Anthony and her comrades in the suffrage
fight)

Anne alone in front
  of the statuary.   The Vote. Women have the vote. They have it each and every one, it is glorious glorious glorious.

Susan B. Anthony
  behind the statue.   Yes women have the vote, all my long life of strength and strife, all my long life, women have it, they can vote, every man and every woman have the vote, the word male is not there any more, that is to say, that is to say.

(Silence. Virgil T. comes in very nicely, he looks
around and sees Anne)

Virgil T.   Very well indeed, very well indeed, you are looking very well indeed, have you a chair anywhere, very well indeed, as we sit, we sit, some day very soon some day they will vote

sitting and that will be a very successful day
any day, every day.

(Henry B. comes in. He looks all around at the statue and then
he sighs)

Henry B.   Does it really mean that women are as white
and cold as marble does it really mean that.

(Angel More comes in and bows gracefully to the sculptured
group)

Angel More.   I can always think of dear Daniel Webster
daily.

(John Adams comes in and looks around, and then
carefully examines the statue)

John Adams.   I think that they might have added dear
delicate Constance Fletcher I do think they
might have added her wonderful profile, I
do think they might have, I do, I really do.

(Andrew Johnson shuffles in)

Andrew Johnson. I have no hope in black or white in white or
black in black or black or white or white, no
hope.

(Thaddeus Stevens comes in, he does not address anybody,
he stands before the statue and frowns)

Thaddeus S.   Rob the cradle, rob it, rob the robber, rob
him, rob whatever there is to be taken, rob,
rob the cradle, rob it.

Daniel Webster (he sees nothing else).

               Angel More, more more Angel More, did you
hear me, can you hear shall you hear me,
when they come and they do come, when
they go and they do go, Angel More can you
will you shall you may you might you would
you hear me, when they have lost and won,
when they have won and lost, when words
are bitter and snow is white, Angel More
come to me and we will leave together.

Angel More.   Dear sir, not leave, stay.

Henrietta M.   I have never been mentioned again. (She
curtseys)

Constance Fletcher. Here I am, I am almost blind but here I am, dear dear here I am, I cannot see what is so white, here I am.

John Adams (kissing her hand).

Here you are, blind as a bat and beautiful as a bird, here you are, white and cold as marble, beautiful as marble, yes that is marble but you you are the living marble dear Constance Fletcher, you are.

Constance Fletcher. Thank you yes I am here, blind as a bat, I am here.

Indiana Elliot. I am sorry to interrupt so sorry to interrupt but I have a great deal to say about marriage, either one or the other married must be economical, either one or the other, if either one or the other of a married couple are economical then a marriage is successful, if not not, I have a great deal to say about marriage, and dear Susan B. Anthony was never married, how wonderful it is to be never married how wonderful. I have a great deal to say about marriage.

Susan B. Anthony
  voice from behind
    the statue.

It is a puzzle, I am not puzzled but it is a puzzle, if there are no children there are no men and women, and if there are men and women, it is rather horrible, and if it is rather horrible, then there are children, I am not puzzled but it is very puzzling, women and men vote and children, I am not puzzled but it is very puzzling.

Gloster Heming. I have only been a man who has a very fine name, and it must be said I made it up yes I did, so many do why not I, so many do, so many do, and why not two, when anybody might, and you can vote and you can dote with any name. Thank you.

Isabel Wentworth. They looked for me and they found me, I like to talk about it. It is very nearly necessary not to be noisy not to be noisy and hope, hope and hop, no use in enjoying men and women no use, I wonder why we are all happy, yes.

Annie Hope.   There is another Anne and she believes, I am hopey hope and I do not believe I have been in California and Kalamazoo, and I do not believe I burst into tears and I do not believe.

(They all crowd closer together and Lillian Russell who comes in stands quite alone)

Lillian Russell.   I can act so drunk that I never drink, I can drink so drunk that I never act, I have a curl I was a girl and I am old and fat but very handsome for all that.

(Anthony Comstock comes in and glares at her)

Anthony Comstock.   I have heard that they have thought that they would wish that one like you could vote a vote and help to let the ones who want do what they like, I have heard that even you, and I am through, I cannot hope that there is dope, oh yes a horrid word. I have never heard, short.

Jenny Reefer.   I have hope and faith, not charity no not charity, I have hope and faith, no not, not charity, no not charity.

Ulysses S. Grant.   Women are women, soldiers are soldiers, men are not men, lies are not lies, do, and then a dog barks, listen to him and then a dog barks, a dog barks a dog barks any dog barks, listen to him any dog barks.

(he sits down)

Herman Atlan.   I am not loved any more, I was loved oh yes I was loved but I am not loved any more, I am not, was I not, I knew I would refuse what a woman would choose and so I am not loved any more, not loved any more.

Donald Gallup.   Last but not least, first and not best, I am tall as a man, I am firm as a clam, and I never change, from day to day.

(Jo the Loiterer and Chris a Citizen)

Jo the Loiterer.	Let us dance and sing, Chrissy Chris, wet and not in debt, I am a married man and I know how I show I am a married man. She votes, she changes her name and she votes.

(They all crowd together in front of the statue, there is
a moment of silence and then a chorus)

Chorus.	To vote the vote, the vote we vote, can vote do vote will vote could vote, the vote the vote.
Jo the Loiterer.	I am the only one who cannot vote, no loiterer can vote.
Indiana Elliot.	I am a loiterer Indiana Loiterer and I can vote.
Jo the Loiterer.	You only have the name, you have not got the game.
Chorus.	The vote the vote we will have the vote.
Lillian Russell.	It is so beautiful to meet you all here so beautiful.
Ulysses S. Grant.	Vote the vote, the army does not vote, the general generals, there is no vote, bah vote.
The Chorus.	The vote we vote we note the vote.

(They all bow and smile to the statue. Suddenly Susan B.'s
voice is heard)

Susan B.'s voice.	We cannot retrace our steps, going forward may be the same as going backwards. We cannot retrace our steps, retrace our steps. All my long life, all my life, we do not retrace our steps, all my long life, but.

(A silence a long silence)

But—we do not retrace our steps, all my long life, and here, here we are here, in marble and gold, did I say gold, yes I said gold, in marble and gold and where—

(A silence)

Where is where. In my long life of effort and strife, dear life, life is strife, in my long life, it will not come and go, I tell you so, it will stay it will pay but

(A long silence)

But do I want what we have got, has it not

gone, what made it live, has it not gone because now it is had, in my long life in my long
life

(Silence)

Life is strife, I was a martyr all my life not to
what I won but to what was done.

(Silence)

Do you know because I tell you so, or do
you know, do you know.

(Silence)

My long life, my long life.

Curtain

DOCTOR FAUSTUS LIGHTS THE LIGHTS

⚡ 1938 ⚡

ACT I

Faust standing at the door of his room, with his arms up at the door lintel looking out, behind him a blaze of electric light.
Just then Mephisto approaches and appears at the door.

Faustus growls out.—The devil what the devil what do I care if the devil is there.

Mephisto says. But Doctor Faustus dear yes I am here.

Doctor Faustus. What do I care there is no here nor there. What am I. I am Doctor Faustus who knows everything can do everything and you say it was through you but not at all, if I had not been in a hurry and if I had taken my time I would have known how to make white electric light and day-light and night light and what did I do I saw you miserable devil I saw you and I was deceived and I believed miserable devil I thought I needed you, and I thought I was tempted by the devil and I know no temptation is tempting unless the devil tells you so. And you wanted my soul what the hell did you want my soul for, how do you know I have a soul, who says so nobody says so but you the devil and everybody knows the devil is all lies, so how do you know how do I know that I have a soul to sell how do you know Mr. Devil oh Mr. Devil how can you tell you can not tell anything and I I who know everything I keep on having so much light that light is not bright and what after

89

all is the use of light, you can see just as well without it, you can go around just as well without it you can get up and go to bed just as well without it, and I I wanted to make it and the devil take it yes you devil you do not even want it and I sold my soul to make it. I have made it but have I a soul to pay for it.

Mephisto coming nearer and trying to pat his arm.

Yes dear Doctor Faustus yes of course you have a soul of course you have, do not believe them when they say the devil lies, you know the devil never lies, he deceives oh yes he deceives but that is not lying no dear please dear Doctor Faustus do not say the devil lies.

Doctor Faustus.

Who cares if you lie if you steal, there is no snake to grind under one's heel, there is no hope there is no death there is no life there is no breath, there just is every day all day and when there is no day there is no day, and anyway of what use is a devil unless he goes away, go away old devil go away, there is no use in a devil unless he goes away, how can you remember a devil unless he goes away, oh devil there is no use in your coming to stay and now you are red at night which is not a delight and you are red in the morning which is not a warning go away devil go away or stay after all what can a devil say.

Mephisto.

A devil can smile a devil can while away whatever there is to give away, and now are you not proud Doctor Faustus yes you are you know you are you are the only one who knows what you know and it is I the devil who tells you so.

Faustus.

You fool you devil how can you know, how can you tell me so, if I am the only one who can know what I know then no devil can know what I know and no devil can tell me so and

I could know without any soul to sell, without there being anything in hell. What I know I know, I know how I do what I do when I see the way through and always any day I will see another day and you old devil you know very well you never see any other way than just the way to hell, you only know one way. You only know one thing, you are never ready for anything, and I everything is always now and now and now perhaps through you I begin to know that it is all just so, that light however bright will never be other than light, and any light is just a light and now there is nothing more either by day or by night but just a light. Oh you devil go to hell, that is all you know to tell, and who is interested in hell just a devil is interested in hell because that is all he can tell, whether I stamp or whether I cry whether I live or whether I die, I can know that all a devil can say is just about going to hell the same way, get out of here devil, it does not interest me whether you can buy or I can sell, get out of here devil just you go to hell.

Faustus gives him an awful kick, and Mephisto moves away and the electric lights just then begin to get very gay.

Alright then

The Ballet

Doctor Faustus sitting alone surrounded by electric lights.

His dog comes in and says

Thank you.

One of the electric lights goes out and again the dog says

Thank you.

The electric light that went out is replaced by a glow.

The dog murmurs.

My my what a sky.

And then he says

Thank you.

Doctor Faustus' song:

If I do it
If you do it
What is it.
 Once again the dog says
Thank you.
 A duet between Doctor Faustus and the dog about the electric
 light about the electric lights.
Bathe me
 says Doctor Faustus
Bathe me
In the electric lights
 During this time the electric lights come and go
What is it
 says Doctor Faustus
Thank you
 says the dog.
 Just at this moment the electric lights get brighter and nothing
 comes
Was it it
 says Doctor Faustus
 Faustus meditates he does not see the dog.
Will it
Will it
Will it be
Will it be it.
 Faustus sighs and repeats
Will it be it.
 A duet between the dog and Faustus
Will it be it
Just it.
 At that moment the electric light gets pale again and in that
 moment Faustus shocked says
It is it
 A little boy comes in and plays with the dog, the dog says
Thank you.
 Doctor Faustus looks away from the electric lights and then he
 sings a song.

Let me Alone

Let me alone
Oh let me alone
Dog and boy let me alone oh let me alone
Leave me alone
Let me be alone
little boy and dog
let let me alone
 He sighs
 And as he sighs
 He says
Dog and boy boy and dog leave me alone let me let me be alone.
 The dog says
Thank you
 but does not look at Faustus
 A pause
 No words
 The dog says
Thank you
I say thank you
Thank you
 The little boy
The day begins to-day
The day
The moon begins the day
 Doctor Faustus
There is no moon to-day
 Dark silence
You obey I obey
There is no moon to-day.
 Silence
 and the dog says
I obey I say
Thank you any day
 The little boy says
Once in a while they get up.
 Doctor Faustus says
I shall not think

I shall not
No I shall not.
    Faustus addresses little boy and dog
Night is better than day so please go away
    The boy says
But say
When the hay has to be cut every day then there is the devil to pay
    The dog starts and then he shrinks and says
Thank you
    Faustus half turns and starts
I hear her
    he says
I hear her say
Call to her to sing
To sing all about
to sing a song
All about
day-light and night light.
Moonlight and star-light
electric light and twilight
every light as well.
    The electric lights glow and a chorus in the distance sings
Her name is her name is her name is Marguerite Ida and Helena
Annabel.
    Faustus sings
I knew it I knew it the electric lights they told me so no dog can
know no boy can know I cannot know they cannot know the electric
lights they told me so I would not know I could not know who can
know who can tell me so I know you know they can know her name
is Marguerite Ida and Helena Annabel and when I tell oh when
I tell oh when I when I when I tell, oh go away and go away and
tell and tell and tell and tell and tell, oh hell.
    The electric lights commence to dance and one by one they go
    out and come in and the boy and the dog begin to sing.
Oh very well oh Doctor Faustus very very well oh very well, thank
you says the dog oh very well says the boy her name her name is
Marguerite Ida and Helena Annabel, I know says the dog I know
says the boy I know says Doctor Faustus no no no no no nobody
can know what I know I know her name is not Marguerite Ida
and Helena Annabel, very well says the boy it is says the boy her

name is Marguerite Ida and Helena Annabel, no no no says Doctor
Faustus, yes yes yes says the dog, no says the boy yes says the dog,
her name is not Marguerite Ida and Helena Annabel and she is not
ready yet to sing about day-light and night light, moonlight and
star-light electric light and twilight she is not she is not but she will
be. She will not be says Doctor Faustus never never never, never
will her name be Marguerite Ida and Helena Annabel never never
never never well as well never Marguerite Ida and Helena Annabel
never Marguerite Ida and Helena Annabel.

There is a sudden hush and the distant chorus says
It might be it might be her name her name might be Marguerite
Ida and Helena Annabel it might be.

And Doctor Faustus says in a loud whisper
It might be but it is not, and the little boy says how do you know
and Faustus says it might be it might not be not be not be, and as
he says the last not be the dog says
Thank you.

Scene II

I am I and my name is Marguerite Ida and Helena Annabel,
and then oh then I could yes I could I could begin to cry but why
why could I begin to cry.

And I am I and I am here and how do I know how wild the
wild world is how wild the wild woods are the wood they call the
woods the poor man's overcoat but do they cover me and if they
do how wild they are wild and wild and wild they are, how do I
know how wild woods are when I have never ever seen a wood
before.

I wish, (she whispered) I knew why woods are wild why
animals are wild why I am I, why I can cry, I wish I wish I knew,
I wish oh how I wish I knew. Once I am in I will never be through
the woods are there and I am here and am I here or am I there,
oh where oh where is here oh where oh where is there and animals
wild animals are everywhere.

She sits down.

I wish (says she conversationally) I wish if I had a wish that
when I sat down it would not be here but there there where I
could have a chair there where I would not have to look around

fearfully everywhere there where a chair and a carpet underneath the chair would make me know that there is there, but here here everywhere there is nothing nothing like a carpet nothing like a chair, here it is wild everywhere I hear I hear everywhere that the woods are wild and I am here and here is here and here I am sitting without a chair without a carpet, oh help me to a carpet with a chair save me from the woods the wild woods everywhere where everything is wild wild and I I am not there I am here oh dear I am not there.

She stands up with her hands at her sides she opens and closes her eyes and opens them again.

If my eyes are open and my eyes are closed I see I see, I see no carpet I see no chair I see the wild woods everywhere, what good does it do me to close my eyes no good at all the woods the woods are there I close my eyes but the green is there and I open my eyes and I have to stare to be sure the green is there the green of the woods, I saw it when my eyes were closed I saw the wild woods everywhere and now I open my eyes and there there is the wild wood everywhere.

Would it do as well if my name was not Marguerite Ida and Helena Annabel would it do as well I would give up even that for a carpet and a chair and to be not here but there, but (and she lets out a shriek,) I am here I am not there and I am Marguerite Ida and Helena Annabel and it is not well that I could tell what there is to tell what there is to see and what do I see and do I see it at all oh yes I do I call and call but yes I do I see it all oh dear oh dear oh dear yes I am here.

She says

In the distance there is daylight and near to there is none.

There is something under the leaves and Marguerite Ida and Helena Annabel makes a quick turn and she sees that a viper has stung her.

In the distance there is daylight and near to there is none.

There is a rustling under the leaves and Marguerite Ida and Helena Annabel makes a quick turn and she sees that a viper has stung her, she sees it and she says and what is it. There is no answer. Does it hurt she says and then she says no not really and she says was it a viper and she says how can I tell I never saw one before but is it she says and she stands up again and sits down and pulls down her stocking and says well it was not a bee not a busy bee no not, nor a mosquito nor a sting it was a bite and serpents bite yes they do perhaps it was one. Marguerite Ida and Helena Annabel sits thinking and then she sees a country woman with a sickle coming. Have I she says have I been bitten, the woman comes nearer, have I says Marguerite Ida and Helena Annabel have I have I been bitten. Have you been bitten answers the country woman, why yes it can happen, then I have been bitten says Marguerite Ida and Helena Annabel why not if you have been is the answer.

They stand repeating have I and yes it does happen and then Marguerite Ida and Helena Annabel says let me show you and the woman says oh yes but I have never seen any one who has been bitten but let me see no I cannot tell she says but go away and do something, what shall I do said Marguerite Ida and Helena Annabel do something to kill the poison, but what said Marguerite Ida and Helena Annabel, a doctor can do it said the woman but what doctor said Marguerite Ida and Helena Annabel, Doctor Faustus can do it said the woman, do you know him said Marguerite Ida and Helena Annabel no of course I do not know him nobody does there is a dog, he says thank you said the woman and go and see him go go go said the woman and Marguerite Ida and Helena Annabel went.

As she went she began to sing.
Do vipers sting do vipers bite
If they bite with all their might
Do they do they sting
Or do they do they bite
Alright they bite if they bite with all their might.
And I am I Marguerite Ida or am I Helena Annabel
Oh well
Am I Marguerite Ida or am I Helena Annabel
Very well oh very well
Am I Marguerite Ida very well am I Helena Annabel.

She stops she remembers the viper and in a whisper she says was it a sting was it a bite am I alright; was it a sting was it a bite, alright was it a sting, oh or was it a bite.

She moves away and then suddenly she stops.
Will he tell
Will he tell that I am Marguerite Ida that I am Helena Annabel.

Will he tell
     And then she stops again
And the bite might he make it a bite.
Doctor Faustus a queer name
Might he make it a bite
     And so she disappears.

Scene III

     Doctor Faustus the dog and the boy all sleeping, the dog
dreaming says thickly
Thank you, thank you thank you thank you thank you, thank you
thank you.
     Doctor Faustus turns and murmurs
Man and dog dog and man each one can tell it all like a ball with
a caress no tenderness, man and dog just the same each one can
take the blame each one can well as well tell it all as they can, man
and dog, well well man and dog what is the difference between a
man and a dog when I say none do I go away does he go away
go away to stay no nobody goes away the dog the boy they can
stay I can go away go away where where there there where, dog
and boy can annoy I can go say I go where do I go I go where I go,
where is there there is where and all the day and all the night too
it grew and grew and there is no way to say I and a dog and a boy,
if a boy is to grow to be a man am I a boy am I a dog is a dog a
boy is a boy a dog and what am I I cannot cry what am I oh what
am I
     And then he waits a moment and he says
Oh what am I.
     Just then in the distance there is a call
Doctor Faustus Doctor Faustus are you there Doctor Faustus I am
here Doctor Faustus I am coming there Doctor Faustus, there is
where Doctor Faustus oh where is there Doctor Faustus say it
Doctor Faustus are you there Doctor Faustus are you there.
     The dog murmurs
Thank you thank you
     and the boy says
There is somebody of course there is somebody just there there
is somebody somebody is there oh yes somebody is there.

and all together they say

Where is there nobody says nobody is there. Somebody is there and nobody says that somebody is not there. Somebody somebody is there somebody somebody somebody somebody says there is where where is it where is it where is it where, here is here here is there somebody somebody says where is where.

Outside the voice says

Doctor Faustus are you there Doctor Faustus any where, Doctor Faustus are you there.

And then there is a knock at the door.

The electric lights glow softly and Marguerite Ida and Helena Annabel comes in.

Well and yes well, and this is yes this is Doctor Faustus Doctor Doctor Faustus and he can and he can change a bite hold it tight make it not kill not kill Marguerite Ida not kill Helena Annabel and hell oh hell not a hell not well yes well Doctor Faustus can he can make it all well.

And then she says in a quiet voice.

Doctor Faustus have you ever been to hell.

Of course not she says of course you have not how could you sell your soul if you had ever been to hell of course not, no of course not.

Doctor Faustus tell me what did they give you when you sold your soul, not hell no of course not not hell.

And then she goes on.

I I am Marguerite Ida and Helena Annabel and a viper bit or stung it is very well begun and if it is so then oh oh I will die and as my soul has not been sold I Marguerite Ida and Helena Annabel perhaps I will go to hell.

The dog sighs and says

Thank you

and the little boy coming nearer says

what is a viper, tell me Marguerite Ida and Helena Annabel I like you being Marguerite Ida and Helena Annabel what is a viper do I know it very well or do I not know it very well please tell you are Marguerite Ida and Helena Annabel what is a viper.

Doctor Faustus says

Little boy and dog can be killed by a viper but Marguerite Ida and Helena Annabel not very well no not very well

(He bursts out)

Leave me alone

Let me be alone

Little boy and dog let me be alone, Marguerite Ida and Helena Annabel let me be alone, I have no soul I had no soul I sold it sold it here there and everywhere.

What did I do I knew

I knew that there could be light not moon-light star light day-light and candle light, I knew I knew I saw the lightening light, I saw it light, I said I I I must have that light, and what did I do oh what did I too I said I would sell my soul all through but I knew I knew that electric light was all true, and true oh yes it is true they took it that it was true that I sold my soul to them as well and so never never could I go to hell never never as well. Go away dog and boy go away Marguerite Ida and Helena Annabel go away all who can die and go to heaven or hell go away oh go away go away leave me alone oh leave me alone. I said it I said it was the light I said I gave the light I said the lights are right and the day is bright little boy and dog leave me alone let me be alone.

The country woman with the sickle looks in at the window and sings Well well this is the Doctor Faustus and he has not gone to hell he has pretty lights and they light so very well and there is a dog and he says thank you and there is a little boy oh yes little boy there you are you just are there yes little boy you are and there is Marguerite Ida and Helena Annabel and a viper did bite her, oh cure her Doctor Faustus cure her what is the use of your having been to hell if Marguerite Ida and Helena Annabel is not to be all well.

And the chorus sings

What is the use Doctor Faustus what is the use what is the use of having been to hell if you cannot cure this only only this Marguerite Ida and Helena Annabel.

Doctor Faustus says

I think I have thought thought is not bought oh no thought is not bought I think I have thought and what have I bought I have bought thought, to think is not bought but I I have bought thought and so you come here you come you come here and here and here where can I say that not to-day not any day can I look and see, no no I cannot look no no I cannot see and you you say you are Marguerite Ida and Helena Annabel and I I cannot see I cannot

see Marguerite Ida and I cannot see Helena Annabel and you you
are the two and I cannot cannot see you.

Marguerite Ida and Helena Annabel

Do not see me Doctor Faustus do not see me it would terrify me
if you did see do not see me no no do not see me I am Marguerite
Ida and Helena Annabel but do not see me cure me Doctor Faustus
do the viper bit the viper stung his sting was a bite and you you
have the light cure me Doctor Faustus cure me do but do not
see me, I see you but do not see me cure me do but do not see
me I implore you.

Doctor Faustus

A dog says thank you but you you say do not see me cure me
do but do not see me what shall I do.

He turns to the dog

The dog says

Thank you

and the boy says

What difference does it make to you if you do what difference
oh what difference does it make to you if you do, whatever you
do do whatever you do do what difference does it make to you
if you do.

Marguerite Ida and Helena Annabel

What difference does it make to you if you do what difference
does it make to you but I a viper has had his bite and I I will die
but you you cannot die you have sold your soul but I I have mine
and a viper has come and he has bitten me and see see how the
poison works see see how I must die, see how little by little it is
coming to be high, higher and higher I must die oh Doctor Faustus
what difference does it make to you what difference oh what
difference but to me to me to me to me a viper has bitten me a
bitter viper a viper has bitten me.

The dog

Oh Thank you thank you all all of you thank you thank you oh
thank you everybody thank you he and we thank you, a viper has
bitten you thank you thank you.

The boy

A viper has bitten her she knows it too a viper has bitten her
believe it or not it is true, a viper has bitten her and if Doctor
Faustus does not cure her it will be all through her a viper has
bitten her a viper a viper.

Dog

Thank you

Woman at the window

A viper has bitten her and if Doctor Faustus does not cure her it
will be all through her.

Chorus in the distance

Who is she

She has not gone to hell

Very well

Very well

She has not gone to hell

Who is she

Marguerite Ida and Helena Annabel

And what has happened to her

A viper has bitten her

And if Doctor Faustus does not cure her

It will go all through her

And he what does he say

He says he cannot see her

Why cannot he see her

Because he cannot look at her

He cannot look at Marguerite Ida and Helena Annabel

But he cannot cure her without seeing her

They say yes yes

And he says there is no witness

And he says

He can but he will not

And she says he must and he will

And the dog says thank you

And the boy says very well

And the woman says well cure her and she says she is Marguerite
Ida and Helena Annabel.

There is silence the lights flicker and flicker, and Marguerite
Ida and Helena Annabel gets weaker and weaker and the poison
stronger and stronger and suddenly the dog says startlingly

Thank you

Doctor Faustus says

I cannot see you

The viper has forgotten you.

The dog has said thank you

The boy has said will you
The woman has said
Can you
And you, you have said you are you
Enough said.
You are not dead.
Enough said
Enough said.
You are not dead.
No you are not dead
Enough said
Enough said
You are not dead.

All join in enough said you are not dead you are not dead
enough said yes enough said no you are not dead yes enough said,
thank you yes enough said no you are not dead.

And at the last
In a low whisper
She says
I am Marguerite Ida and Helena Annabel and enough said I am
not dead.

Curtain

ACT II

Some one comes and sings
Very
Very
Butter better very well
Butcher whether it will tell
Well is well and silver sell
Sell a salted almond to Nell
Which she will accept
And then
What does a fatty do
She does not pay for it.
No she does not

Does not pay for it.
By this time they know how to spell very
Very likely the whole thing is really extraordinary
Which is a great relief
All the time her name is Marguerite Ida Marguerite Ida
     They drift in and they sing
Very likely the whole thing is extraordinary
Which is a great relief
All the time her name is Marguerite Ida
Marguerite Ida.
     Then they converse about it.
Marguerite Ida is her name Marguerite Ida and Helena Annabel
who can tell if her name is Marguerite Ida or Helena Annabel
Sillies all that is what makes you tall.
To be tall means to say that everything else is layed away.
Of course her names is Marguerite Ida too and Helena Annabel as
well.
     A full chorus
Of course her names is Marguerite Ida too and Helena Annabel as
well.
     A deep voice asks
Would a viper have stung her if she had only had one name would
he would he.
How do you know how do you know that a viper did sting her.
How could Doctor Faustus have cured her if there had not been
something the matter with her.
Marguerite Ida and Helena Annabel it is true her name is Marguerite Ida and Helena Annabel as well and a viper has stung her
and Doctor Faustus has cured her, cured her cured her, he has
sold his soul to hell cured her cured her cured he he has sold
his soul to hell and her name is Marguerite Ida and Helena Annabel
and a viper had to bite her and Doctor Faustus had to cure her
cure her cure her cure her.
     The curtain at the corner raises and there she is Marguerite
Ida and Helena Annabel and she has an artificial viper there beside
her and a halo is around her not of electric light but of candle light,
and she sits there and waits.
     The chorus sings
There she is
Is she there

Look and see
Is she there
Is she there
Anywhere
Look and see
Is she there
Yes she is there
There is there
She is there
Look and see
She is there.
There she is
There there
Where
Why there
Look and see there
There she is
And what is there
A viper is there
The viper that bit her
No silly no
How could he be there
This is not a viper
This is what is like a viper
She is there
And a viper did bite her
And Doctor Faustus did cure her
And now
And now
And now she is there
Where
Why there
Oh yes there.
Yes oh yes yes there.
There she is
Look and see
And the viper is there
And the light is there
Who gave her the light
Nobody did

Doctor Faustus sold his soul
And so the light came there
And did she sell her soul.
No silly he sold his soul
She had a viper bite her
She is there
Oh yes she is there
Look there
Yes there
She is there.
    Marguerite Ida begins to sing
I sit and sit with my back to the sun I sat and sat with my back
to the sun. Marguerite Ida sat and sat with her back to the sun.
The sun oh the sun the lights are bright like the sun set and she
sat with her back to the sun sat and sat
    She sits
    A very grand ballet of lights.
Nobody can know that it so
They come from everywhere
By land by sea by air
They come from everywhere
To look at her there.
See how she sits
See how she eats
See how she lights,
The candle lights.
See how the viper there,
Cannot hurt her.
No indeed he cannot.
Nothing can touch her,
She has everything
And her soul,
Nothing can lose her,
See how they come
See how they come
To see her.
See how they come.
Watch
They come by sea
They come by land

They come by air
And she sits
With her back to the sun
One sun
And she is one
Marguerite Ida and Helena Annabel as well.

They commence to come and more and more come and they come from the sea from the land and from the air.

And she sits.

A man comes from over the seas and a great many are around him

He sees her as she sits.

And he says

Pretty pretty dear
She is all my love and always here
And I am hers and she is mine
And I love her all the time
Pretty pretty pretty dear.
No says the chorus no.
She is she and the viper bit her
And Doctor Faustus cured her.
The man from over seas repeats
Pretty pretty pretty dear
She is all my love and always here
And I am hers and she is mine
And I love her all the time.

Marguerite Ida and Helena Annabel suddenly hears something and says
What is it.

He comes forward and says again
Pretty pretty pretty dear she is all my love and she is always here.

She sings slowly
You do or you do not.

He
Pretty pretty dear she is all my love and she is always here.
Well well he says well well and her name is Marguerite Ida and Helena Annabel and they all say it was a viper, what is a viper, a viper is a serpent and anybody has been bitten and not everybody dies and cries, and so why why say it all the time, I have been bitten I I I have been bitten by her bitten by her there she

sits with her back to the sun and I have won I have won her I
have won her.

She sings a song
You do or you do not
You are or you are not
I am there is no not
But you you you
You are as you are not

He says
Do you do what you do because you knew all the way through
that I I was coming to you answer me that.

She turns her back on him.

And he says
I am your sun oh very very well begun, you turn your back on
your sun, I am your sun, I have won I have won I am your sun.

Marguerite Ida and Helena Annabel rises. She holds the viper
she says
Is it you Doctor Faustus is it you, tell me man from over the sea
are you he.

He laughs.
Are you afraid now afraid of me.

She says
Are you he.

He says
I am the only he and you are the only she and we are the only we.
Come come do you hear me come come, you must come to me,
throw away the viper throw away the sun throw away the lights
until there are none. I am not any one I am the only one, you
have to have me because I am that one.

She looks very troubled and drops the viper but she instantly
stoops and picks it up and some of the lights go out and she fusses
about it.

And then suddenly she starts,
No one is one when there are two, look behind you look behind
you you are not one you are two.

She faints.

And indeed behind the man of the seas is Mephistopheles and
with him is a boy and a
girl.

Together they sing the song the boy and the girl.

Mr. Viper think of me. He says you do she says you do and if you
do dear Mr. Viper if you do then it is all true he is a boy I am a
girl it is all true dear dear Mr. Viper think of me.

The chorus says in the back,

Dear dear Mr. Viper think of them one is a boy one is a girl
dear dear viper dear dear viper think of them.

Marguerite Ida and Helena Annabel still staring at the man
from over the seas and Mephisto behind them.

She whispers,

They two I two they two that makes six it should be seven they
two I two they two five is heaven.

Mephisto says

And what if I ask what answer me what, I have a will of iron
yes a will to do what I do. I do what I do what I do, I do I do.

And he strides forward,

Where where where are you, what a to do, when a light is bright
there is moon-light, when a light is not so bright then it is day-
light, and when a light is no light than it is electric light, but you
you have candle light, who are you.

The ballet rushes in and out.

Marguerite Ida and Helena Annabel lifts the viper and says
Lights are all right but the viper is my might.

Pooh says Mephisto, I despise a viper, the viper tries but the
viper lies. Me they cannot touch no not any such, a viper, ha ha
a viper, a viper, ha ha, no the lights the lights the candle lights,
I know a light when I see a light, I work I work all day and all
night, I am the devil and day and night, I never sleep by any light
by any dark by any might, I never sleep not by day not by night,
you cannot fool me by candle light, where is the real electric light
woman answer me.

The little boy and girl creep closer, they sing.

Mr. Viper dear Mr. Viper, he is a boy I am a girl she is a girl
I am a boy we do not want to annoy but we do oh we do oh
Mr. Viper yes we do we want you to know that she is a girl that
I am boy, oh yes Mr. Viper please Mr. Viper here we are Mr.
Viper listen to us Mr. Viper, oh please Mr. Viper it is not true
Mr. Viper what the devil says Mr. Viper that there is no Mr. Viper,
please Mr. Viper please Mr. Viper, she is a girl he is a boy please
Mr. Viper you are Mr. Viper please Mr. Viper please tell us so.

The man from over the seas smiles at them all, and says

It is lovely to be at ease.
    Mephisto says
What you know I am the devil and you do not listen to me I
work and I work by day and by night and you do not listen to me
he and she she and he do not listen to me you will see you will see,
if I work day and night and I do I do I work day and night, then
you will see what you will see, look out look out for me.
    He rushes away
    And Helena Annabel and Marguerite Ida shrinks back, and
says to them all
What does he say
    And the man from over the seas says
Pretty pretty dear she is all my love and she is always here.
    and then more slowly
I am the only he you are the only she and we are the only we,
    and the chorus sings softly
And the viper did bite her and Doctor Faustus did cure her.
    And the boy and girl sing softly.
Yes Mr. Viper he is a boy she is a girl yes Mr. Viper.
    And the ballet of lights fades away.

Curtain

ACT III ⸌ Scene I

Doctor Faustus' house
Faustus in his chair, the dog and the boy, the electric lights
are right but the room is dark.
    Faustus
Yes they shine
They shine all the time.
I know they shine
I see them shine
And I am here
I have no fear
But what shall I do
I am all through
I cannot bear
To have no care

I like it bright
I do like it bright
Alright I like it bright,
But is it white
Or is it bright.
Dear dear
I do care
That nobody can share.
What if they do
It is all to me
Ah I do not like that word me,
Why not even if it does rhyme with she. I know all the words that
rhyme with bright with light with might with alright, I know them
so that I cannot tell I can spell but I cannot tell how much I need
to not have that, not light not sight, not light not night not alright,
not night not sight not bright, no no not night not sight not bright
no no not bright.

   There is a moment's silence and then the dog says
Thank you.

   He turns around and then he says
Yes thank you.

   And then he says
Not bright not night dear Doctor Faustus you are right, I am a
dog yes I am just that I am I am a dog and I bay at the moon,
I did yes I did I used to do it I used to bay at the moon I always
used to do it and now now not any more, I cannot, of course I
cannot, the electric lights they make it be that there is no night
and if there is no night then there is no moon and if there is no
moon I do not see it and if I do not see it I cannot bay at it.

   The dog sighs and settles down to rest
   and as he settles down he says
Thank you.

   The little boy cuddles up close to him and says
Yes there is no moon and if there is a moon then we do not bay
at the moon and if there is no moon then no one is crazy any more
because it is the moon of course it is the moon that always made
them be like that, say thank you doggie and I too I too with you
will say thank you.

   They softly murmur
Thank you thank you thank you too.

They all sleep in the dark with the electric light all bright, and then at the window comes something.

Is it the moon says the dog is it the moon says the boy is it the moon do not wake me is it the moon says Faustus.

No says a woman no it is not it is not the moon, I am not the moon I am at the window Doctor Faustus do not you know what it is that is happening.

No answer.

Doctor Faustus do not you know what is happening.

Back of her a chorus

Doctor Faustus do not you know what is happening.

Still no answer

All together louder

Doctor Faustus do not you know do not you know what it is that is happening.

Doctor Faustus.

Go away woman and men, children and dogs moon and stars go away let me alone let me be alone no light is bright, I have no sight, go away woman and let me boy and dog let me be alone I need no light to tell me it is bright, go away go away, go away go away.

No says the woman no I am at the window and here I remain till you hear it all. Here we know because Doctor Faustus tells us so, that he only he can turn night into day but now they say, they say, (her voice rises to a screech) they say a woman can turn night into day, they say a woman and a viper bit her and did not hurt her and he showed her how and now she can turn night into day, Doctor Faustus oh Doctor Faustus say you are the only one who can turn night into day, oh Doctor Faustus yes do say that you are the only one who can turn night into day.

The chorus behind says

Oh Doctor Faustus oh Doctor Faustus do say that you are the only one who can turn night into day.

Faustus starts up confused he faces the woman, he says,
What is it you say.

And she says imploringly,

Oh Doctor Faustus do say you are the only one who can turn night into day.

Faustus slowly draws himself erect and says

Yes I do say I am the only one who can turn night into day.

And the woman and the chorus say,
He is the only one who can turn night into day.
And the dog says
He is the only one who can turn night into day, there is no moon
any night or any day he is the only one to turn night into day,
and the little boy says
Yes he is the only one to turn night into day.
And the woman then says
But come Doctor Faustus come away come and see whether they
say that they can turn night into day.
Who says
says Doctor Faustus
She says
says the woman
Who is she
says Doctor Faustus
The answer
Marguerite Ida or Helena Annabel
She
says Doctor Faustus
Who said I could not go to hell.
She she
says the woman
She she
says the chorus
Thank you
said the dog
Well
said Doctor Faustus
Well then I can go to hell, if she can turn night into day then I
can go to hell, come on then come on we will go and see her and
I will show her that I can go to hell, if she can turn night into day
as they say then I am not the only one very well I am not the only
one so Marguerite Ida and Helena Annabel listen well you can-
not but I I can go to hell. Come on every one never again will
I be alone come on come on every one.
They all leave.

Scene II

The scene as before, Marguerite Ida and Helena Annabel
sitting with the man from over the seas their backs to the sun, the
music to express a noon-day hush.

Everybody dreamily saying
Mr. Viper please Mr. Viper,
some saying
Is he is he Doctor Faustus no he isn't no he isn't, is he is he is he
all he loves her is he is he all she loves him, no one can remember
anything but him, which is she and which is he sweetly after all
there is no bee there is a viper such a nice sweet quiet one, nobody
any body knows how to run, come any one come, see any one,
some, come viper sun, we know no other any one, any one can
forget a light, even an electric one but no one no no one can forget
a viper even a stuffed one no no one and no one can forget the
sun and no one can forget Doctor Faustus no no one and and
no one can forget Thank you and the dog and no one can forget
a little boy and no one can forget any one no no one.

(These words to be distributed among the chorus)
and the man from over seas murmurs dreamily
Pretty pretty pretty dear here I am and you are here and yet
and yet it would be better yet if you had more names and not
only four in one let it be begun, forget it oh forget it pretty one,
and if not I will forget that you are one yes I will yes I will
pretty pretty one yes I will.

Marguerite Ida and Helena Annabel stiffens a little
Well will you yes I will, no one can know when I do not tell
then so that they cannot know anything they know, yes I know,
I do know just what I can know, it is not there well anywhere, I
cannot come not for any one I cannot say what is night and day
but I am the only one who can know anything about any one,
am I one dear dear am I one, who hears me knows me I am here
and here I am, yes here I am.

The chorus gets more lively and says
Yes there she is
Dear me
says the man from over the seas.
Just then out of the gloom appears at the other end of the

stage Faust and the boy and the dog, nobody sees them, just then in front of every one appears Mephisto, very excited and sings

Which of you can dare to deceive me which of you he or she can dare to deceive me, I who have a will of iron I who make what will be happen I who can win men or women I who can be wherever I am which of you has been deceiving which of you she or he which of you have been deceiving me.

He shouts louder

If there is a light who has the right, I say I gave it to him, she says he gave it to her or she does not say anything, I say I am Mephisto and what I have I do not give no not to any one, who has been in her who has been in him, I will win.

The boy and girl shrilly sing

She is she and he is he and we are we Mr. Viper do not forget to be. Please Mr. Viper do not forget to be, do not forget that she is she and that he is he please Mr. Viper do not forget me.

Faustus murmurs in a low voice

I sold my soul to make it bright with electric light and now no one not I not she not they not he are interested in that thing and I and I I cannot go to hell I have sold my soul to make a light and the light is bright but not interesting in my sight and I would oh yes I would I would rather go to hell be I with all my might and then go to hell oh yes alright.

Mephisto strides up to him and says

You deceived me.

I did not

says Faustus

Mephisto.

You deceived me and I am never deceived

Faust, you deceived me and I am always deceived,

Mephisto, you deceived me and I am never deceived.

Faustus

Well well let us forget it is not ready yet let us forget and now oh how how I want to be me myself all now, I do not care for light let it be however light, I do not care anything but to be well and to go to hell. Tell me oh devil tell me will she will Marguerite Ida and Helena Annabel will she will she really will she go to hell.

Mephisto

I suppose so.

Faustus

Well then how dear devil how how can I who have no soul I sold it for a light how can I be I again alright and go to hell.

Mephisto

Commit a sin

Faustus

What sin, how can I without a soul commit a sin.

Mephisto

Kill anything

Faustus

Kill

Mephisto

Yes kill something oh yes kill anything.

Yes it is I who have been deceived I the devil who no one can deceive yes it is I I who have been deceived.

Faustus

But if I kill what then will.

Mephisto

It is I who have an iron will.

Faustus

But if I kill what will happen then.

Mephisto

Oh go to hell.

Faustus

I will

He turns he sees the boy and dog he says

I will kill I will I will.

He whispers

I will kill I will I will.

He turns to the boy and dog and he says

Boy and dog I will kill you two I will kill I will I will boy and dog I will kill you kill you, the viper will kill you but it will be I who did it, you will die.

The dog says

Thank you, the light is so bright there is no moon tonight I cannot bay at the moon the viper will kill me. Thank you,

and the boy says

And I too, there is no day and night there is no dog to-night to say thank you the viper will kill me too, good-bye to you.

In the distance the voices of the boy and girl are heard saying

Mr. Viper please listen to me he is a boy she is a girl.

There is a rustle the viper appears and the dog and the boy die.

Faustus

They are dead yes they are dead, dear dog dear boy yes you are dead you are forever ever ever dead and I I can because you die nobody can deny later I will go to hell very well very well I will go to hell Marguerite Ida Helena Annabel I come to tell to tell you that I can go to hell.

Mephisto

And I, while you cry I who do not deny that now you can go to hell have I nothing to do with you.

Faustus

No I am through with you I do not need the devil I can go to hell all alone. Leave me alone let me be alone I can go to hell all alone.

Mephisto

No listen to me now take her with you do I will make you young take her with you do Marguerite Ida and Helena Annabel take her with you do.

Faustus

Is it true that I can be young.

Mephisto

Yes.

Faustus

Alright.

He is young he approaches Marguerite Ida and Helena Annabel who wakes up and looks at him. He says

Look well I am Doctor Faustus and I can go to hell.

Marguerite Ida and Helena Annabel

You Doctor Faustus never never Doctor Faustus is old I was told and I saw it with my eyes he was old and could not go to hell and you are young and can go to hell, very well you are not Doctor Faustus never never.

Faustus

I am I am I killed the boy and dog when I was an old man and now I am a young man and you Marguerite Ida and Helena Annabel and you know it well and you know I can go to hell and I can take some one too and that some one will be you.

Marguerite Ida and Helena Annabel

Never never, never never, you think you are so clever you think

you can deceive, you think you can be old and you are young and
old like any one but never never, I am Marguerite Ida and Helena
Annabel and I know no man or devil no viper and no light I can
be anything and everything and it is always always alright. No
one can deceive me not a young man not an old man not a devil
not a viper I am Marguerite Ida and Helena Annabel and never
never will a young man be an old man and an old man be a
young man, you are not Doctor Faustus no not ever never never

    and she falls back fainting into the arms of the man from over
    the seas who sings

Pretty pretty pretty dear I am he and she is she and we are we,
pretty pretty dear I am here yes I am here pretty pretty pretty
dear.

    Mephisto strides up

Always deceived always deceived I have a will of iron and I am
always deceived always deceived come Doctor Faustus I have a
will of iron and you will go to hell.

    Faustus sings

Leave me alone let me be alone, dog and boy boy and dog leave
me alone let me be alone

    and he sinks into the darkness and it is all dark and the little
    boy and the little girl sing

Please Mr. Viper listen to me he is he and she is she and we are
we please Mr. Viper listen to me.

Curtain

AN EXERCISE IN ANALYSIS

⸙ 1917 ⸙

A PLAY

I have given up analysis.

Act II

Splendid profit.

Act III

I have paid my debt to humanity.

Act III

Hurry.

Act IV

Climb. In climbing do not be contented.

Part II

Run ahead.
Run on ahead.

Act II

Have you a knife.

Act III

Do not see soldiers ahead they swim.

Act IV

So they do.

Part III

When we wheel where there is a turning. That is the meaning of wheel.

Act II

Acts are longer.

Act III

Places resemble their mother.

Act III

They have the beauty of their father and the intelligence of their mother.

Act IV

A long time.
Who is the packer.
Miss Morton comes first.

Part II

Extra size plates.

Act II

Believe in saying divided duty. Believe in saying a delay divided is divided between a mother and Mrs. Turner.
Can you wish me that.
I can wish you winds.
All winds make water.
I can wish you water.
I can wish you a drawing of a little goat in a great deal of work. Work is pleasant to me.

Act II

In acting again we are acting offensively.

Act III

He doesn't like the poor in Barcelona they do not like the poor.

Act IV

What did she see when she saw men swimming.

Part III

Examples.

Examples and examples.
All examples of children.
Now to ask guns.
Now to ask colors.
She was settled for it. For life. For me.

Act II

Come again for three days come again for three days come again for three days.

Act III

All the ways of pigeons. All ways and deception. She did not deceive me. Do not deceive her cousin. Her cousin makes powder. Heat.

Act IV

Can you counsel me.

Part IV

I want to know something and Miss Douglas won't tell me. May I ask it. Do you feel strong.
When.
When you write.

Act II

And memory. Do you believe in memory and in credibility. Do you have winter weather here.

Act III

We do not allow Mr. Douglas to be contradicted here. We do not desire that he should feel himself beginning to be about to be wrong.
Then you agree with what ever he says.
I do not say that this is so I say so.

Act IV

Now I understand.

Part V

Can you match streets.

Can you believe in parks.
Do you like democracy.
Have you a king in Greece.

Act II

There are plenty of places in which to be idle.

Act III

Not all of them are agreeable.

Act IV

Not when there is likelihood of invasion. We live here.

Part VI

Can you forgive me.

Act II

Can you see that I have heard that the meaning of extravagance is in doing that again.

Act III

Doing that again.

Act IV

I partly said author.

Part VII

This is a reasonable food.

Act II

This is not an unreasonable carriage.

Act III

There is plenty of rubber in America.

Act IV

And in Europe.

Part VIII

In the middle of the river there is not always water.

Act II

Not in Spain.

Act III

Nor in Mexico.

Act IV

Nor in Arizona.

Part IX

Please me when you do please me.

Act II

And in there.

Act III

Where.

Act IV

In the room.

Part X

When can you believe me.

Act II

When can he believe me.

Act III

When can they say they wonder.

Act IV

When shall we have another.

Part X

Recollections.

Act II

To a duchess.

Act III

A dowager duchess.

Act IV

A husband.

Part XI

A husband and a wife.

Act II

Splendid leaves.

Act III

He introduced me.

Act IV

They introduced me too.

Part XII

Can you recollect missing him.

Act II

Can you follow me quickly.

Act III

He was a boy.

Act IV

You are once more an American.

Part XIII

Can you remember what she said.

Act II

Can you remember him.

Act III

He will be glad not to have married Sylvia.

Act IV

He will never be needed in the business.

Part XIV

He will never be needed in that business.

Act II

He is ashamed of his message.

Act III

She is ashamed of her system.

Act IV

He is never neglected.

Part XV

I am awfully sorry.

Act II

Thanks so much.

Act III

We ask for him.

Act IV

We can send butter.

Part XVI

We cannot send butter.

Act II

Mrs. Turner can come.

Act III

In the winter.

Act IV

Remember the weather.

Part XVII

A kind way.

Act II

A very kind way.

Act III

I am really in search of a flavor.

Act IV

So am I.

Part XVIII

Can you see numbers.

Act II

Can you read about numbers.

Act III

And four.

Act IV

Smiles.

Part XIX

I can see what I hear.

Act II

I can hear too.

Act III

So can I when I wish.

Act IV

So can Mrs. Turner.

Part XX

More silky than ever how do you do it.

Act II

Houses.

Act III

Can we see the set.

Act IV

The set of what.

Part XXI

I borrow you.

Act II

Why do you have that.

Act III

Because it pleases me.

Act IV

You said you would not be married.

Part XXII

Plenty of space to put things together.

Act II

Here is plenty of space.

Act III

There is an excuse.

Act IV

There is no excuse.

Part XXIII

We went to-day.

Act III

We went there to-day.

Act III

I cannot repeat what they say.

Act IV

Neither can I.

Part XXIV

Can you speak to me.

Act II

Can you speak to me here.

Act III

Can you speak to me about it.

Act IV

Can you speak to me about anything. Can you speak to me.

Part XXV

Can you complain to-day.

Act II

Can you.

Act III

Do you know about wishes.

Act IV

I do know all about it.

Part XXVI

Can you recollect me.

Act II

What were the opportunities of meeting you.

Act III

What have you sold.

Act IV

Why are you so certain.

Part XXVII

I want to be simple too.

Act II

Of course you do.

Act III

Can you come at four.

Act IV

Yes indeed.

Part XXVIII

Can you understand me.

Act II

I can understand you very well.

Act III

Do you agree with Miss Crutwell.

Act IV

I do not.

Part XXIX

Can you be to blame.

Act II

Can they be to blame in this.

Act III

Can they request a question.

Act IV

Can they see they are polite.

Part XXX

No they cannot feel the purpose.

Act II

No they cannot have time.

Act III

No they can be observant.

Act IV

No indeed for me.

Part XXXI

I do not like such a declaration.

Act II

Do not tell me about birds.

Act III

What is a bird.

Act IV

We have suffered.

Part XXXII

I can cure anything.

Act II

So can most fishes.

Act III

And birds.

Act IV

And water-fowl.

Part XXXIII

There is plenty to blame.

Act II

The introductions.

Act III

Waiting.

Act IV

And memory.

Part XXXIV

Please be mannish.

Act II

Please do.

Act III

Please do be a sailor.

Act IV

Please be womanish.

Part XXXV

A bird.

Act II

There are many parts to the bird.

Act III

She knows.

Act IV

So do I.

Part XXXVI

I am not amused.

Act II

It was a copy.

Act III

It was a copy.

Act IV

It was a copy.

Part XXXVII

Do not make a mistake.

Act II

Take care.

Act III

Have a pleasant time.

Act IV

Remain there.

Part XXXVIII

I express an opinion.

Act II

You express an opinion too.

Part XXXIX

Can you say that you excuse me.

Act II

Can you say that you excuse him from the room.

Act III

Can you say anything about it.

Part XL

She doesn't mind.

Act II

She does not mind.

Act III

Neither does she mind.

Act IV

We do not mind him.

Part XLI

Leave us in that way.

Act II

Was she the first one to say do you smoke.

Act III

Was he the last one here.

Act IV

To be here.

Part XLII

Can you see very much.

Act II

Can you see very much here.

Act III

Here and there.

Act IV

Can you paint that, the color of that house.

Act V

Yes I can.

Act VI

Thank you.

Part XLIII

Satisfy them.

Act II

Do satisfy them.

Act III

Do they make that noise.

Act IV

They do or they do not.

Part XLIV

Can you finish.

Act II

And make a mistake.

Act III

And not make a mistake there.

Act IV

And have a treasure.

Part XLV

Of course I have a treasure.

Act II

Of course I have so much thought.

Act III

Do not be ungrateful.

Act IV

To me.

Part XLVI

Can you believe me when I swim.

Act II

Can you trust me.

Act III

Can you have a wife.

Part XLVII

Please do not mention that address.

Act II

To me.

Act III

Do not believe me when I tell you that it is so.

Part XLVIII

In the sense that as.

Act II

Spread it.

Act III

To Hungary.

Act IV

And New York.

Part XLIX

This was what I meant.

Act II

Oh did you indeed.

Part L

The next time we go we will go together.

Part LI

Please me.

Act II

Do please me.

Act III

Please me pleasantly.

Act IV

Yes I will.

Part LII

Can you sing.

Act II

I have asked you that before.

Act III

I can ask you again.

Act IV

You can if you like.

Part LIII

Can you not vary it.

Act II

By what.

Act III

By making changes.

Act IV

Oh yes.

Part LIV

Why do you wish me to eat differently.

Act II

You mean less quickly.

Act III

I mean what I say.

Act IV

Yes it is true.

Part LV

Can you come together.

Act II

Can you come together.

Act III

Can you come together.

Act IV

Can you come together.

Part LVI

Can you come together.

Part LVII

What is the name of the bedding.

Act II

It is different.

Act III

Of course it is different.

Act III

Then don't explain.

Part LVIII

Can you be foolish.

Act II

You mean in your thoughts.

Act III

In recommending a novel.

Act IV

Get all the books you can.

Part LX

Not disappointed.

Act II

Not in there.

Act III

Call me.

Act IV

Call me Ellen.

A CIRCULAR PLAY

⚹ 1920 ⚹

A PLAY IN CIRCLES

First in a circle.

Papa dozes mamma blows her noses.
We cannot say this the other way.
Exactly.
Passably.

Second in circles.

A citroen and a citizen
A miss and bliss.
We came together.
Then suddenly there was an army.
In my room.
We asked them to go away
We asked them very kindly to stay.
How can Cailloux be dead again.
Napoleon is dead.
Not again.
A morning celebration.
And a surprising birthday.
A room is full of odd bits of disturbing furniture.
Guess again.

The third circle.

Round as around as my apple.
An apple is out of season
So are raisins.
We rise above it.
A circle is contained in there.

Four times three.

Canned fruit and sugar

139

Plates at Toys
Coal and wood.
Hat blocked.
He is blocked by a driver.
I forget.
Little silver clasp for necklace.
Circles.
We can be won to believe that the President saw through the trick.

Miss Mildred Aldrich is isolated. Is isolated with the President.
A circular play.
Cut wood cut wood.
I hear a sore.
Stop being thundering.
I meant wondering.
He meant blundering.
I have been mistaken.
No one is so certain.
She is certain.
Certainly right.
Can I be so sorry.
How can I turn around. I will leave it to her to decide how to arrange it.

Circle Hats.

My color.
Their color.
Two
One
Two won.
I can think so quickly.
Silent and thoughtful. Crimson rambler and a legion post legion, a poor post legion. Crimson rambler or star.

Circles.

It is a good idea to stare. We had our photographs taken, not intentionally but we happened to have seats in the front row near the arena and so when a photograph was taken we were in it.

In a circle.

The Inner circle is one in which we hope to engage places.
We were so sorry.
A great many people realise this better.

In the morning.

Good night.

Encircle.

A dog with a rabbit.

How can you tell a treasure.

We can tell by the reaction. And after that. And after that we are pleased.

The idea of circle.

I bind myself to exercise myself only in one way.

Beauty in a circle.

A beauty is not suddenly in a circle. It comes with rapture. A great deal of beauty is rapture. A circle is a necessity. Otherwise you would see no one. We each have our circle. How old is America. Very old.

The Circle.

The work can you work.

And meat

Can you meet

And flour

Can you flower

Calligraphy. Writing to a girl.

A great many say we have wives and children to-day.

Can you be angry at women.

Another circle.

I believe that they are pleased with us.

For a circle.

Prizes.

When you win prizes.

Explain winning prizes.

A growing plant is given to us.

Mrs. de Monzy has adopted a child.

A mildred circle.

The balcony is airy. You can put five persons on it. Do little children have hernia. Are they born with it. Babies smile. Have a care of a vermillion.

A circle higher.

Jennie dance to Marguerite. Vera dance alone. And what can you say about tuberculosis.

It was not a circle. Amelia and Susan were not scared. They said we are refreshed by the news. I can never forget the slaughter.

Eggs and eggs.

A dog stares.

Mrs. Whitney before her door.

Circular saws.

Did you speak of offering, did you speak of offering me.

Offer is a word used.

Oil well is a well.

Try fish exclusively.

Jessie Jessie said.

Do have a line.

Or go ahead.

Go ahead of him.

Discharge blessing.

Mrs. Wells lives in Palma da Mallorca.

We are going to dinner Thursday.

She is the first to profit here.

Circle sings.

At first in circles.

Jessie Jessie is not messy. She has her old carriage.

I knew that bird. I was deceived by the star-light. The morning makes mention of the sun and the dirt of Lockey and all of that of Caesar. Dear Caesar I am always willing to wear Caesars. Not down or away but stay.

An inner circle.

And inner circle again. Do tease me. Nose kisses and thirds. I have been deceived. No you have been refused. I have refused ten spots as one. But not as ten. As ten. But not as too. Dear thought and receipt.

A climbing entrance.

This is a circle.

Legally a circle.

When the Russians speak.

When did you hear from me last.

This is the way we settle.

Circle one.

Has he been rude.

Did he touch me.

Circle two.

Can you be careful of money. Can you believe in roses. Can you make mint like lilacs that is the leaves.

Nelly can.

Circle three.

Red on it.

It is strange to distribute it to the women. They can see around it. It makes them young.

Does it around.

Round they are.

Circle Four.

She can admire me always. She can always admire me.

Do not try circles exclusively.

Four circles.

He was a disappointment to me. I could not understand the reason for the waiting. Do we prefer seven or fourteen. Do we like sixteen times fifty. We are all agreed that we like the letters of Henry James.

Consider a circle.

In the car there are four three if you like and outside two, four if you like. Four necessarily more than. Two necessarily more than two.

Four if you like.

Expressly a circle.

Were we at home. In messages, in sending messages, in quarreling, in shooting, in endangering, in resolving and in destroying there is a course of events. Honeysuckle grows and peas. Can you sing together.

Not a circular saw.

I saw what I saw.

Believe me to be an offender. Offend me and I do not wish to hear from Ollie. Can you explain that contraction.

A mystery.

Sing in a circle.

Messages are received all the time. Frank says. Mildred. An afternoon.

Leave a circle.

Leaves in or circle.

In travelling to California what do you say to me. I say oh have you been thin.

Leaves or a circle.

I leave you there.

Do not despair.

I recollect that there is no hurry. Why do the Indians make China. They make Indo china.

Leaves for to-day.

A circle in royalty.

Royal circles are distinguished by their color.

Remain in a circle.

A distinction. Have they changed their minds. He looks very well. We were surprised that he did not resemble Mr. Mirrlees. You meant the Frenchman.

A Neapolitan noble is a neapolitan noble. And women are that. Do you know the brother. Poor brother he is dead. He was killed in the army.

Let us circle.

We circle around.

Not a fragrance not a common gift not an address. A change of scene.

She was glad to come to Paris.

A little boy in a large circle.

An island is not round by much.

Commence again to encircle water.

Sleep a credit to me or.

Or what did I say.

A circle stretches. From San Francisco to the sun. From Tangier to the moon. From London to the water.

From Bird to lessens.

Can a circle enlist.

Can a circle exist.

Can we be all tall.

50 pounds and 40 pounds makes 80 pounds. We paid for thirty pounds. I paid for it all.

Crushed circle.

Red or cranberries.

Strawberries or meat.

Sugar or potatoes.

Roast beef or water.

Melon or rehearsed.

Take a street.

One does not run around in a circle to make a circular play.

Do not run around in a circle and make a circular play.

It is not necessary to run around in a circle to get ready to write a circular play.

I used to be able to do this very nicely.

Once more I think about conversations.

Conversations conversions, Hindustani and remorse.

I necessarily gather a circle.

I gather in a circle.

And now to play.

Play for a circle.

Do stand proudly.

Do paint well.

Do call hearers.

Do believe in roads.

Do have dark currants.

In a circle.

They gathered to say.

Figs.

Butter.

Pine apple cloth.

Hurt oranges.

And melons.

In July we are in the midst of summer.

Will be happy to-day.

Inner circle.

How can I finish.

Now think.

I think of a reason.

Often soften.

A Negro.

A splendid custom and a splendid interest.

I believe in whirrs.

Fourth of July.

Strawberries.

Flags strawberries and yellow flowers.

Now we really circle.

Action.

When we first see Sylvia we ask where have you been.

When we first recall them we say and your mother.

We expect them soon.

Early in July.

With tobacco.

But no dream.

This is the way we act.

Come in.

How do you like Morocco.

Very well and the weight is splendid.

In a circle.

A father and mother and a son.

Mother father son and daughter.

Can I recall nations.

Around the grass.

             Relieved for a circle.

Cause an excitement.

The cause of an excitement is this, the language is not the same, the door is not the same the bed is the same the door is the same the window is nearly the same and the pencil is of silver.

In bringing a thing into the country can we ask is it of gold. A country is not in a circle it is near and in the distance.

Let me amuse you.

           Round circles.

Realise that you have to write a letter.

And teeth

Teeth are sincerely regretted.

I want to urge winter.

           Encircle Alice.

I have not met their wife.

And how can Alice pay.

She makes Herbert work like a Turk.

           Sing fifty.

A circle of her children.

Can you be sorry he went.

Can you be sorry that she went away.

           Now we come to the circle.

Frederick.

A Palm.

Jacky.

Leaves.

George

A diary.

Marion
Wishes.
Mabel
Reckless.
And Harriet,
Dear Harriet.

Sing circles.

Can you believe that Mary Ethel has plans.
Indeed I do and I respect her husband.
Do you dislike her children.
I have not always had a prejudice against twins.
To be catholic to be african to be Eastern.
Have you always had a prejudice against twins.
Tomorrow we go.
If you say so.

Circular watches.

Methods.
How do you recognise hats.
How do you marry.

Circular glasses.

Indeed indeed we speed.
And what do you feel now.
How wonderfully charming are the appearances.
And then you are satisfied.
And even rested.
Circular eye glasses.
Swing into the circle.
See it comes to-day.
Make a swing on Monday.
We made ours Thursday.
In an hour.
The singing bird is singing in the cuckoo tree. Singing to me
oh singing to me.

Circular sets.

Glass candlesticks and glass mandolins and perhaps glass
candles and roads.

In circles.

Do they make you sad or sympathetic or more nearly ruddy.

Repeat north.
More circles.

The action of a circular play consists in reasonably enlarging doors. Doors can be made circularly.

Also we can go to Saint Cloud.

We can also have prejudices against voices.

How many more wish to come in.

Circles circle to-day.

Now I want to tell about whimsies.

Whimsies consist in pleasing a wife in instantaneous reference, in pleasure, in fatigue and in resolution. Also it means no errors nor indeed any disturbance. Principally a peculiarity is no peculiarity.

And how do I neglect circles.

I consider whether I tie or whether I neglect to tie.

Dogs are contagious.

And I mean cats.

Not freely.

Circular addresses.

Mrs. Persons was hurt because we said she had not left her address.

She was also embarrassed by the mention of the date in addition to the name of the week.

Can you imagine addresses.

I know nothing more difficult than to imagine addresses.

How old can you be.

You can be very old and very well preserved.

And addresses.

Dresses and addresses.

Circular dresses.

Rescue.

Let us breathe in matches.

And really lilacs.

And most of all we are religious.

Can you think of a Jew.

Please be a religious circle.

A religious circle earnestly pleases those who protest those who attach that meaning and even those who regather fowl. How can you say they were killed. In my country we do this we leave it there and in a way a rabbit is not necessarily there.

Oh how you love to Knead.

Bread.

Think of the brown bread.
Think of tigers.
Think more of Indians
And think how easily we can finish.
What
The white flour.
Of course the white flour.
There is white flour.
                    Conceive that as a circle.
Do you mean to please.
I reason like this. A proceeding which necessitates that recollection perfection selection and protection rhyme and that stupefaction action satisfaction and subtraction rhyme and that dearer clearer freer and nearer follow one another a proceeding which not any one dislikes stamps a play as a wonderful beginning.
Tea.
Before tea.
Let me express about the noise let me say that he is easily dissatisfied.
Listen to me.
Circles are cheery.
We have no noon.
Indeed we draw two pictures one with glasses one without. Every time they shake the table cloth near the window a glass falls out.
How can you be surprised by news.
Suppose one tells you he was furiously angry at his son. Another says it was his wife who was his pride and yet another assures you that after all he was born in Paris. Only a mercenary would work so hard.
                    News of circles.
Where is she where is she where is she.
Wish she.
She wishes for Robert Dole and William Haynse.
Where is she.
She is not readily mistaken.
Mabel Stern can she burn.
I can break a pear.
Clamor for me.

I reminded her that I need not give her flowers. Them flowers. I need not give them flowers. Give flowers to them I need not give flowers to them. I need not have given flowers to them.

Circular dancing.

Dole keeps a dancing club. He is an American from the United States of America. He was never in Europe before the European war. Since then he has remained. He has prospered he has seemingly prospered. William Haynse acts as his orchestra. He plays the piano. They do not have a mechanical piano. William earned a great deal more money before they put a tax on music not in music halls but in restaurants. He is fond of Pepper.

And Mr. Lambert.

Mr. Lambert appears.

Sing a song of sight.

Circulating songs.

How bright are Frank and Nellie.

Very bright.

And Lou Flower. Not so at night. Not so very bitter at sight. Not so monstrous for the height. Not irregular at all.

Let us encircle let us encircle graciously.

Can you see the moon can you see it seen can you see a boy of sixteen.

And if I answer yes can you guess how many candles out of six make a mess.

None of ours.

Oh yes they do in cooking.

Electricity we say makes it very light to-day. To-day the sun is shining tenderly.

A circlet of kisses.

Can you kiss to see.

Some see.

Can you kiss me.

I see.

Can you hear of kissing me.

Yes I see where you can be.

Do I sound like Alice.

Any voice is resembling.

By this I mean when I am accustomed to them their voices sound in my ears.

Can you say the page to-day can you say the pages. Sleeping in the day is like Klim backwards.

Klim backwards is milk just like silk.

Is milk a can.

Circles are candy.

Irregular circles.

Can you think with me.

I can hear Alice.

So can a great many people.

In Terra Cotta Town.

I named roses wild flowers.

Circles.

Fourteen circles.

Fifteen circles.

I wonder if I have heard about those circles.

PHOTOGRAPH

✔ 1920 ✔

A PLAY IN FIVE ACTS

For a photograph we need a wall.
Star gazing.
Photographs are small. They reproduce well.
I enlarge better.
Don't say that practically.
And so we resist.
We miss stones.
　　　Now we sing.
St. Cloud and you.
Saint Cloud and loud.
I sing you sing, birthday songs tulip belongs to red cream
and green and crimson so that the house chosen has a soft wall.
Oh come and believe me oh come and believe me to-day oh
come and believe me oh come just for one minute
Age makes no difference.
Neither does the Vieux Colombier.
Why do you think of that at all.
I describe a different house.
So does Gabriella.
Twins.
There is a prejudice about twins.
Twins are one. Does this mean as they separate as they are
separate or together.
Let me hear the story of the twin. So we begin.
　　　　　Photograph.
The sub title. Twin.
Two a twin.—Step in.
Margot.—Not a twin.
Lilacs.—For a twin.

Forget me nots.—By a twin.
Twin houses.
We are considering twin houses. I say.
Have I read all about twins.
And now to walk as twins walk.
Two twins have two doors.
One twin is a bore.
I exercise more. I walk before the twins door.
Dozens above the eggs dozens above.
Afternoons seen.
Mrs. Roberts.
Mrs. Lord
Mr. Andrew Reding.
Miss Nuttall
Mrs. Reading
Come in and be lame.
Come in together Alsatian.
A language tires.
A language tries to be.
A language tries to be free.
This can be called Twinny.
She had cne god-daughter
Burning.
We are very bitter.
We are bitter.
Railroads are mistaken
They insult us.
Now I can occasion remonstrance.
Miss Nuttall was born in America.
Mrs. Roberts was also born there.
Mr. Andrew Reding went to America.
Mrs. Reading was born in America.
Mrs. Lord was born on the boat
Now indeed this is not what I meant to say for this does not
describe my feeling.
My feeling is that one comes in more frequently than another
and yet they always come together. This is not exactly so. They
do come together but some come more frquently than others and
we like to see them all.
I can sigh to play.

I can sigh for a play.
A play means more.

Act Second

Two authors. Rabbits are eaten.
    Dogs eat rabbits.
Snails eat leaves.
Expression falters.
Wild flowers drink.
The Star Spangled banner.
Read the notices.

Act III

A photograph. A photograph of a number of people if each
one of them is reproduces if two have a baby if both the babies
are boys what is the name of the street.
Madame.

Act IV

We say we were warm. Guess McAdam.
We say we talked about them.
Joseph moan, Edith atone, the bird belongs to the throne.
Birdie sing about an intention.
Did you intend to depress me. Certainly not I asked for a
translation. Do not compromise my father. Zero.
Baby was so interested in one part of the story. And I, I was
interested. And what can pearls mean. Pearls can mean some sort
of reason. It is very reasonable. I am very sleepy and burned.
Burned by the sun to-day.
Stand up to sing.

Act V

I make a sentence in Vincennes. It is this. I will never reason
away George.

PAISIEU

✸ 1928 ✸

A PLAY

A WORK OF PURE IMAGINATION IN WHICH NO REMINISCENCES INTRUDE

Not Paisieu a play.

Arbuthnot or hollowed is constant eggs and grasped.

Failure in white clouds.

Arbuthnot

Geronimo

A tall infirm on account of distance and around.

Germaine and a child.

Follow an example.

Poplar chestnut and oak trees and not maiden hair fern, not planted Arbuthnot Geronimo Caesar a plainly fairly watered plain. Germaine and her child.

Father and more than a pleasant hope of celerity.

An exceedingly gay cover for the having perfectly corrected withstand in presentation.

To do like it.

Act in a venture.

When to be used to it or plant of clouds and definite trees are among enduring it being covered with a cloud by reason of failure in liking to turn back on the view.

View point.

Act on in measuring. Faded olive is better than black.

ACT ONE

Geronimo in season.

ACT ONE

Seasonable dishes.

Scorpions butterflies and scorpions are non-existent so she could be easy.

ACT ONE

Its beginning in twenty twenty two.

Nobody counts poplars.

Nobody counts poplars.

Nobody.

Counts.

Poplars.

Nobody counts poplars as counts counts poplars.

Next.

Poplars and act as at went in presently preening incoherent ally.

Philip in rain.

Pointed in a absently mentioning whenever oppositely done with out.

The Rhone fails. The Rhone fails.

Not at all.

Geronimo and painted.

Germaine and her child with alive although a couple of whether it is as mart as Martha the confidant of Martha Butta Do do please not remember.

A do be a do be at do be at do be at do be at at all. Cut cut leather which is not bound. Cut leather which is not bound. Dove tail. Cut leather.

Susan and Honor.

An oxen is one out of two with a widow land in collusion.

Indicative indent.

Neither in winter nor summer. Never take never. It is too far in.

Geronimo invited

How do you do may be.

The sun which is covered.

Our grows.

Scene II

Effect of poplar saving set settle. Chadbourne and relight.

How are you.

Relegate.

After attic.

Not to be influenced.

Weigh whatever.

Geronimo in rejoinder.

It is very easy not to be accustomed to you.

It pleases him because it seizes him.

John Allenby in return

With may call tolerating in refrain come there might does fare needless consuming our mention.

Willow masses have buried soon.

Leon who has tried.

And a waste in means it.

Garfield Arthur. Who has hurt a shawl.

Ought other than the recipient be surprised.

May imagine.

Mosses are curious to the Plantagent as a land.

Germaine and her child.

They go around the Rhone. This is pervade.

Geronimo we were smile.

Distant Dismay Ismay is main gettatable in position.

Herbert is a cousin of Hildebrand William.

Having seen. Having. Seen. Having not scented seen.

It is useless to know the difference between a cat and a dog because it is playful.

Because it is seriously a resort by fasten fastener.

Bilingual means by having.

Henry and Geronimo and regional.

Fairly a calendar.

Arthur is right.

It is easy.

Scene III

Gregory Alice photographed in earrings.

Ideally. What.

Better have a cake in water.

A cake in water in care of Gertrude Geronimo.

Advise a gardener for maple trees.

Disuse of in between.

Did indeed twitter.

Color collaboration.

Ernestine Fabrini. Have counted what it cost.

And Jenny Lane. Have knelt.

Rudolph Geronimo. Is never mistaken.

Edna Mencken teases in private.

Lightly come.

To be too pearly.

It is never to be safe to see that.

It is.

Never.

To be safe

To see that.

A race of lend lent whose to indulge who and Raymond Hughes.

Geronimo makes a middle.

In will.

A shanty.

A little oblige oblate narrow nearly Nancy a farmer and a lieutenant's wife. A lieutenant who has made a place for them.

Call Caesarien an obligation.

It is unavoidable will.

Geronimo makes mended marshes with partly a day.

Thaddeus Henry has been appointed ahead.

Never to remember or a crane. Ethel and Mary have a shrine. They like their belying it made in have lakes.

They go convinced.

Windows and removed all loops.

A banister may be best with a ground-work.

Mary Louise and to be sure.

Mary Louise met a wedding and was entitled to an estimation of by the way.

James has been hours in the beneath their changing.

Does did denial make a rendition of truly at better than allow.

Geronimo has all patience here.

Scene in a marsh

One two appointments which are kept.

They only use a name to call if they change.

Mary Louise, Mary and Louise.

It is a day in perusal.

How are hours able discharge gained and sustain blaming aroused left hen folded in streams. Streams are broken out.

Geronimo is curiously careless.

Hurried after is a frame for a marsh willow.

Missing alike when they are trying this can count are right.

Geronimo felt the need of our support.

Eldridge Godfrey.

As if he was dead.

Benjamin and his cousin.

Astonishing to find who some where satchel seen is.

Maybe they wish and watch without in an angle fastened by their closing in an hour which is unsatisfactory to be actively duly laid in absolved from adapting left as a rope for them.

Mary Augustine France Perrine.

Reminiscences are trafficked in being ranging by their after partly laying in joining their division. Imagine her saying anything.

A scene between Geronimo and the division between with winding and gaining and very well in planting and end planting their careful women.

It is so much to have grain winnowed winnowed by the fan.

He replies you are a realist and you live in the imagined lives in them.

He said. You make it clear that tenderly as you adore me you do not care for the kind of women who resemble me you think very badly of them and so in all because of course I have no prospect of proposing that request of being joined there.

She said. If they went there and they came back who then could have their money back.

A matter of fact is that there is a blue sky of different colors. A blue sky of different colors.

Scene in preciseness

Whole button come can couple with all division in antics of required lame and dew.

Germaine and her child.

Germaine and her child.

Very pretty if older.

No need to no need to no need to need to need to.

Thank you.

Germaine made it be all that they did.

Scene IV

He had after all fifty names to his credit. He thought of half of them and may be made a mistake.

This may be why they did double trouble to deny.

Geronimo and count

It is the difference between very quickly and very quickly.

Go back come back.

A gardener's wife is a gardener's wife and she has four children.

They say that there are some which have been needed.

Herbert William Harvey had four children.

Had he had four children.

How can he have four children.

Two boys and two girls three boys and a girl a boy and three girls three boys and two girls that makes five that is what there were.

Geronimo called them and they were very considerate.

They are to be known at once.

Geronimo Germaine and her child Marry Perrine Hubert William Harvey and the rest of them all do have a railway in sight.

Never mention any thing seen.

Definition made a hand.

Bay below marsh medal go does dapple all about when characteristic double in our bite with covered made in paths of lettuce which has needed rain but ask for rain.

About in son of many money. She will come to be rather very finely moulded.

Hot what wintered for the land be inside of colored gains with green if burned with green.

Lay lain Gerald Geronimo comes rather as a well.

Nearly with having no need to thank severally as they bring capes.

Gerald Geronimo come to mother.

Robert Widow name the general

Charles Partner come for me.

Paolo Poplar do be incased with a merriment as marsh.

They found they fare they do this too.

Scene in which Geronimo visits Germaine and her child and they laugh about it.

Mary Auguste France Perrine makes it a duty to be seen and to be sure to do about it all make it in pain.

Patently a distant in a marsh. There is no distance in a dry marsh.

Germaine makes it in his way if he likes thirds. He is called let them speak as if whenever they are never having it come there.

Never eat never eat never eat it.

Gerald Geronimo can be mistaken for some one else.

Scene V

Geronimo and Kate Sebastian.

To bell welcome.

They may be a dainty into two field made mention.

Double ours.

Widows widowed with recommended dahlias and thousands. Recourse.

Geronimo needs Mr. Genny.

He has him.

Geronimo very well and thank you her recollection.

Double doubt of double box.

Howards who have held.

Windowed without a marsh meadow and place pleases in dependence of in all in so much that when inculcated a remained of personal resist to most.

They can be not said to mean everything.

Having passed all that time without knowing their name it is not necessary.

To be called to be.

Geronimo may misuses lain as a mantle which when it came it came later.

A little boy bringing grapes on a plate.

Scene VI

Gabrielle Geronimo interferes between Alice and Helen.

Alice and Helen Helen is the one who was supposed simply sacredly to time.

Timed in their care.

Geronimo has need of regain relieve around this in contribution.

Who can think things.

One or two if the sun sets behind a cloud does it set.

Scene VII

A pound of their announcement.

Geronimo in willing.

Does it sound the same when it is said as different.

Leaving Joseph Geronimo with Fred.

Leaving Mary Rose with Anderson John Anderson their son John.

Does it.

Joseph Geronimo leaves starting to their change.

May happens in chances for needless their pinning.

Do they always have to look as marshes if lakes have swimming. Does curl later latest in galaxy combined may it be for the next to an instance.

Buy across.

Gone interdict a clarified with it in other gainsaid in politeness with rested in in gentleness that no one.

Pets praises.

He made no mistake.

Herbert when he came.

Being very in the main their hap hazard.

Echo in echo.

Need there be in when in courses as if a water-fall was in a hole.

Never leave two leaves marshes at in all.

Thanks for it as in by kept call.

Remember a marsh by the willow.

A very big marsh which with very little ones would be one two three all out but she.

Working without seeing is better than at maintaining their matter of fact in a tree. Thrifty. Combing and at a time.

Geronimo has patiently been settled where it is no matter of course.

Like lines.

Fascinated like lines.

Joseph Geronimo may know the names and the days and the ferns if it is by then.

Come went in calling disuse to be made with in very much when with their in there back again with it laid for that which in carries they can couple around in interminable during done with by their same as it.

Same as it near which following coughed allow lain recompense taught.

Joseph Geronimo fell and was very much hurt. He had a stick in his hand but he did not fall on it he was happily very well able to go and fancy that it was his turn.

Right about it farther and very caked with out joining in a partly with all lain with a showing of whenever in a reminded in point of all. Do be exhausted too.

Mary Rose can be called Mary. Mary Rose after all.

It is partly why a balustrade is made of their roughness is made of their made of there in through absently counselling.

Balustrade is made of stone of iron of wood of cement of whiling marble away.

We think of their eating.

Scene VIII

It is for them it is for them it is for them all.

Scene IX

Marsh and marshes

A marsh a marsh of great extent and marshes they when dry are needed as being left to dry not as fodder but as bedding.

They are reliable.

As often as ever.

Never to attempt to sever their withdrawal in around and not see or seize when they sparingly display this in call of standing behind fours. They are not afraid when they are there but welcoming applicable relate relating to it a half at a plan.

Joseph has held horns and not at all trees not at all when

rescinded and defended and different and intended. Joseph being right. Joseph Geronimo a lesson.

ACT II

Faster boil water.
Geronimo in endless.
Why in why hide in.
Come to them see.
Has to them literally.
Arthur Geronimo lends them a house and they see that it is so.
Edward Sebastian has pairs of oxen on a train to use side by side idly beside.
With whenever window.
Widow with Mauricette and Sebastian.
Arthur Geronimo loves to think it is so.
With or without ours.
It is a difficulty to do it rapidly.
There are no actions without a fire out of doors.
Leave live it to me.
Pariah arrive are how are hard it welded calls preclaiming innumerable discover in a main land pier.
Cut pay much for four fixed named joint in remake part it partly in substance do knit and do sit and do sew.
Owned add double come to be with after every lack of custom.
It is called a tunnel in a wall.
Any hour of these with.
Within abundance.
Never having seen.
Bird and their parents.
She was a girl who was tall.
They made a stain.
Made with appoint.
Laughter in rendered with around.
It was a disappointment.
Having left the sand she which was that she that she did not want ever to see it again from that side.
Weak ways of clouds.
Always arrange.
Arthur and Rene, Harry and Remy Geronimo.

We are pleased that you are pleased with marshes.

And doves name respected mountains.

And do pigeons name happily see their mountains.

Arthur and Rene Geronimo.

Mauricette is never bound to be all never bound to be all but she is called to their being known as seldom secreted.

Without ours.

Never look around and see.

With when wending in a mine.

They call replenish replenish.

Having promised not to not to have it fortunately a completion of remarkable aim to be shown their in their resistance, can a horse be led by a change with differing.

Never remember of course.

A winnowed horse is strange in their reentering with without does and display they can carry it in maintenance by liking for their fairly well do as inclined.

No temptation to be very whispered in requital.

There is no difference.

With sweet William.

Cry and mine mine as there are as as many.

How has a house been here.

Here in the house.

Once and more.

Coupled with plains.

How are over with rather with added made to fasten in and state theirs for them.

Never having seen any one it is best to have it all in an amount with counting that it is with them which they were lain.

It is not remain remain doors.

Where are why where there indecently make farther as in cutting.

It is wetter in the marshes than they were.

No one has to be a way to go Geronimo.

Scene II

It is very wise to have a tree surrounded by seats made by hand and pieces. The tree that is used is only left with not theirs most. They have now six seats ten seats. One only has been when they went.

This has started as in this winter.

They are followed without farther.

Geronimo is made allowed.

Alfred and Edith Ferdinand and Gustave Geronimo in sequence.

To be she is to be disappointed in dismantle with aims.

No one is afraid of cows followed by goats sorrow to have seen it.

Never will see never will see never will see will seen.

Around their exactly.

Without their house. Hurry without their house.

In an interval in veiling their maintain incline does manipulated following read reading made about covertly rather than with the embroidress.

Geronimo, the embroidress.

Will cut grass leave a trace. It will on the air.

Welcome how after as many hours of interval it is made permanently withstood.

Never mean the name.

William Geronimo has plenty of time.

Think in stitches.

Wilfred Geronimo has plenty of time.

Ages will vary very well. Hopeless of ages which will vary very well.

Harry Geronimo tells that it is a bulwark.

A round about within with vary indubitable not unlike that.

A minor obstacle intervened and an abridgement of a wonder be known lamed in fervent should join.

Joseph Geronimo is hours to-day.

The whole return is when they said if they did. Like very many meadows they were never better than ever with then leaned about reply commence in tacitly just come as in denial for the fortune to be fare for the mischance if an allowed daughter with a very little well well how is she. Germaine and her daughter who is very nearly will will it come to this marsh marshes. Used were used to it well will went were to were to used to where went were used were went to it. Germaine has been selected as arrival of arrival of marshes. Arrival of marshes.

Joseph Geronimo can always change his name.

Need it be some where in on our account.

Arthur Constance sharpened with aid.

Arthur France Geronimo is curtailed in his preparation in advance where they were they were of their account within August.

ACT III

Howard Geronimo is curtained and the marshes but or birds.

If three are eighty-two four are forty-nine.

Please have please please have saves them.

Henry Geronimo speaks without reading, our have not hindered Alice Geronimo sir.

Coupled cups of christening in Rudolph Geronimo waited distances black berries are called wall or ripe.

Letting there have been their hare which is without allowance.

What is the difference between interruption.

Come with in abundant out of door oven.

There was back which is the same as blacken.

Germaine and her baby loved to be a cradle in felt in the same without their once is coupled leave out that having parasol in decision which of it which can be satisfactory left to their larger out in from with it.

They have come back again.

From here to here.

Geronimo let having fairly more add once.

Geronimo has forgotten something.

Eight cows are stopped from proceeding.

Who prefers rocks to marshes.

Little clouds to Saint Francis.

Arthur to Evelyn.

Scene II

They were wistful.

It is that she has stated while they were ready now.

Integrally ready now.

But in the niece which may reference about mountain in sewn.

Next.

Weakness.

Alarmed.

Ivy on fire.

With unprotected glass.

No observation no observation.

Rosellen Geronimo is away.

Everything in waiting.

Felicity Stone is nearly at one with their being what they have as if they like.

Felicity Geronimo had learned to have it made by hand.

The embroidress.

The marshes.

The Mountain.

The partly owned vineyard and with it.

Fred Geronimo was awfully glad that it was possible.

Must know the difference between bowing and not.

Arthur France Geronimo is the son of a widow.

Consider it at at measured.

Mildred do do have almond an almond.

Without a while.

Scene III

If you have it take it.

The window prize is blessed beside, if you have been whatever they must let it be considered meant, considered.

It does help.

Charles darken like their sakes.

Well now Mister.

Carolus Geronimo is covered by their being thought with them. It is an amount.

Herbert quickly was quite very much with by not had become signed as obligation in further it is called why do you like to be very comfortably here.

Very made in vain.

Arthur Geronimo craves a word of love.

A fog is a rain and grapes are valuable. Geronimo did hope to be like it it could be called fairly with a pressure.

Arthur Geronimo takes articles.

Marshes are made late, they are made with edges believe.

The only thing that is that with is two trains.

Be likely with very many prepares.

Arthur Elizabeth and Helen Geronimo met Camille Berard
and asked him about hours.

With whether on account.

Scene IV

A bid for grapes and pears has been received.

Scene V

Please Kate.

Gilbert Geronimo felt it to be so.

Oars ours chiefly seen beside with languish for the sake of
intended to go very quickly.

Who has had hatted reminds of lean meant like with a defined
leader.

Demand.

Never to have rather looked out at scenery.

Winifred Geronimo caught walks that is to say many any way
were without them. They may be candied without a distant sentence of allowance with named more than alike refer ably not by
apter anticipate does well.

Winifred Geronimo and partly their all.

Winifred awoke.

Does seeing others remind one of that or is it bewildering.

William and Everest Geronimo meant that marshes are made
before meadows.

Marion Geronimo is ridiculous.

Francis Geronimo has become common-place.

Winifred Geronimo has a little dog named Cleo and she has
hopes of having at least more.

Ducks are a pleasure to another.

Plenty of Amy's fancies are without.

Away by butter.

Delay and said.

They must be a better than to without doubtfully reminded.

Scene VI

Winifred Arthur and Germaine have her.

Scene VII

Made Mary.

How are hours.

Genevieve Butler knew Christian Geronimo.

A wedding is a certainty.

Genevieve Butler answered in inviting.

Christian Geronimo to Germaine's wedding.

Difference in delaying everything some prefer marshes from here and some prefer marshes from there.

Was a grandchild a woman thank you for thinking.

Joseph Geronimo led.

At an advantage. They were conducting it under them. Dotted with searching.

Walter and his restiveness at most when dismay comes to be their portion.

Howards are happily without birds it is amazing that a praying mantle prays.

Be what ever eight cakes are they choose farther than much which is fancied with or without lending itself to that.

Double delivers bestowed following an attempted with hired indubitable named and reside come reversed in their intention tears make marshes heave without not at length with joined as it was.

They differ in color and more without choice.

Has she no curiosity.

Has he no curiosity.

Did he say that there would be no rain but a dark cloud would give drops.

Now Winifred and Fred they are both as instead he went with his brother.

Scene VIII

Letters and which which meant which.

Arthur Geronimo never stops walking.

Neil Geronimo may be.

After all may have marshes better before than why after they had heard that it was a bother.

Whether bother.

She loves liberty and right.

Once more it was as much as they wanted. Without their leav-

ing it alone. That they might do what they liked. With everything
as they had it. As it is known without their being any trouble
about it, as much of it as they liked. Without all of it being more
than which it could not be fastened in partly leaving all more than
they did. It is very well to have it known as that.

Six o'clock. Names name announce. Coming more than for
which compels the mainly assorted to be surely fattening aimed as
considerable with hour come to be nine.

What is the difference between useful and marches. What is
the difference between useful and marches and marshes.

One forty one.

Marguerite Geronimo name unknown.

Henry and Camille Geronimo may have agate as a moon stone
may have agate as a granite may have an unstated rain.

Walter Badenoch Geronimo is understood.

Scene IX

Heard bells or hare-bells as a delicacy.
Failure as such.
Why should a student love a rope walk as sitting. Do not take
any notice of it.

Scene X

After Albert what happens.
It might be why they were their own.
With wideness a banner of included the while.
Harriet Howard Hilda Freedman Geronimo in pronouncements
one more in permitting time. Two and two in thank you.

Scene XI

There are hours of excitement.
When made of whenever.
Camille Geronimo in order to do and to go and to go so and
to do so. He is to do so and to go.
Camille Geronimo lets it be why they have permitted with
out it Camille Geronimo.
Single-sided despatched in remain.
Camille Geronimo enjoyed himself.

Out hour aloud.

In dividend.

What does he mingle within in.

Never to notice the difference in trees.

Never to notice their difference in trees.

Annie Swan bent to their wishes.

Alfred Geronimo is sure that a dog can bark at a cow.

Can let them lift them they do not mind them when they cannot let them lift them.

Camille Geronimo finds it a circumstance.

In which patience is a virtue.

Camille Geronimo lets it like it when made of their without it being of any doubt.

Wives of circumstance.

Germaine greeted the step mother of her brother when he brought her child and liked it.

Germaine comes to carrying anything which is what is meant by coming.

Without doubt.

Winifred Geronimo and can have to have it do as it is more than before then.

He having been used to it mistakes it for it.

Bertram Geronimo refused to very much as it was.

Scene XII

Esther Henry seen.

Henry Henry seen.

Benjamin Geronimo seen.

How can it about it be matter if it did.

Back to Geronimo and exchange it for it. About how often.

Once if they asked who was it then with then tell then.

Once when they asked allowed her. Edith Geronimo or not.

Edith and Francis Geronimo made it bequeath. Bequeath is forward.

A add and not for theirs in and Elliot Geronimo in search.

Putting theirs into adding erasing.

It is not out of them where with outlet do be announced.

A smoke does not always mean a train it means a field.

There is no difference between a shadow and sweating.

William Geronimo brings mention and leaving.
Arthur Feneon Geronimo lauds him.
Why do they say that they do not like walnuts because they have never said it to-night.

Scene XIII

Helen and Esther Geronimo were after having been in.
At a distance is a lake.
Because marshes are not between it.
Alice Geronimo presents delicacies in an admiration with pinks.

Scene XIV

Katherine Tardy. Virginia Geronimo and in wills made marshes.
Katherine Tardy and Virginia Geronimo were known at noon.
In marshes Katherine Tardy Virginia Geronimo were known at noon in marshes.
Katherine Geronimo Virginia Tardy were known at noon Katherine Geronimo and Virginia Tardy were known at noon in marshes.
Katherine Tardy and Virginia Geronimo were known at noon in marshes for the rest there was prevention of planting poplars. Josephine Geronimo and Virginia Tardy were present at the planting of poplars in the marshes.
A hillside was burnt.
Helped to help themselves for veneration in sending wells to violently dismay them. How sweetly marshes grow lavendar pinks and without lilies.
This is the use of their having Germaine dismay in because of their preventing it with more however like it.
Edith Geronimo is without a witness.
Papers are very well all very well when they are deferred to by them when they are deferred to by them, paper is all very well when they are deferred to by them. Papers are all very well when they are deferred to by them.

ACT III

Marshes are without doubt not only very attractive but not

dangerous after a very long time without the water in them having been replaced. They can be so found politely.

Scene II

Scene in behalf of quantity.

Vincent Geronimo held it well in hand.

Sent in behalf of quantity.

Further than they can be belated.

Vincent Geronimo chose lending it.

Vincent Geronimo left alone in that because it is plenty of without in their a chance coming in two in the reason that they have.

Vincent Geronimo they were to be sought without them.

Does Vincent Geronimo know the difference between eighteen and eighteen.

Does Vincent Geronimo know the difference between eighteen and eighteen other things not being taken into account.

Left allowed her.

Principally pursuasive as if pinned in reft commence intrusion.

Winifred went with Vincent and Virgil Geronimo to prepare a letter to their mother.

She yawned.

Penfold was a name which Vincent Geronimo knew Mrs. Penfold said and it was true that Vincent Geronimo was just then with them.

Which was true.

They made a plan to think of them.

Vernon Geronimo made shares of their leaving without it.

Vernon Geronimo interrupted hourly.

Vernon, Wilfred and Elisabeth Geronimo met Katherine and was it that they had hoped to know what it was that not by it can be and mind, Lizzie do you mind what it is that is asked.

Vincent Geronimo feels the absence of Mary Louise not that it is of any importance as her place has been taken.

Does which and dulled made which she knows that is is the same and she was that which was a pleasure.

Makes theirs a study of which theirs which.

Very likely.

Scene III

In made in a single in made them.

What is it.

What is it marshes what is it.

In made in a single in made of them.

It with all fairly with all with it all fairly, with it with it all fairly in with it in with it in with it all fairly.

It is in with it all fairly represented in with it all fairly with it in it all fairly represented with it in it all fairly.

Lucien and Florence Geronimo. Lawrence and Lawrence and Florence and Lucien and Simon Geronimo gently.

Lucian and Florence shirred about with them in this.

Names and hearing names without abound.

That is not very well known.

It is without about what is there when at in case of mainly further.

Had Winifred known Florence.

Pauses with capture.

Laying it down makes it might do.

However.

However laying it however moreover it was without any might which if it is all as it is as with their chance in the middle.

Winifred Geronimo is appointed.

She can be left to it very next to the acceptance of in line as it is asked.

While in there they were there while they were there.

Add in added in added in add in added in marking marking in marshes.

Virginia Geronimo was met.

Winifred Geronimo hereby with all.

Scene IV

A disappointment it is a disappointment not to reach the same to them it is a disappointment not to reach it to them.

The grain spelled just the same.

Glaudia Geronimo waits for Francis Geronimo when he asks her to do so.

All about which when they gather that they have all told that they went. Is it delicacy that they delicately that they have left that as that which they will find it very likely that it is of the because of the flavor of raspberries.

Delight delightful delicacy delicately, deliciously delightfully delicately delicacy.

If they have left it delicately for them to have it to do delightfully delicacy delicate delicately delicious or deliciously.

They were delicately leaving it delicately for them to do delicately for them to do delicately they left it to them delicately for them to do it was a delicate thing for them to do to have done it for them to do.

Florence Geronimo pronounces it as it is said. Said it as it is said. Florence Geronimo pronounces it as it is said it is said as it is said so.

Arthur Geronimo sells dishes dishes are made to wait.

Philip Geronimo plants poplars in marshes poplars which are very tall trees if they are made to be are made to be fruit trees are made to be fruit trees.

Philip Geronimo has sold poplar trees which are made to be fruit trees to him.

What is the difference between the oldest and partly Negro. Philip Geronimo or was it as he said.

Scene V

Philip Geronimo has served in an army.

Maddelena Geronimo is meant to be wielded or so.

Mattie Geronimo is an advantage.

Minnie Geronimo turns to throw it where there is no mistaking it for the difference between a pink which will be or whether they were reliable.

Edith Geronimo likes it with an effort made to make it stop smaller.

Annie Geronimo made it for them.

Scene VI

There are passes in a mountain and if a tree can be used they will put it where they are.

Leave where they went. Leaves are where they are where they went.

Leaves where they went.

There are beside that there is dew and so in the evening and so they are careful not to come too early in the morning.

Scene VII

Consent consent.
She is to consent.

Scene VIII

Howard Mather Geronimo in very much which they had.

Does it does marshes dally with pleasure. Is it a pleasure to pass by a branch of a marsh will they be for this as once and bedding.

Have thanked that have thanked that thanked bedding.

Adelaide Stone Geronimo prefers damp weather it is better.

Anna Firth Geronimo is possessing possessing placing painting planning seeing seen bedding.

Cows have bedding cut in marshes for that reason.

Refused explaining cutting bedding for cows for the reason that marshes for the cows cutting bedding for that reason.

Agatha's husband was first a general then a doctor and now will she have given a pleasure to her daughter who has intended seeing what she is saying.

Agatha Henry Geronimo is patiently in shoes, shoes are worn when there are additional adding in time. Nowadays nobody does not wear shoes.

How can they like this naming this with it all which with out do notify clauses come to their however they can do not differ in likelihood.

A dove which has been a sea-gull in she knows a lark when she sees many of them.

Alice Geronimo partly does not at least by that disturb in dismay loses from as can ship with shipped comfort a capable capacity of use that on account admirable.

It is how not to know that they can get with a point let left consume fragile deploy display that the not a forget-me-not which is an aster to say day daisy.

Winifred Geronimo married Albert Geronimo.

Scene IX

Genevieve Geronimo with or with whether they thought they were with whether. They thought that they with whether.

Genevieve Geronimo straightened it out.

Without their finding it out.

Not what he finds but what he likes that makes the difference. Hour alike.

Bertha Geronimo has a mother named Danny.

They with their right make hay while they are able and as they wish to finish early.

They are right as they wish to finish early.

They are right to finish early.

Scene X

They make Saturday come soon and will they like it after some have not come.

Nestle beside above where it is.

It is made with them to of having for furnishing of course.

Thank you very much for an island of a church and trees island on land.

With whether they are whether they are this one if it was an eager in measure that they can be black and white. An object a little dog called Basket a magpie in the air.

Bravig Geronimo wishes them to be where they will be an inheritance without them.

There is no difference between coming up and going down if she asks them.

Ethel With Geronimo makes it fairly certain that it is without their doubt. Around. She would say to satisfy.

Edith Elizabeth Ellen Geronimo has planned to be alone without poplars she has planned to find it without doubt as they know.

One two one two button her shoe one two one two.

Scene XI

Haphazard in a in between their doubling it.

If it looks like it when they were there.

If it looks like it when they were there.

Remember just where they like where they were with them in

about with while they were inquired with more for their sake as little as they can be to be for them a share as they like it which they do.

Lucy Adrian Geronimo does dislike Lucy Mildred Geronimo but only by having been without the name. A name is always cut in orange slices.

Lucy Geronimo makes it very dearly for them by their having meant to lose all their grapes very dearly for them by their having meant to lose all their grapes which may be by the time it changes which if it could be called presented by a out loud out of their alas which can be left to them by the time.

It is however.

Stop and take her away.

Scene XII

With at first two and enemy.

Never mind a wide cloud.

They need them with him.

Adela Geronimo called it a little with help of whenever it is withdrawn.

It is easy to tell which was there as well as mistaken about Johanna.

Johanna Geronimo comes to conclusions.

Without egress they come to a vineyard in which grow grapes.

There is mindful of an evidence of kings which have been stated.

Jenny Geronimo has heard very well.

Scene XIII

Out of cows eight are milked.

Out of the cows eight are milked.

Scene XIV

Does as you do.

They with their crane.

Leave however alike.

Just when they are denounced.

Having asked them would.

Collar and collars are without a parlor, parlor.
It is very easy to have eaten.

Scene XV

Does she mind covering.
Does she mind covering.
With does she mind covering.
With with does she mind covering.
Success with success.
Good God.
The good wood is when there is a willow which is alone.
Philadelphia Geronimo made a landscape.
Three please they offered you grapes grapes which are in
clusters and not warm enough to attached to wasps.
If the farmer calls his things merchandise he is used to it.
Wilmot Geronimo makes a plan to leave Wednesday.
Edgar Winifred Geronimo makes a painting of a hippodrome
leave amply their excuse accustom in change.
With them.
Will they ask Helen Geronimo to go. With them.
Went with them.
The difference between their willing and abate.
This is the better that they are in amount.
Transcription in around.
Follow him with however as they only.
Further farther either whether point exhibition of roses with-
out a basket.

Scene XVI

Advantage of hearing about Eugene Geronimo.
Edgar Arthur Henry Edward Allen Russell Geronimo whistles.
How kind a young man in black supports a heavy young woman in
light color.
They can be followed by a dog with it.
She can tell whether it is as much as they tell that they can
without that it is that they tell can candied with allowance that
they tell if without that whether that they tell this in reason that if
sewn that they tell that it is hours aloud without well with seem
that it is in commence with confess that they seem that they tell

now than which if they come that they tell make it have that it is
that with seen that with what that they shall that they mean that
they tell with when if more to have come at last that it is that they
tell. A family can never be photographed together. Is is what is
fortunately in amount, Geronimo can reflect make it that if beside
it is never better just as much ready of more than with it as best
known that in the summer they do not come autumn with a plain
that if at all however looking down with road at least as might in
behalf rained in collapse just in with additionally not in a given
with never having to have it happen that they came when they
were there. Hour Geronimo has been called satin. This in attention.
Alike remain added addition for the other surprise in front with a
chamber. To shut. It is not a drying in the top of their chance. She
says that the sun does not set yet because it is behind the mountains. Geronimo. Or before. William Geronimo makes a prize for.
Him.

AN HISTORIC DRAMA
IN MEMORY OF WINNIE ELLIOT

⚹ 1930 ⚹

Characters

Ashley who has lost his money.
Harry who still has plenty.
Nuña an heiress.

Place
The door-way of a building.

Humphrey.   I have a wife and child. I have the wife to have the child. The child is mine.
    A brief interval and they have changed with them. Waiting for them to find them.

Abel.   Should their name be often called so that they will turn.
    A place where none of them have been. It is a well known but not an interesting city.

Ashley.   I am terribly frightened when I am in.

Harry.   This could pain me.

Humphrey.   I have not met him.
    A street in a city that is supposed to be pretty.

Amelia.   I am waiting.

Humphrey.   Because you have been here before.

Amelia.   They will choose me.

Ashley.   As well as who can.

Harry.   I come away.

Amelia.   While I stay

Humphrey.   Or they will go.
    A room where they had known him.

Humphrey.   I am a father of a boy. She knows.

Act I

Inside of a room

Nuña.   Why Ashley

Ashley.   You are pleased Nuña

Nuña.   Why of course Ashley

                      Leaving together

Humphrey.   Are you coming along with me

Harry.   Not if you are going to be waiting.

                      Out of the house

Humphrey.   It is alright to leave a light.

Harry.   Alright.

Ashley.   In an hour.

Harry.   Of which they obtain for them as much.

Humphrey.   With their widening.

Ashley.   In written obedience.

Harry.   Much as much beguiled.

Nuña.   After this they were all very well and tranquil. They were much rested.

                      In the house.

Nuña.   It is other. With which it is a grain.

     Would they attach me to them.

     Or go there with them.

Ashley.   How are you.

Humphrey.   Or how do you do.

Harry.   A house is perfect.

Nuña.   But you bother them

                 A street where they are building

Ashley.   For it they will not be able. To have it. Or is it just like that.

Harry.   May be they will be alike with it.

Ashley.   It is often why they mean it.

Harry.   But just as well.

               A building which is not finished.

Nuña.   We are able to appeal to that at once.

Harry.   But just as well.

Nuña.   With them. They will go.

Harry.   By the time that it is better to go.

Nuña.   Just what they do not like

Harry.   As an excuse in pieces.

Nuña.   But just as really well. As part of that time.

                      After they left.

Humphrey.   All who are able will be able to pass.

Harry.   It is a very delicate matter.

Humphrey.   Which I arrange or give away.
Harry.   Oh yes.

Partly at the door

Humphrey.   I have been not amused but very well able to be careful.
Nuña.   Just at once.
Humphrey.   It is obtained.
Nuña.   Or there clearly.

At the door

Nuña.   They will mean
Ashley.   In words or prose.
Harry.   Or well-attended.
Humphrey.   With them nor especially.
Harry.   It is not easy.

Before a building

Ashley.   They will be moved about
Nuña.   By chance.
Humphrey.   By force of circumstances.
Nuña.   With each one at a time.
Harry.   Just as plainly.

At a corner building.

Humphrey.   I should be back at five.
Humphrey.   And so I will.
Humphrey.   I am as careful as I ever was.
Humphrey.   Which was very careful until. I cannot avoid being as careful still. They will not wish to wait. But I will join them. I live in an interesting part. When they come. If they do. Or altogether.
Humphrey.   It is known that I have been married to need my boy. I was not astonished to have one. But I am very nervous. About everything.

In a building

Ashley.   I am in a building.
Harry.   And so am I but not in the same building.
Nuña.   I have been often out of doors where there are mountains. If you say in the mountains.
Ashley.   If you say.
Harry.   But just the same.
Nuña.   It is very well known. That they. Are everything.
Ashley.   With which they like.

Harry.   I do.

Inside of several buildings

Humphrey.   It is neither.
Humphrey.   Which they allowed.
Ashley.   In which I came there. To be here.
Harry.   And came.
Humphrey.   Full of which. It is remarkable that they do.

In between one building

Ashley.   Which they have they will disgrace me.
Harry.   With which they will outline.
Nuña.   But which they will not go. Nor feel. Better.
Harry.   Should it be alike.

Near a street.

Charles.   Ashley will be here.
Harry.   If he can.
Ashley.   If I can.

Behind a tree

Nuña.   Will whom.
Harry.   With it.
Humphrey.   But will it be with him.
Nuña.   Or more. More not at once. A little more.
Harry.   I have been very pleasant all the time.
Humphrey.   I can wait. Not here. By me.
Harry.   Just immediately.
Nuña.   In which arrangement I acquiesce.

By the house.

Humphrey.   It is not because not only. That there is sense.
Ashley.   Do which they will yield in a double doubt.
Harry.   It is as well that it is all gained.
Nuña.   Just as well.
Ashley.   For them in as a best name.
Harry.   How are ours equaled.
Nuña.   Do their best.

Near the door

Harry.   It just made known
Nuña.   With them to-day to be.
Ashley.   Nor we have ours.
Humphrey.   They could like it. By coming here again.
Nuña.   They will do like it.
Ashley.   They will do it more and why.

Harry.	Theirs is kindness.

          Just as near the door

Humphrey.	Two are where they always are.

          In front of a building

Nuña.	No she says no to me.
Ashley.	When they are coming.
Harry.	Will whoever pleases come here.
Ashley.	If they like it.
Harry.	But which will they place.
Nuña.	Once in a while.
Harry.	By their being kind.

          A distance from the door

Amelia.	But just what is when they do.
Humphrey.	All of it to be carried and seen.
Amelia.	In it.
Humphrey.	My arrangement.

          Near a corner

Nuña.	This is where I could have gone.
Humphrey.	Which is what they liked where they went

          Back of a lighted square

Harry.	It will be.
Ashley.	When they like it by the time of seven.
Nuña.	At once.
Amelia.	She will not join any one
Humphrey.	But which is it like.

          In front of a tree in a city.

Humphrey.	It is nice to plan again for a change.

          Sitting inside of a room

Nuña.	He heard me come to be well at noon.

          In front of a building

Ashley.	They will amount to at most.
Harry.	With well.

          In front of a building

Ashley.	It is their to be cost.
Harry.	All as much as exjoin.
Nuña.	They think things in singing.
Humphrey.	I have often wondered as I have a child what should have been its name.
Harry.	It might have been called after myself.
Ashley.	I think riches to be kept and spent.

Nuña.   With it at noon afternoon.

Humphrey.   For ever feel well.

Inside a house.

Harry.   She was instructed.

Humphrey.   Who helped her here.

Ashley.   For them when they come

Amelia.   By this at a time.

Nuña.   Will they add.

Humphrey.   She may be alright.

Harry.   With them as lent.

Ashley.   Just without noise.

Amelia.   By which.

Nuña.   In place of a little way.

In front of a building.

Humphrey.   It will not shine as mine but I am worried. Because it
              is I who have a child who is a boy.

In front of a tree in a city.

Ashley.   I have been known to be alone and lonely.

Harry.   They will come to have everything ready.

Nuña.   They will like to have it offered.

Amelia.   Which is why

Nuña.   That they like

Ashley.   As well as a noise.

Near the rest of the trees in a city.

Humphrey.   She will like who will they like with me as they can
              with all which it is organized like that.

In front of a building.

Harry.   With there. It is quite well there.

Ashley.   Should I be known.

Nuña.   With them with me.

Amelia.   As which if they like twice.

Nuña.   With just as much the same.

Harry.   They will be there in time.

Ashley.   For which they have whom.

Humphrey.   It made it tell. It has been what with it that it made
              it tell.

Near the room

Humphrey.   Will it be made yet.

In front of a building.

Nuña.   It is made ready for it yet.

Ashley.	They will have it there.
Harry.	It will be made ready.
Amelia.	Just as much as all of it.

In a room.

Nuña.	Leave it to whom it may concern
Harry.	That they will think that they have seen
Humphrey.	In any mistake.

In front of where they are building

Ashley.	I never thank any one so much
Amelia.	By this they cross.
Nuña.	In place of which they may be as much.
Harry.	As with them more.

Near the tree near the corner.

Ashley.	She will determine some day.
Harry.	It will be better that they came
Nuña.	With whom they came
Amelia.	With which they had friends.
Humphrey.	But which is it of where they wanted to be given that.

In front of the corner of the building.

Humphrey.	It should never not be an anxiety to be careful of having not been anxious to have withstood their having denied which they never do.
Harry.	It can be by no means parallel.
Nuña.	Or which they cover to believe it is his for them.

In the room

Amelia.	She will gain what they give.
Ashley.	To be uninterrupted.

In front of the building

Nuña.	With it it was about it.
Harry.	Not with how they confer to come.

In front of their building

Humphrey.	Should always for it be what is for a having them come not in but it is not to be had as for expected.
Amelia.	She will like close.
Ashley.	With them he came
Harry.	Can I be like as well.
Nuña.	Yes to be less made or. They can.

WILL HE COME BACK BETTER. SECOND HISTORIC DRAMA. IN THE COUNTRY.

1930

Ashley. Will be respected.
Amelia. They will call.
Harry. Has by her name
Nuña. This once for all.
Still in the country
Humphrey. We should be thought to be here.
Back in the country
Humphrey. But she will know what they have said.
Amelia. Of course she will.
Nuña. But will they tell.
Ashley. Just what they will have. To tell.
Harry. But not only they will.
Nuña. What they have to tell.
In the country.
Ashley. Should they shut the shutters.
Near the country.
Amelia. Will they happen to be after it is often near.
Ashley. She may be a couple more in time.
Nuña. Could it be a place. Like it.
Harry. But will it after it is after all like it.
In the country
Humphrey. Should they come more than there nearly.
Back of the country.
Humphrey. But please like it. They are all there.
The country.
Harry. As acquired.
Ashley. Or she should.
Nuña. Choose it for it applied.
Amelia. They will be in me.
Humphrey. For leave as guide to given.

　　　　　　　　　　　　In the country.

Harry.　　　　Should why they be the pleasure.
Ashley.　　　　For this to them as that.
Nuña.　　　　By going to them for a leaf
Amelia.　　　　It is by each according.
Humphrey.　　Noon may make their pet.

　　　　　　　　　　　Near the country.

Humphrey.　　Just by their nearing all goals.
　　　　　　　They will lead all golds.
　　　　　　　But they will lead all gold
　　　　　　　Just as they mean all folds.
　　　　　　　By that appointment let them.

　　　　　　　　　　Next to the country.

Ashley.　　　　But which they will mean
Harry.　　　　By which they will mean

　　　　　　　　　　　In the country.

Nuña.　　　　By which they will mean me.
Amelia.　　　　By it which they can mean.
Harry.　　　　By it which they do say
Ashley.　　　　By which they do and does whether.
Humphrey.　　In call a known
Harry.　　　　It is not known to be hers
Ashley.　　　　Well very well plainly.

　　　　　　　　　　　In the country.

Humphrey.　　Well is undoubtedly well made.
Ashley.　　　　Did no one.
Harry.　　　　Better with two.
Amelia.　　　　With any not with it too.
Nuña.　　　　Appoint in belating.

　　　　　　　　As well as in the country.

Ashley.　　　　Twenty times are buried.
Harry.　　　　May be I like it.
Amelia.　　　　With which they do.
Nuña.　　　　So but be nearly better
Humphrey.　　They shall see the region which they chose.

　　　　　　　　　　　The country.

Nuña.　　　　Should it be a country.

　　　　　　　　　　Near the country.

Ashley.　　　　Just think why.
Harry.　　　　They think why

Nuña.   But it is not here now
Amelia.   Just why not.
                        Near the country
Humphrey.   Do I mean near the country they come near the
                country they come.
                        In the country.
Harry.   Should it be shown.
Ashley.   Could it have come
Amelia.   Would it be known
Nuña.   Or would it have come
                        In the country
Humphrey.   They know ninety-nine just as well.
Ashley.   Should it be an antagonism
Nuña.   They may play
Amelia.   With him and with me.
Harry.   They may be here just as I am.
                        Near the country
Humphrey.   We are welcomed by their choice this is why they are
                as we know.
                        In the country.
Humphrey.   Whose does it as they mean.
                        Near the country.
Ashley.   For which near them
Amelia.   They will be never the less with her for him.
Nuña.   She may be with them with her for them.
Harry.   They may be hurried there without them with him.
Humphrey.   It is as well to be chosen for the sake of her being
                there without them.
                        Near the country
Ashley.   It may be better to be even better than with her.
Harry.   She may be rather may be with her.
Nuña.   Or which she will without with her
Amelia.   They may be with or with without them.
Humphrey.   Not in unkind they will not feel it all be with her
                which they know.
                        In the country.
Harry.   It is often beaming that they hate the place
Ashley.   Or hurry can they
Amelia.   By which it is all caught.
Nuña.   By all of which it is all bought

Humphrey.   But which will change they mean with may.

                    By the country.

Ashley.   To be not only however they are more.

Harry.   Not however they are not not even all.

Nuña.   But which they will in their half unison.

Amelia.   But they will

                    For the country.

Amelia.   It is by ours.

Ashley.   With me not in that case

Harry.   But which in why not by it.

Humphrey.   All they will have relief which is theirs bv not only
              for the time by it very likely settled in August.

                    In the country.

Amelia.   They may be like a name

Ashley.   Not when they hear they have.

Harry.   All could it be like it.

Nuña.   Left where it is.

Amelia.   For them.

                    In the country.

Amelia.   She may search

Ashley.   With only without may.

Harry.   It is not only may they.

Nuña.   It is only may they.

                    The country

Nuña.   It is only that is only.

Amelia.   It is only not that it is this not only

Ashley.   They may more they may not more not only

Harry.   May they own not only.

Humphrey.   Should they not just not when felt that they should not
              jointly leave it to be not only but not for them.

                    Near the country.

Nuña.   To be best known lean and leaving with it may they
              come.

Amelia.   It is nearly with them nearly with them and with them
              they nearly come.

Ashley.   Should they nearly be with them when they nearly
              come.

Harry.   They may be nearly with them.

Humphrey.   Should they be not with them when they come with-
              out them which is the way they do and can come

In the country.

Ashley. They will not come
Harry. Yes they will not come
Amelia. They will come for them
Nuña. They will not come with them

In the country.

Humphrey. They may be like which they have been when not to engage them to have been to not come

Near the country.

Ashley. She may be ashamed to show that she draws away.
Harry. May be she is just like that.
Nuña. May be she is not not only with them.
Amelia. May be she is not. That may account for this.
Humphrey. They may be not. As like as not. They may be as alike as this.

In the country.

Ashley. They may inquire why they mean this
Harry. They may be meaning to have been where they have been with when they mean did they have to mean not that they did not mean not why they won.
Nuña. They may mean. That they mean to be one of them one who did not mean not to win.
Amelia. They will know just the edge of which they have.

By way of the country.

Humphrey. They will be not pained but careful to please be coming after they have been where they went before they knew that not only but more than also that they would be right to be coming.
Harry. They may be obliged to be coming
Nuña. Or which they were.
Ashley. They will not without which they will as well as shall will not or kindly.
Amelia. May like it at a glance

In the country.

Ashley. Just when they mean
Harry. May they by best not alone
Nuña. With well and end to feel
Amelia. My or leaving mine. Mine is or mine.
Humphrey. Will they be each one in there alone

Nearly in the country

Nuña.	Should it be best.
Amelia.	But which should it be
Harry.	They are here
Ashley.	Which they will be now here.

Entirely in the country

Humphrey.	Should it be known as next best.

In the country

Ashley.	However many have it in their power to do so.
Harry.	Just why not
Nuña.	More than more or.
Amelia.	It is why they are joined

In the country.

Ashley.	Not in the country.

In the country

Harry.	They are not in the country.
Ashley.	But yet they are not in the country
Amelia.	They are in the country but not yet
Nuña.	They begin among them in the country
Humphrey.	They should be known when they are not in the country.

In the country

Ashley.	They are not in the country
Harry.	They are not when they are not in the country
Nuña.	They are there when they are in the country
Amelia.	They are not by their being with in the country
Humphrey.	They are with their leaving being now near being in the country

Finis

THIRD HISTORIC DRAMA

⸙ 1930 ⸙

On the way back.

Ashley.   They could be just as welcome as they ever were.

From the lion.

Ashley.   It is too bad that they are capitally thought to be numerous.

Nuña.   Or who could after they made up their mind.

In place of a lion.

Humphrey.   If in reproduced ought ought it to be all or ought. There to be a change.

Afraid of a lion.

Harry.   He is not afraid of a lion.

Nuña.   Which is it. A lion

Amelia.   With which they are not accustomed

Ashley.   But will they be told.

Humphrey.   Be whichever is. But to be disappointed. For him to be.

Having been writing to go with them.

Humphrey.   They will not go with them that is they think not.

Harry.   Should all of it be taught to be writing.

Having left the country where they were

Harry.   Just why they change the chance.

Harry.   Just why they change the chances.

Coming back again

Nuña.   Will two be known

Ashley.   But two be here.

Harry.   But two beside

Amelia.   But two but two and known beside

Humphrey.   For them a welcome.

Having gone back.

Humphrey.   With for them.

Harry.   That they declined a part of it.

Nuña.   That they will wish for it.

Amelia.   Just by chance.

Amelia.   Just by chance.

Ashley.   May can they remain always.

Amelia.   In whether they can

               They go away from danger.

Amelia.   Could they ever believe it.

Nuña.   Here she is

Ashley.   Is it

Harry.   Mine it is

Humphrey.   When. They met.

               They are near danger.

               Made precious by danger.

Humphrey.   Be ever present at a time

Harry.   All like it.

Nuña.   With whom they come

Amelia.   By which they like.

Ashley.   Added to make it is not mine.

Humphrey.   But at present to be pleasant

Ashley.   Once for them.

Harry.   Or even once for them

Amelia.   Or not even with them

Nuña.   Even more once for them

Humphrey.   Should be shouldered

               Near danger.

Amelia.   When they owed a boat.

Nuña.   They took care

Ashley.   To go there

Amelia.   When they took care.

               In danger

Amelia.   It was when they took care

Nuña.   That they took care

Ashley.   They were out there

Harry.   When they took care

               In danger

Humphrey.   To look like care of which they look alike to look to take care

Harry.   They took very good care to go there

Ashley.   Just as they took care.

Amelia.   In they take care.
Nuña.   Just as they in they took care
Humphrey.   They took their care.
                           In danger
Humphrey.   Just when they took care there.
                           In danger.
Harry.   Shall they stay and stick to it and not go away
Ashley.   Not at all, they will be here when they go away.
Nuña.   But she may like whatever they do not say
Amelia.   They will change a chance.
Nuña.   Just why is it that it is dangerous at once
Harry.   Because to have it is why they come to be here
Amelia.   Just why they come often which is there for that pur-
               pose.
Harry.   May be they will not only hear it but see it
Humphrey.   Just when is it that they could be more than they
               could in not only it alone.
Harry.   It is not it in here
Humphrey.   It is not where they have been only made often to be
               changed to their intention as not only because with
               inherent result of their just joining.
Ashley.   It may be she may be here.
Harry.   May they be often in a wish.
Amelia.   She may be because of their being known
Nuña.   Or all alike.
Ashley.   Fortunately for four more.
                           Near danger.
Ashley.   Why could they have it.
Harry.   Why could they like it.
Nuña.   Why could they go there
Amelia.   Why could they be there
                           Out of danger
Ashley.   They did what they liked
Harry.   Which is not what they could have
Amelia.   But which they could have
Nuña.   But which they could have.
                           In danger.
Nuña.   How like it is to danger.
Amelia.   And they like it with me
Ashley.   They may like with them will they come

Harry.	They will or they will not come with me.
Humphrey.	They will be known to have been in danger without which they will not have been.

Nearly in danger

Nuña.	How many have fastened them in so that they can come in in which case they will be in and they will not be often needed not to have been more than for which they have been
Amelia.	It is kind to be like and liked.
Ashley.	For them.
Harry.	Yes not without for them

Not in danger.

Harry.	May they be in there with might they be not there which they might not be there.
Ashley.	Just as well
Nuña.	They may just as well
Amelia.	With kindness
Humphrey.	Laid more than lain.

In no danger

Amelia.	Have they known when they have been in danger.
Nuña.	Or which they are alike.
Harry.	May they be placed as a panic.
Ashley.	May or makes it be dark as night.

Awake to danger.

Nuña.	They may be the cause of their not leaving many more here.
Amelia.	But which they like to please.
Harry.	Just made at once
Ashley.	In three or two.

In danger

Harry.	Should they be with and without which they should be with as much.
Nuña.	Names may be faced.
Amelia.	May be they like.
Ashley.	What they have in there which they are nearly more than they like to.
Humphrey.	They will account of course.

In danger.

Ashley.	She may or sooner they can be known
Harry.	Just with them

Nuña.   Only be where with them
Amelia.   Just like it.

                          In danger
Nuña.   Who can or may they know riches now.
Amelia.   It is a day to learn.
Ashley.   Just may he join.
Harry.   Just as arranged and might they.
Humphrey.   Every day in danger.

                          In danger
Harry.   They may be sound to find.
Ashley.   Just when they do.
Nuña.   Who do
Amelia.   All ours who can do more than they can do
                      More danger
Humphrey.   It is well known
Amelia.   That they will all come here with them

                      Finis

PLAY I [–III]

⸙ 1930 ⸙

Pierre Revel and Louis de Kerstradt.
Subsidiary characters Blanche Lavielle and Genevieve Butler.

Pierre Revel   In reply they come as presently.
Genevieve Butler   In season or in out they account for much.
Louis de Kerstradt   In reply they come as preference and presently
      Louis de Kerstradt and Pierre Revel alone.
  It is in our reply that we have chosen.
  They will be wise in disappointment.
  They will there will be weddings.
  It is not in doubt of presently
  That they are avaricious.
  In presence of in attach.
      Louis de Kerstradt and Pierre Revel alone and interrupted.
  No one feels agony in three.
  They plan a change.
  They must be avaricious.
  They must storm and beckon
  They will be all winter and not told.
      Blanche Lavielle comes in calling.
  I have been incoherent in a measure.
      Genevieve Butler comes in hurriedly
  They are careful as they might.
  Have left it to be made a place
  Of which they know
  That she is occupied.
      Louis de Kerstradt names them it is very common to use
that form of expression.
Pierre Revel.   Has met a young man fencing.
      He paints as well.
  He is now understood hourly.

Pierre Revel and Louis de Kerstradt.
Is there a difference between being old.
Who might you think would ask candy
To be pernicious
Or candied fruit.
Who is hourly asking.
May they be alike.
It is of no use to think well of them.

Pierre Revel hovers with Louis de Kerstradt and Blanche
Lavielle.
We might hope to ask them
Curtain falls.

PLAY II

Nogent Christian and Germaine Pichot and William Hart-
man and Grace Church.
Nogent meets William Hartman and prays.
Who says prayers.
If she were at all as taught.
Thirty three as out in her hope.
It is well to have gone longer
Without her.
Nogent Christian and William Hartman.
Am I told.

Scene II

Germaine Pichot and William Hartman.
She went alone why because it is idle to ask her.
Nogent Christian and Germaine Pichot and Grace Church.
They are seldom in wielding their or wish.
Nogent Christian and William Hartman
It is in authority for in which.

Scene III

Germaine Pichot and Yvonne Christian.
Who made her like it.

I made her like it
Because I told her to like it.
 Germaine Pichot, Nogent Christian, William Hartman and
Grace Church.
 For them with all of it in a hurry.
 Nogent Christian
They might be anxious for us.
 William Hartman and Nogent Christian.

PLAY III

In which
Louise the Wife.

Characters.
 Louise, James, Isadore and Jenny.
Louise meeting with pleasure.
 How do you do
 She says the same to you.
Louise and Isadore who have not detained James.
 Will you pardon me.
Louise the wife.
 She remains alone in order to give orders.
Louise and James.
 We are here with them.
Louise and Jenny and Isadore.
 We need hearing for this to be for them.
 And they will like
 They will have it alike
 In their dependence
 And independence
 When
 They will prepare which
 They will admire
 And for which they will care
 Very much.
Louise and Jenny and Isadore look at the door.
 When they are able to care to have it done.
James comes in.
 I like it very much.

Scene II

They need to be necessary for their name.
Louise adding
    She may be there for me.
Louise and Jenny and James.
    They move about without them.
    They will have approaches in their admittance
    They will both them for them
    It is hazardous to have plants.
    She may be cautious.
Louise and an addition.
    They will hope that they are satisfactory.
    It makes no difference in moaning.
    They will meet a grave peril.
    They will hope for theirs.
    They will like it.
    They will be subdued.
    They will nourish
    They will happen to give it
    They will come
Jenny Isadore.
    They will come and they will be welcome
Jenny Louise Isadore and James
    Who has had the happiness of thinking of it.
    I have.
    And with them
    As it is done
    Aloud.

Curtain

THEY MUST. BE WEDDED. TO THEIR WIFE.

✦ 1931 ✦

A PLAY

Any name. Of which. One. Has known. At least two.

      Josephine

      Ernest

      Therese

      Julia

      and

      Guy and Paul and John.

Of all these. Two or more. Except Guy.

And this. By. One brother.

Two separate brothers. Of two. Separate brothers.

They must hurry and get. Their wagons. With their harvest in.
Before the rain. Can. Pour.

      Also.

It would be well. If. No. Hail fell.

To hurt. The other things. That have been planted.

Act I

Three brothers. Of which. One. Saved. The two. One. By one.
From drowning.

Act I

Reminding. Of. The names. Which. Have been chosen.
Josephine Ernest Therese Julia Guy Paul and John.

Act I

Josephine.   Has been known by that name.

Ernest.   Has meant more. Than. That claim.
Therese.   Will be faintly neat. And they close.
Julia.   Name which welcomes a valley.
Guy.   It is a funeral. To be. Well.
Paul.   She says. It has. Charm.
John.   Will they cover. Endeavor.

All in a barn.

Act I

Scene I

Mary.   Why will. They hope. That she. Is the mother of Etienne.
Josephine.   Because. I am married.
Ernest.   Why will they hurry.
Therese.   They smile quietly in a gain.
Julia.   May she. Have heard. Birds.
Guy.   He saved my life.
Paul.   And mine.
John.   I claim. No. Shame.

Scene II

They see a river. Which. Runs through a marsh. One might think. That the mother was unhappy. But not at all. She has hopes. For her future.

They have. Not forgotten. The sister. And daughter. Neither. Will they. Like it.

Marcelle.   Who has known. When. He. Can smile.

All who remain. Come in.

He is. Sure. To dance. Well. If not. Now.

And so. The month. Of July. Opens. And closes.

Scene III

This scene is in a place where. They are.
Violet.   Oh will you. Ask Him. To marry me.
Marcel.   He laughed.
Josephine.   After many opposite to. It.
Ernest.   Politeness.

Therese.   I am older. Than a boat.
            And there. Can be no folly. In owning. It.
            There can. Be no. Hesitation. In. Working.
            Like. And. Unlike. May. They. Come in.
They all wish. That they. Had been there. When. They would.
Have been. Surely. Not. So frightened.
            After this. They may be proud. Of themselves.

Scene IV

She may be wearing a gown newly washed and pressed. Not in
any other language this would be written differently.
Josephine.   Oh Josephine.
Ernest.   May be a victim. Of himself. He may be delightful. Or
not. As it happens.
Therese.   Will always know. That she. Is not a disappointment.
Nor whether. There. Will be. Her. Share.
Julia.   Julia could be called Julia Arthur only this. Would make.
A dog. Uneasy.
Guy.   Would it. Be possible. To believe it. Of three.
Paul.   She says. He is charming.
John.   He rescued. Them. One by one. From. Drowning.

Scene IV

All of them having come to the door.
This is now. Scene IV.
They all. Talk. As if. It were alarming.
Also. As if. They expected. Him. Not to be. Charming.
They also. Make preparations. For an. Exception. They will.
Gladly. Wait. For his. Impatience. And. For his reception. They
will also confuse. A bird calling. With a dog. Squeaking.
            And so. They resume. Their. Usual. Expression.

Scene V

Will she be alive. And will. They thrive.
They may best. Be. Best. And. Most.
Josephine is not. Astonishing.
Ernest.   Is obedient. And. Developing.

Therese.   Is quiet. And not. Depressing.
Julia.   Is harmonious. And. Impatient. And willing.
                    Guy Paul and John.
               May. Or may not. Come.
They will. Hope. That it is. Their wish.
Which they welcome.

Scene I

Pretty soon. They will think. Of some one.

Scene I

It is going on nicely.

The place in which they stay is this one which surrounds. In the midst of suspicion that they will leave without them they may be an audience. As a reception of a difficulty they may manage to stammer. They will. Incline. To oblige. Only one. When they stare.

This is how millions mean.

This is a little a scene.

Just when will they go by adapting.

Nor may they be merrily there. To share.

Justly. In why.

It is a round movement this. Because. Declared.

For it. It is. A wonder. Because. They. Were. Spared.

Might it be agreeable if it were a mistake.

Josephine.   May not attend. A. Wedding.

Ernest.   Has been widened. By attention. To misers. In their misery.

Therese.   Is always sure. To have. The key. In her bag.

Julia.   Julia is known as forlorn.

John.   An elder brother who regrets the illness of his father because it deprives them of traveling as a vacation.

Guy.   Who has not been drowned Although he was very nearly not saved.

Paul.   Whom she says always has. Charm.

They will come together to vote as to whether they will be often. Without weddings. All who look. Are wealthy. As found.

Josephine hesitates.   More than they do. She chooses her air.

Julia.   Has been not only better but really well.

Therese.   Is patient and calm.
Ernest.   Purposeful.
John.   Devoted.
Guy.   Unknown.
and Paul.   Pleasant vivacious and quarrelsome.
    Bitterness is entertained by them all.

Scene I

Josephine.   Will leave.
             Patience will yield.
             She will employ.
             They will enjoy.
Josephine.   Josephine is called. And she has. Displaced. Xenobie.
             Also. She has well said. That. She will not stay. That is.
             She. May be. There. All. Are. Pleased.
Josephine.   All. Are. Pleased.
             And kisses. Two. On either cheek.
             May be accepted. Or. Refused.
             By. Two. Josephine.
Julia.   Julia loves to be. Above. With her. Yes. With a pleas-
             ure. They will. Be their care. Or. Julia. Other. Than.
             With them. Or. Another. Julia. Has made it clear. With
             them. Here. Julia.
Therese.   Will blindly keep. Not only. But. Also. With welcome.
             As from. The time. With one. Welcome. Indeed made.
             In the. Interval. With them. Therese. Can. In face. Of.
             Therese.
Ernest.   Should it. Present. Presently. There. May. Should they.
             Form coldly. With. And. An amount. A. Clergy. All
             who should. Place grace. Or. Disgrace. They may be
             forty to four fairly. It is well always to mistake a name.
John.   Did all. See John.
             All who. And. Whom. Would come and soon see
             Josephine. See John.
Guy.   They may recognise places.
Paul.   All who did know Julia said Julia would try.

Scene II

    They add gayety and gayly.

Scene III

Josephine.   Meant Joseph was once free.
Did he think for them.

Scene IV

Therese   May she be thought well of, by all who are made clearly in their prayers as brother and their brother. She may shut. It. Without them. By the time. That they. Are cautious. In this case. No. One. Is mentioned.

Julia.   Julia who has won Guy to be welcome to them. Welcome to them. Julia who has been unwilling to be unwelcome to them. Julia who has been unwilling to be with them unwelcome for them. Julia who has been with them welcome for them. With them. By them.

Julia and Guy.   One. Two. Three.

Ernest.   And a pause. A pleasure. And a pause.

John.   A pleasure without a pause without them.
Scene in which they second them.

Scene I

It is our right. To be. Our delight.

Scene I

Just why they would.

Josephine.   Differs from Fanny and Catherine.

Ernest.   Therese differs from Josephine and Mercedes.

Therese.   Ernest. Fastening. Audibly. Ernest. Fastening. They in conclusion. Audibly. Josephine.

Julia.   May they. Who by. And by. Who. By and by.

Julia.   May they. Who. By and by.

John.   Webster. Was a name. That was spoken.

Guy.   All who call a wall.
Very well I thank you.

Guy.   All who tell that. It is. Brightly. A concert.

Guy.   Who have been happy.

Paul.   Forget-me-not.

Scene II

Act I

Forget me not.

Josephine.   They have hurt them. By. Leaving.
                Are they afraid of leaving.

Josephine.   Have they minded sleeping.
                And been bothered. By sleeping.

Josephine.   Have they heard of meant. With them. Mentioning
                and trembling. Both lost.

Therese.   It is always at last.
                Ernest. Should have been. First.
                They will. Have been. Made. By them.
                For him.

Ernest.   Do they mind him.

Julia.   As all. He was disturbed.

John.   It makes no difference. It is not that.
                It makes a difference.
                Because. Of which.

Guy.   Orphans. Profit. By mischance.

Paul.   I call. For all.

They all   May be they do.
come together. Will they.

They have   For them. To think.
known each   Whichever
other.   It is very clearly.
                Autocratic.
                And angrily.
                As well. As they say.

Act II

They may very well be equal.

Scene I

Josephine.   I like it as it has been begun.

Scene II

Josephine.　A very beautiful day succeeds in summer.

Scene III

Josephine.　May we be well. Forgotten.

Scene IV

Josephine.　I should be thankful. That. He. Has made it possible.
Therese.　I. May be silent. And. Simple.
Julia.　Come smile. And be. A. Half. Of. Will.
Ernest.　How are Howards. Known. Alone.
John.　Disturb. Them. As. Known.
Guy.　Do not distress. Or cause distress.
Guy.　Or cause distress. Do not distress.
Paul.　A brother. Paul has. No brother.
　　　　The time comes for one of them.

Act II

Josephine.　Who has held Josephine.
Julia.　Who has beheld Julia.
Therese.　Who has been Therese.
Paul.　Who has loved Paul.
John.　Who has learned of John.
Ernest.　Who has followed Marcel.
Guy.　Who can think well of Guy.
All together.　And all the same they will be disappointed.
Josephine.　May has met. With wet. Weather.
Josephine.　And they will think well. Of me.
Josephine.　For them to close. At once. Is a. Mistake.
Josephine.　I have thought of three.
Julia.　Be relieved of perplexity. And for which fortune and fortunately in thoughts of plunder. For the same. In there. In. Perplexity. With. Guidance. It is a hope. That they have made. With them. Their mistake. In guidance.

Julia.	It is easy to see a shadow. And with. And will he. Withdraw.
Julia.	They may be often. Exactly. They. Answer.
Julia.	It is our aloud. All of which. They. State.
Julia.	It is not. By that time. That. They are. In error.
Julia.	By that time. Which. They have called. As hospitable. As their. Or. Are there. All in told. And having. Told.
Julia.	Should it be hurt.
Julia.	Coming.
Therese.	Esther. Should it. A volume of. White. And relieving. All. As it. Was it. A color.
Therese.	Should she allow.
Therese.	Them to go.
Therese.	Where they would if they went.
Therese.	It is. Obliging.
John.	Do they.
John.	Believe in a mining for them.
John.	They have broken nothing.
John.	I say. Nothing.
John.	They have.
John.	Nothing here with them.
Guy.	Believe it all.
Paul.	One of them call.
Ernest.	May attach mention.
Ernest.	They sometimes say. Honorable mention.

Scene II

Josephine may establish who may.

Josephine.	They will announce declare.
Josephine.	A will wonder where.
Josephine.	More say more. See.
Josephine.	With this. And. With. Me.
Josephine.	As. Best. Us.

Scene II

Josephine and Therese.	She led. More. Than. Their. May be helped. To. Send her.

Josephine and Therese.	Will she be. With them. Will she. Be. Dismayed. Excuse. Will she be disenchanting. Just made. In sofar. Justly made.
Josephine and Therese.	Insofar justly made to prepare. For them with them alone.
Josephine and Therese.	It is. A pleasure. To see. Delicacy. Which makes it. She is. Sweetness itself. As she. Appears.

It is pleasant that balsamine has a fragrance.

Josephine and Julia.	May she be tall. And true. May she also. Be new. May she. Also. Be. One of few. May she come. To see. Them.
Josephine and Julia.	Very nicely.
Julia and Therese.	They have not met. To meet. Will they. Be surely. As. Will they be. Better. With. Them. As made it. Be all. Fortunately for them. It is pleasant to have a white table. Only naturally.
Therese and Josephine.	May be. In why. Of. They. Mention their wonder. Of. About. Well.

Funnily too hot.

Therese and Julia.	Should have been. As they were. Inviting.
Julia and Ernest.	More. Will be precious. As. Well.
Julia and Ernest.	For them. To have. In time.

Julia
    and   Always helped.
Ernest.

Julia
    and   A little. Once. At a time.
Ernest.

Julia
    and   Once. At a time. A little. As helped.
Ernest   Much of the time. They do.
    and   Refuse. Crowns.
Therese.

Josephine
    and   By their help. Are they anxious. For it.
Therese.

Josephine
    and   In no hurry.
Therese.

Scene II

Josephine.   It is very inappropriate. To have it. Made. With them.
    By them.
Therese.   Or as they feel well.
Therese.   Which it is. No. No. Which. With. An applied. In
    their. Credit.

Josephine
    to   No wonder. That. They greet. With pleasure. Their.
Therese.   Boat.
Therese   Have many heard. Of dances. Dancers. Make dances.
    and   And.
Francis.   Dances. For themselves.
Therese
    to   Josephine speaks first. It. Is widely. Unknown. That
Josephine.   they are. Troubled.
Josephine
    to   It is mine.
Ernest.
Therese
    to   It is mine.
Ernest.

Therese
to
John.

With whom.

Therese
to
Guy.

Claude is a name and also Ernest.

Therese
to
Ernest.

Should they manage. To urge. Them.

Josephine
to
Ernest.

Or with their yellow. Wishes. Or. Cravats.

Josephine
to
Guy
and
Therese.

It is of very extraordinary importance. That. They. Give this.

Therese
and
Josephine
to
Ernest
and
Guy.

Should they be often induced. Induced. Introduced. Should they. Be often. Induced. To change more. Than formerly.

Therese
and
Josephine
and
Julia
to
Edward.

It is in vain. That they count. The amount. For which. They manage. To leave. And open. More often. Themselves. To their lambs.

All of
them
together.

Little dogs resemble little girls.

Julia
to
Ernest
and
Guy.

They may have chances.
They. May. Have chances.
They. May. Have. Chances.

Julia
    to
John   They may have had chances.
    and
Guy.
Julia
    to   Or with it.
Guy.   They may have been there.
Julia
    to   With them.
John.

Scene II

Julia
    to
Guy   It is a. Wheelbarrow. That makes. One anxious.
    and
John.
Julia
    to
Guy   They may know. That. One is one.
    and
John.
Julia
    to
Guy   In made. To punish them. With one.
    and
John.
Guy
    to
Julia   It is. An anxious thing. To say. The month. Of May.
    and
John.
Guy
    to   With which. They will. Please. Me.
Julia.
Guy
    to   After all. It was not what. I had expected It. Was you.
Therese.

Guy to Therese.	It was you. And. They. Will have pleasure. In that case.
Therese to Julia.	Will all. Who will. Make it. A pleasure too.
Therese to Guy.	They will be anxious. That they have. Seen me.
Therese to Julia and Guy.	All of a wall. Is wet. When they. See me.
Therese to Julia and John and Guy.	Or has been. And now. Is dry. This has been. Because. Of the action. Of the sun. On water. And pleasure. And quiet. And a noise. Which. When. It came alone. After.
Therese to John and Guy and Julia and Ernest.	Was not what they. Would have. As an interference. And my niece and nephew. Knew. That. Aloud.
Ernest and Josephine.	All who may know. A march. Will know. That willows blow. When they mean.
Ernest and Josephine.	It is all. Made at all. By them. As. They mean.
Josephine and Ernest and	It is mine. When. Is it. Mine.

Guy.
Josephine
  and
Julia
  and   When is. It mine.
Ernest
  and
Guy.
Josephine
  and
Julia
  and   When is it. Mine.
Ernest
  and
Guy.
Josephine
  and
Julia
  and
Ernest   When is it mine.
  and
John
  and
Guy.
Josephine
  and
Ernest   When is it mine.
  and
John.
Josephine.   Or which. Is mine.
Josephine.   Is it mine.
Josephine
  and   They may be. Thought. As well.
John.
Josephine.   Naturally.

Scene III

Julia
  and   It is three.
Guy.

Julia.	We three. It is. Three.
Julia and Therese.	No one. Has known. They know. That hail. Can hurt. What. It falls. Upon.
Josephine.	I have been. With. I mean.
Julia.	And with. Josephine.
Therese.	It is. Of no importance. To be timid.
Josephine.	With them. They are. Induced.
Josephine.	To introduce. Mind. Them.

Scene IV

Guy.	It is an advantage. To hope. That it. Is true.
John.	Who can. Be seen. By two.
Guy.	Be welcoming. Them. As they come through.

Scene V

Therese.	Has curtains. And has. Refused. Curtains. Has wells. And. Has. Refused wells. Has aprons. And. Has not. Refused aprons. Has wealth. And has not either. Refused. Or not refused. Wealth.

Scene VI

Therese.	Shall be. Met.
Julia.	In. On their. Account.
Josephine.	May calculate. Four. To a measure.

Act III

It may be beautiful to resemble them most.

Therese.	Is occupied in writing.
Josephine.	Is occupied at once.
Julia.	Is not warned to be cautious.
John.	Is sensitive to impressions.
Guy.	Is managed by singing.
Ernest.	Is variable because of their at all.

All who mention what is left to leave them and so they sit quietly while the curtain goes up.

Scene I

Josephine.	Many many have been here.
Julia.	To see me.
Therese.	When this you see believe in me.
John.	With pleasure.
Paul.	Has charm.
Ernest.	Is not betrayed.
Guy.	More than enough.
Josephine.	Replaces one.
Julia.	Replaces one.
Therese.	Replaces one.

One and one and one.

Scene II

Cora.	Which one of it. Should.
Dora.	Or could.
Josephine.	Or. Would.

Scene III

Josephine.	Play well. For Dora.
Therese and Cora.	May they. Call Cora. She may come. For her.
John.	Favor Freddy.
Ernest.	And believe well. Of. A melody.
Guy and Paul.	And think. And. Swim. And meditate. And. Destroy. And think. Well again. Of. Their. Joy.
Josephine and John.	It is of no use thinking of this. As they amount. To the same.
Therese and Guy.	She may be. Angrily. With them. They. May be.

Julia
   and   Should it be. Well. For them. To like it.
Paul.   Would it be. Well. In them. To. Like it.
Cora
   and   It is inestimable.
Ernest.   They remind them. Of their amusements.
Josephine
   and   Confine riches.
A Place.   Confine. Riches.
Josephine
   and   Confine places. In. That way.
Cora.   Confine. The place. In that. Way.
Josephine
   and   Compare love. To them.
Guy.   Compare love. With them.
Josephine
   and   They will compare. Their.
Ernest.   They will. Compare. Their.
Josephine
   and   They will. Compare. It. With their. Advantage.
Paul.
Paul
   and   They will even. Compare.
Josephine. They. Will even compare.
Paul
   and   Compare add. And they. Compare.
Josephine Comparison.
   and   They will compare. Adding. With. Seen.
Adding.   Them.
Josephine
   and   It is astonishing. That asking.
Nichole. Is it. A name. For a. Woman.

Scene IV

Josephine. Julia may be. With. And succeeding.
Julia.   Cora is not. Patient.
Josephine. They may align. Making.
Julia.   Just made. Harbingers.
Julia.   Of a. Reason.

Josephine	
in	They may dance together.
pleasure.	

Scene V

Josephine.	She might be late.
Josephine.	Or rather more. At. Their behest.
Josephine.	In a chance. Of an allowance.
Josephine.	Just when. They went. And well. Alone.
Julia	
and	
Cora	They will. Will. He.
meeting	May she.
Guy.	They will.

Scene VI

Practicing.

John.	Could know all.
Guy	
and	They will call.
Paul.	
Ernest	
and	One.
John.	
John.	They may. And could. Count.
John	
and	It was. It was. Too.
Ernest.	
John.	Two more.
Walter	
and	The youngest. For. Water.
Paul.	
Paul.	May they. A wall.
Walter	
and	
Walter	Will they. Or. Will they.
and	Be tall.

Paul.	Because they. Are. Tall.
Paul and Guy	She may be.
	They may. Be. As. They. May. Be.
Paul.	With it. She might. Be united.

Scene VII

Josephine.	Can be. Respectfully. Left free.
Julia.	She may be. Respectfully. Free.
Guy.	She. May be. Respectfully. Left free.
Paul.	She may be. Respectfully left free.
Josephine.	May be. Respectfully left free.
Josephine.	May be. With three Josephine Julia and Guy.
Josephine.	May be. With them. With the. Three Josephine Therese John and Guy.
Josephine.	She may be. One of. Three. Josephine Julia John and Guy.
Julia and Guy.	They may be. Very sleepy.
	And again. They may not be.

Scene VIII

Therese.	But and budget.
Joseph and Therese.	But and budget.
Therese and Guy.	Be careful of three.
Julia and John.	May they repair places.
Cora and Guy.	It is very easy to be fearful.
	And they will provide themselves with it.
Therese and Paul.	They will either ease with ease.
	Or not with ease.

Julia
    and   Not without an easy access.
Ernest.   Not with and with it.
Cora
    and   They use names.
Hilda.
Julia
    and   It should be wide.
Therese.   With them.
Therese
    and   Wild with them.
Julia.

Scene IX

Julia.   I. Julia.

Scene X

Therese
    and   Twenty or three.
Guy.

Scene XI

Josephine
    and   It may be a dish. Or which.
John.   It may. Be a wish. Or. Which.
Therese
    and   It might nearly have been a stain.
John.

Scene XII

Julia
    and   By choosing. A mine.
Josephine.   They will. Find time.
Josephine
    and   But will it. Have been. A net.
John.   No. At once.

John.	It is not certain or sure.
and	Of having an older brother. Or daughter.
Guy.	It should be tried.

Act IV

Scene I

Therese.	Who will. Who will. It will. They may. If they will.
Therese.	A circumstance that was not intermitting in embrace. Their. Clarity.
Therese.	She should be sent. That is. It is. She that is. They are sent.
Therese.	No. When. They are. Welcome.
Josephine.	It is a bandage. She will. Be very. Anxious. To know. That she. Is. All well.
Josephine.	She may be often. All made ready. And then. It rains.
Josephine.	She can be all. Ready. And when. She has gone. She has hesitated. But really. She had better. Go.
Josephine:	She may be. Unaccountable. If there has been. No difference. For that. Which. It is not at all. Extraordinary. To have happen.
Josephine.	She may be. Without doubt. Better prepared. Than ever. They were. But it will be. All of it. At. One time. And assiduously. In their. Rebound. She may not be worthy. Of all. They wish.
Josephine.	It is of course. Of no account. Not for them.
Julia.	All changes. Are made. By liking. It. Best. By liking. It best. By liking it best. All changes. Are felt. By liking it best. All changes are felt by liking it best.
Julia.	She may. Easily. Be anxious to please.
Julia.	They will turn around. If they think. They hear a sound.
Julia.	It is. A disadvantage.
Cora.	Do be pleasantly with me. To see. Do be pleasantly to see. With me.
Cora.	They in that in it that they.
Cora.	It is an extra or an. Extra order.
Cora.	It if she may. Have it. To-day.
Cora.	Should they. Have it. To-day.

Therese	
Julia	They will. And may. Have heard. Them say. They
Josephine	will. Have been. When. They. Went away.
and	
Cora.	
John.	It is. No doubt. Alright.
John.	No doubt about what they were doing.
John.	In. At once.
John.	By themselves.
Paul.	It may be at all.
Paul.	All change. To have them call.
Paul.	Our having it. They having it.
Paul.	Which they.
Paul.	Once for all.
Paul.	It is. Of no importance.
Guy.	Shiny as they will.
Guy.	Exchange it.
Ernest	
and	Fairly one two three.
Guy.	

Scene II

Therese.	She may be clouded. Or cowed.
Julia.	And they will trace. And. They will shape. Their destiny.
Guy	
and	It is well. To carefully tell. In the meantime. That.
Walter.	They may be often closed to have it. Closed to them.
John.	May they be precious to us.
Josephine.	As they. Are telling.
	All who told. Are with our consent.
	Left carefully. To be. Attentive.
Paul	
and	It may be. That they. Are willing. To be an authority.
Ernest.	About vainglory.
Guy.	She may be. Attached jealously.
Josephine.	For they may like. It all. To be suddenly. Left only. To them. As they may like. When they have it all about. Them.

Therese.	Children are told to be. About to be. Happy. They are equally. Careful.
Julia.	Made to call them in a minute.
Ernest and Paul.	Neither of them are drowned have been drowned.
John.	With them.

Scene III

William can call call Cora.

Scene IV

With welcome. As they deplore. Their arrival.

Scene V

Should be anxiously careful.

Act II

Therese.	Be well. And frightened.
Therese.	Let no one deceive. By. Smiling.
Therese.	Make my claim. Mine.
Therese.	Which they will. Incline. To mean it.
Julia.	With whether. It is. All. A purpose.
Josephine.	By which. They will. Be. Without.
Julia.	Just as much. As a desire.
Therese.	By waiting. Or. For. As well.
Julia.	They may. Be patient.
Josephine.	And. A value.
John.	By. Or. Rather. Or. A calling.
Guy.	They will add. We. In plenty of time.
Ernest.	With all of it. And. Wait.
Guy.	Just by. It. As. They. May. Accuse.
Paul.	A blessing. To be. Promise.
John.	About.
Therese.	With. Mellow.
Josephine.	About. As they. Change.

Julia.	Very likely. They will. Very likely. Take place.
Josephine.	It will very likely take place.

Scene II

By the time that they are welcome they wish.

Josephine.	They wish for it.
Paul.	They. Will. Be pleased. To have it.
Guy.	To wish for it.
Julia.	With them. They must. Be. At once.
Josephine.	Not only chosen.
Therese.	Very well. I thank you.

Scene III

Therese.	Very much. They will.
Julia.	Very much.
Josephine.	Will the will. Violets. Very much.
Julia and Josephine.	Which they please. Play. As. They find it. A very pleasant dish. With.
John.	And without sea shells.
Guy.	But would they affect us.
Paul.	Adversely.
Ernest.	If they do they lead to having seen. A very enormous. Spider in the morning.
John.	Never mention a name.
Guy.	It is in vain. That they. Or we. Mention a name.
Paul.	For their pleasure.
Guy.	As early as they measure.
Paul.	And once again. They sing.
Paul.	As they mean. Sunshine.
Josephine.	She may be taught. That if. She can tell it. As twenty. Or ought. She to be obliged.
Julia.	To be fairly anxious about it.
Josephine.	Or fairly well. Anxious about it.
Therese.	May she come in.
Julia and Josephine.	She may come in.

Scene IV

Julia.	It is rightly. That is it. Or. That it is. Or that. Is it.
Josephine.	By which. They wish.
Julia.	And full of. Might they. Be. Without. A calling of. More than they. Further.
Josephine.	Should have thought likely.
Therese.	It is. A credit. And a pleasure.
Paul.	To wait for. Her.
Guy.	With pleasure.
Ernest.	Beside this. Will they be willing to have it as well a give it beside this.
Paul.	Manifestly. As to origin.
Marguerite.	Has been introduced vainly.
John.	And never again.
Paul.	Will they.
Paul.	Have any.
Paul.	Of one.
Paul.	Of them.
Paul.	Not ever again. Will. They have. Any. Of one. Of them.
Ernest.	It is. In time.
Julia.	When they thank.
Josephine.	As much as they like.
Therese.	When they thank Josephine as much as they like.
Therese.	When they. Thank me.

Scene Three.

Therese.	Will.
Therese.	See John.
Therese.	Will see John.
Therese.	Soon.
Therese.	She will see John soon.
Therese.	Believe all who call.
Therese.	That they come.
Therese.	When they.
Therese.	Call.
Therese.	They will come.

Therese.	When they call.
Therese.	They will come.
Therese.	When they.
Therese.	Call.
Therese.	They will see John.
Therese.	When they.
Therese.	Call.
John.	May be. Without. A pleasure.
John.	They may be. Without. A pleasure.
Guy.	Unless. Hunting. That is. Shooting.
Walter.	Is a pleasure.
Paul.	They may easily. Learn.
Paul.	That there. Is no. Hope.
Paul.	Of their coming.
Paul.	In the morning.
Paul.	As well.
Paul.	As they.
Paul.	Will come.
Paul.	But not be able.
Ernest.	To come.
Paul.	Because Tuesday Thursday and Saturday.
Paul.	Afternoons.
John.	Are partly.
John.	When they.
Paul.	Are not. At liberty.
John.	And often.
Paul.	With them.
Julia.	They may be pleased.
Julia.	To be. Allowed.
Julia.	To play. Theirs.
Julia.	As with them.
Therese.	An account.
Therese.	For which they please.
Therese.	An account for which they please.
Julia.	Be added. To. Effrontery.
Josephine.	Or with them.
Josephine.	As. A plain.
Julia.	But begging.
Therese.	Or may be.
Therese.	On account of their bother.

John.	But with it.
John.	Or. Better.
John.	Than with it.
Therese.	It is. Their. Pleasure.
Therese.	As plainly.
Therese.	As their pleasure.
Therese.	May be. Useful. For them.
Julia and Josephine.	Forty make. Forty four. A conundrum.
Julia.	It is a pleasure to witness.
Josephine.	That they are balanced.
Therese.	And preserved.
Julia.	As more than. They mind.
Josephine.	As it will. Allow.
Josephine.	Them to be. At ease.
John.	But do they need. To surprise them.
John.	Or even itself.
Guy.	They may be happily.
Guy.	At their ease.

Scene Two.

Guy.	They recollect. That they were. Apprised.
Guy.	Of which. They were determined.
John.	In place of their inattention.
John and Paul.	May be. An authority.
Therese.	Has never known. John. To know. Paul.
Therese.	How many Johns are there.
Therese.	But which. Acceptably.
Julia.	But all of it. Amounting.
Josephine.	To their hope.
Julia.	In which they share.

Scene One.

John.	Makes no mention. Of annoying.
Therese.	Of annoyance.

Julia.	Of being. Annoyed.
Josephine.	Of preparation.
Paul.	Of trouble.
Guy.	Of withstanding.
Ernest.	Or affecting them. In opposite ways.
Julia.	They will not annoy them.
Josephine.	They will wonder. Why they have not left.
Therese.	The answer is simple.
John.	May have been it may have been.
John.	Important.
Ernest.	And they may have been. Advised.
Guy.	Because it is.
Walter.	Their hope as well as their wish.
Therese.	Reminded by understanding.
Julia.	As well. As apart.
Josephine.	Which is why. They are favored.

Act III

Therese.	Crowned in glory.
Therese.	Crowning glory.
Therese.	Trained Therese.
Therese.	With them with seen.
Therese.	With lace.
Therese.	Crowned with lace.
Therese.	With grace.
Therese.	Gracefully remembered.
Therese.	Silently respected.
Therese.	Separately placed.
Therese.	Saving it. In place.
Therese.	Of lace.
Therese.	They will surround. It.
Therese.	By leaving. It.
Therese.	Saving it.
Therese.	With. Their. Saving it.
Therese.	And they will. Be. Accepted.
Therese.	As having done it.
Therese.	Quietly. And they mean.

Therese.   My name.
Julia.   They make pleasure.
Josephine.   For them.
Julia.   For them.
Julia.   With them.
Julia.   They make.
Julia.   And give.
Julia.   Pleasure.
Julia.   To them.
Josephine.   For them.
Josephine.   Before.
Josephine.   Or because.
Josephine.   Of them.
John.   When.
John.   With them.
John.   They may.
John.   Give pleasure.
John.   To all.
John.   Or any.
John.   Of them.
Paul.   Because.
Paul.   With all.
Paul.   They will give.
Paul.   Pleasure.
Paul.   To some.
Paul.   Of all of them.
Guy.   They may make.
Guy.   It.
Guy.   A pleasurable occasion.
Guy.   For them.
Ernest.   And they may.
Ernest.   Abide.
Ernest.   By their.
Ernest.   Leaving it all.
Ernest.   There with them.
Ernest.   For them.
Ernest.   Or.
Ernest.   Without.
Ernest.   Them.

Scene II

Therese and Julia.	She may. Add what. They have. Here. And they will. Be disappointed.
Therese.	May they. Have been.
Therese.	Nor. May. They have been there with. And.
Therese.	Without. They know. Best.
Therese.	What. Day. They choose.
Julia to Therese.	Please see. To it. And please. Be very much. Please. Pleased.
Julia to Josephine.	Plainly as well. As. If. They. Have to have it. Back.
Julia to Therese and Josephine.	They may be. With them. Or. They may be. Since they have come. They may be. There.
Julia to Josephine.	It is. Not useless. To have them. Come to. Be there. With them. As. They well know.
Josephine to John.	May you like feathers. No one mentions anything.
All together.	A turkey can be killed. By a dog.

Scene III

Julia.	She asked. For. Their wish.
Julia and Josephine.	But it was a pleasure to give them whatever. They wished.
Julia and Josephine.	It could be. With. A pleasure. That. It. Could be. Easy. To give. Them. Whatever. They wish.
Julia and	They wish. That. They.

John.	Will not. Bother. Not to. Deprive them. Of it.
John and Josephine.	But it might be. A denial. To not. Give them pleasure. For them. To give them. Not. A desirable. Pleasure. As they. Come too.
Guy and Paul.	Should be hurt. If they came. Through. The way. That. By the way. That. Will they. May. Have. It. As a pleasure.
Guy and Therese.	Have never seen. That they like. May they. Beg. Them. To be disinterested.
Guy.	Should naturally mean.
John.	That they will. Love. To come along.
John and Julia.	They have not met. Yet. Nor will they.
Julia and John.	It is politeness. Or their perusal. And a pleasure. To have been. Away. As. Long.
John and William.	Long. May they. Be about it. So long. May be natural.
John and Ernest.	To remember. That they. Bought. A boat.
John and Ernest.	With tears. And prayers. They knew that. The birds. Who have been known as not being shown. As a brown. Swan.
Julia.	May be they do but. Without it.
Julia and John.	She meant that Mary a river, Mary, a day and Mary, is a care.
Julia and John.	They remember. That. There are four. When two. Are two more.
Josephine.	Having never seen them again.
Josephine.	Not. To have. Gone away.
John.	But very freshly.
Therese.	They do. Or do not. Marry.
Therese.	In order to please them.

Act IV

Guy.	Should clearly make a mistake.
	Antagonise clearly. Or they will.
Guy.	Please whether. They will. Antagonise. Clearly.
Guy.	They may join. Thoughts. By union.
Guy.	Clearly.
John	They may. Place. Pressure. And
and	Perhaps. Explain. That. They must.
Julia	Please. Them.
and	Place. Them.
Guy.	
John.	And for this. And.
John.	Asking.
John.	Or else.
John.	They may. Make pleasure.
Paul.	A pastime.
All	They may.
four	Place more.
join in	There where they have.
saying.	More than they. Yet had.
John.	In no way. Do they resemble.
John.	Them.

Scene I

John.	Forty. Is an address.
John.	For them to think well. Of winning.
Guy.	Should be succeeding.
Paul.	By which. They climb.
Paul.	As well. On.
Paul.	As when they are sent out.
John.	In and about.
Guy.	To succeed. To rocking.
John.	In a pleasure. They have weeded.
John.	Weeds thickly. As a memory.
John.	In feeling.
John.	Exhausted.
John	But she may be. Easily.
and	Troubled. Not by. Their success.
Guy.	Just as they would fruitfully.

	Know exactly how. They should count.
Guy.	And blunder.
Guy.	Or fortunately.
Guy.	Or blunder.
John	They may be more.
and	They may not be.
Paul.	More hurried.
Therese.	Should be reminded.
Therese.	That fellow-ship.
Therese.	Means accomplishment.
Julia.	But she may be less there.
Josephine.	As if unknown.
Julia.	By their sheer hope.
Julia.	Of letting. It be as likely.
John.	But which may be thought.
Guy.	Just when. They shall. Devise.
Paul.	That they will authorise.
Ernest.	Them to go.

Scene II

Julia.	I told you so.
Therese.	With their address.
Therese.	But which they will.
Therese.	But she. May be. Very well fitted.
Therese.	To be clothed. For the winter.
Therese.	To be. Admittedly. Not. In pretension.
Therese.	Nor as well.
Therese.	She will.
Julia.	Adhere. To her family.
Therese.	She will.
Josephine.	Be even pleased.
Therese.	To have them come.
Josephine.	To have been. Left. To them.
Therese.	As they will manage.
Julia.	But which they.
Josephine.	Will suggest.
Julia.	It is an appointment and a disappointment.
Julia.	They will deny. That they will.
Julia.	Be with them.

Therese.	Nor very selfish.
Josephine.	As well as will.
Julia.	But they may plan.
Josephine.	And will. And can.
Therese.	In which way.
Julia.	They say.
John.	That they listen with interest.
John.	To what is said.
John.	Is being said.
Guy.	But may.
John.	Having lost. Nothing.
John.	As well. As. Being.
John.	For them. It is. A pleasure.
Guy.	Should. When. They would.
John.	In. Finally. Leaving it.
Guy.	As well. As delight.
Paul.	They will rest. There.
John.	As much. As in. In their interest.
Guy.	But which. They will. Provide.
Guy.	As an instance.
Guy.	Of their. With willing.
Guy.	Should have. As. Well. As. Have been.
Guy.	As much. Thought well.
Guy.	Of. In an instance.

Scene II

Therese.	May talk. Of it.
Therese.	And take. More. Of it.
Therese.	As they will. Please. Be with it.
Therese.	Here. With it.
Julia.	For them. To have no one.
Josephine.	Or just more. Than ever.
Josephine.	More than. Alike.
John.	Should.
Guy.	Which they mean.
Paul.	Maintain.
Ernest.	One. At one time.

Finis

A PLAY OF POUNDS

⸙ 1932 ⸙

At a made at once.
She made him.
Nor she made him.
Introduces weeks and made mistakes.

Scene I

Looked through the book and there was one missing.
Now she made him.
Look through the book and there was one missing.
Had not made him.

Scene one

There is nothing as annoying.
Looking through the book.
And there is one missing.

Scene one

Humility leave to beckon further or she may will be neglected.

Scene one

It is very welcome to announce ours as master-pieces.
They all come

Act one

It is remarkable that she will listen to me.

Scene one

Do you find this as remarkable or austerity.

Act one

She will feel one as one. Or.

Scene one

Remarkably.

Act one Scene one

Shall she be astonished by toiling.

Scene one

Or theirs in hope.

Scene one

A genius or joining.

Scene one

Which may they feel in.

Scene one

Coming excellently.

Scene one

Who has been heard to doubt that they are told, they are cold, they receive it coldly.
Or they are awkward.

Scene one

Shall it be an obligation.

Scene one

Act II

Try this instead.

Act one

She may be.
Having thought of Andrew. And Bartholemew.
Or forgotten.

Act one

Scene one

They may make servants of one and one.
And leave one.
To have one.
And think and mean.
Or how old are James and children.
One two or three.

Scene one

All who make cake are welcome.
All who select something.
She shall be taught as willing.
Or may do is meant as telling.
And they will delight in adding.

Scene one

Shall it be just as she chose.

Act II

All taught, all and everything.
I like very well that she is faithful.

Act one

Scene one

I can be thought to be sweet and all.
Can be as light.
Or with it.
For more than girls.

Scene I

Should should be often bought.

Scene I

I do not think he was amiable.

Scene I

I do not think he was amiable.

Scene II

Just as well.
For it because.

Scene one

All of. The time.

Scene two

It is that they used to. Be always. Very much their care.
And mine. If you like.

Scene two

Shall it be please. And them.
Or often with. A helping all more than then.

Act I

It has happened to be that it has. Why then. Happened. It has
happened to be.

Act I

Scene I

What is the difference.
Between happened to be and it has just now or just or just
then it has happened to happen or to have to have had to had to
happen or to me.

Scene one

They like not to

Scene one

To blame

Act II

It is going or not going to be pretty.

Act II

Should sudden summons be a thought.
Or will she be with us if she is bought.
Or they clearly must go.
As well as if they went.
Or violence with their violets as may be shown.

Act II

Scene one

Should how many.
Or will they listen
To me.

Act one

All who may wet a while their hold.

Scene one

It is a difference between sweetly and well.

Scene one

Should it.

Scene one

For theirs.
Ocean or shall they.
It is quiet to behave kindly.

Scene two

All who were ready to add and a land.

Scene two

Buy me a party or partly we relate.
What they have no wish or rather to do.
Of course it is easy for them them.
Which ever may there be no difference between more.

Scene one

I have suddenly thought.

Act one

It is abler
To have been
Or maybe
Left better. He left better.
She could not leave better.
Difficulty is not deft or better.
Deliver or deliberative.
Different is a does or do dove a verb.

Act one

Order

Scene one

Other or whether or other than one another.

Scene one

About which. They may.

Scene two

It could be history too.

Scene three

It is difficult to be a third.
I like to see her ideally lie there.

Scene four

What is the difference between a pretty one.

Act one

Forty is too old thirty is too old twenty-nine is not too old.

Scene one

Should she. Be willing to let her think. That she could with impunity may she not neglect whether. They will balance or eat. Without their pleasure. For this. To-day.
Can it be better to improve. Or not.
But politeness adds. Will she. Admire.
May they reply frequently.

Scene one

Shut or well shut it.

Scene two

A pleasure of their advantage. May should grope.

Scene one

I will be awfully pleased to be very. Able to make cake.

Act II

This or though with or though.

Act II

She may live by a pound or care for them more or just as well.

Scene one

Could it be why they were awake.

Scene one

Or pleasantly waking. Wakened. Or awaking.

Scene one

Between a sign or either light or add her.

Scene one

A light is not smoking. Or vacant or smoking.

Scene one

Better to be left to be happy.

Act I

It is always by them a blessing. Be very well.

Act I Scene one

Or none.

Scene one

I should delight but not in fright. Which they may please come in.

Scene one

How happy it is always to be ready

Scene one

At or patient. Not in rule. Awhile.
It is very often vacant to be plainly acquainted.
A tall dog is not a long dog. And vice versa.

Scene one

Nobody can know for them to care.

Scene one

A part of which they think I love them do they. They will esteem a pleasure.
Should it be with a pleasure.
Or made nicely.
Or prepared.
They think over.

What they may have given to them.
And so on their account.
And easily not find it at all.

Scene one

Or may they be thought to like absent in branches.
And their attack.
And their pleasure.
It is made merely. At one of three.

Scene one

Calling ought as pairs of plainly.

Act I Scene two

Should make it do or did she hear me.

Scene one

For this how are ours fortunately.

Act II

It is thought that they were never careful

Scene one

Indeed they must have been given to be pleased with care for it.

Scene two

Our acceptance.

Scene one and scene two

For more or for more of for acceptance

Scene one Act I

They shall think well of me.

Act I

They may have learned to mind what they are likely to see for which they drag. And they may have been brought to have riches and no richness in all their thoughts. They will do well to tell us little.

Scene one

It is all who may come to their aid.

Scene two

Please be with pleases
They will be with and pleases
Or should. They be seen
As coming all more than all.
Once at a time they think as well.

Scene two

Or made arrangement.

Act I

They will lessen then for one.

Scene two

All who. Joined them with a ribbon.
A ribbon is a noun to stare.
All beloved with care.
For which foolishness they will join rich men.

Act I

Please be patient.
With a petition.
It is better than their counting.
As much as really.

Scene one

Pleasurable.

Act I

I cannot think that it will be managed.

Scene one

By pressure. Or exchange.

Scene two

Or even customarily

Scene two

Or as a little

Scene two

They will like

Scene two

Intermediate. Or blaming.

Act I

It is my time to be right.

Act I

Who has whom been one.

Act I

If they do.

Scene one

May they be said to make it stay.

Scene two

In there wish.

Act one.

She does not care.

Scene one

But she must be

Scene two

Encouraged.

Act one

Scene one

Should it be brought.
If it is brought I will use it

Scene one

Nor need they mind

Scene one

If they like.

Scene two

But just as well badly.

Scene one

With them as a blessing.

Act one

Scene two

She may be used to having it.

Scene three

Or having it to finish.

Scene three.

Just may they well.
Be frightened.

Or not careful.
Or easily well

Scene two

They may be left to have it help.

Scene two

Them.

Act one

Scene one

Just with

Scene one

With them or just alone.

Scene one

Who is or who is helped
By their having
Or having been.
Left to be outlined
As well.

Scene one

All who call
Or they wish

Scene one

Should be or if they had been well.

Scene one

As much as ever

Scene one

If they were inclined.

Scene one

Or coming afterwards.

Scene

Just whenever

Scene one

They like.

Scene one

All just as it happened.
All of which it is
All more than not as they like
With and better not better
Or without it
Just or as it happened.
It is so easy
To be dazzling

Scene one

They make it do

Scene one

By their if they mind.
That it is stolen.

Scene one

All day

Scene one

In which

Scene one

It is better to be prepared

Act one

Scene one

For fortunately oh will you.

Scene two

For fortunately.

Act two.

They will be scarcely through.
They will be or will not be at all scarcely or scarcely through.

Scene one

She may be caught to be cautious.
Or will she change from better to worse.
It is of no importance to remain.

Scene one.

Will they be caught to be out loud.
Or would they ask

Scene one

It is richly held
To be not all for it
Because
Idleness is no blessing

Scene two

She does not very carefully care.

Scene two

It is a feeling

Scene two

It is their wanting

Scene two

Which they have of one

Scene two

By their use.

Scene two

Or all

Scene two

Of it.

Act II

Would it matter
If they were curious.

Scene two

Should they be weakened
By places.

Scene two

All who are cared for

Scene two

All who

Act I

Scene two

Should they be as well as
And in which they are.
As well as
If they were known.

Act two

Scene three

They will be a wide difference

Scene three

Between which they or as if they had better.

Scene three

But well alarmed.

Scene three.

Just which

Scene three

They are.

Act I

Scene one and two

All who are very careful may be precious
And they will think it best.

Scene two

To make more

Scene two

As they

Scene two

Are obliging

Scene two

Or merely all
Which
When they come.

Scene one

All nearly frightened

Scene one

Because of any one

Scene one

Or presently.

Act I

Scene one.

Would it be any good to like it as well.

Scene two.

Or for which they may as well like it.

Scene three

Made in without a place

Scene four

Just whatever they meant

Act two

Scene one

Which is made for the place.

Scene two

As many place it in that way

Scene three

Usually they like it more

Scene four

As well. Or which they care.
They are careful made to be may be.

Scene five

She hopes that she will be again
Recognized as carefully

Scene six

Or whether they are prepared.

Scene seven

Or failing sometimes.

Scene eight

With all of it may she be cared.
To go there whether she could like it.

Scene nine

More than ever even if she could not.

Act II

Nobody is welcome who has bought with them more than ever there are three there about them

Act II

Scene one

A common place which is their in with it

Scene two

Should all be all made to be all ready or as when it is made to be ready.

Scene three

To wear it at all

Scene four

Or.

Scene five

A shawl.

Act one

She may be to tell her in order.

Scene one

For them

Scene two

As much as they neglect

Scene three

A plan. Once in a while.

Scene four

Which when they went. They were very well willing. By their us. In a change.

Scene five

Yes. I made it.

Act one

When I was happy I was well off.

Scene two

Or whether when I was happy I was happy with as well well off.

Scene three

When I was happy I was as well off.

Act II

No one in and on can be crowded.

Scene one

Or may be

Scene two

They would be just as well willing.

Scene three

May might in excitement.

Scene four

They are very widely precious.

Scene five

Or just as precious

Scene six

Widely as precious just as precious more than it could be used.

Scene seven

Precious to them not only.

Scene eight

For them precious to me.

Scene nine

It was well used and used to it.

Scene ten

They may be without it.

Scene eleven

Made more with before then.

Scene twelve

It makes no difference now.

Act II

Should she. She should.

Scene one

Finally as a set. They may finally regret.

Scene two

They repeat. Or should it be casually.

Scene three

Three is an artifice.

Scene four

More than they like.

Scene five

A wish is as much as they complain.

Scene six

More than they like.

Scene seven

Fairly an artifice

Scene eight

Or in time to admire.

Act II

Will they be rich or in between.
Not as they like it.
For them is there a difference.

Act I

Hush much may it be that they ask the same of them.
Or often as they are willing.

Scene one

Which is a source of a kind of our pleasure.

Act II

Scene one

Avoidance is a valley of pleasure.

Scene two

They will be alright

Scene three

In making more.

Scene four

Or two.

Scene five

It is very well counted

Scene six

Or they made a mistake

Scene seven

In little pieces

Scene eight.

It had been just as well or more of it which they had or not at
all

Scene three

It is a pleasure that the hair will curl.
Even if at all. They are I am late.

Act III

It is all they have in resting often.

Scene one

As if they are called.

Scene two

If they would

Scene three

Be patient.

Act II

With and with counting

Act II

She is only owned by not leaving and resting

Act II

Scene one

She will leave this as one

Scene two

For seconds only

Scene three

As they might one

Scene four

May four

Scene five

And or one.

Scene six

In which they with hers fix

Scene seven

As much as one.

Act III

It is kindly to be about ought.

Scene one

Or widening now

Scene two

Should always call

Scene three

May they be frequent or frequently in many and place.

Scene four

Which they think of as restless.

Scene five

But as once in a while.

Scene six

By them with which they are again.

Scene seven

All little likeness to them was lost

Act I

Scene one

If she does.

Scene two

It is that is.

Scene three

That they will have come to them.

Scene four

One as one.

Scene five.

Could she be acquainted with their name.

Scene six

If they knew their name as their name.

Scene seven

Or will they interfere.

Scene eight

With which they have here.

Scene nine

As well as yes.

Act I

Will they come and will they welcome.

Scene one

Will they come and will he be welcome.

Scene two

Or will he be called away

Scene three

Or will he be not able to stay

Scene four

Or will he trouble them to ask him

Scene five

To be welcoming.
It is very happy to be often there

Act II

She may be always tractable or able or welcome if she is able.
To be welcome

Scene two

And no neglect makes her welcome.

Scene three

Nor ever. No neglect makes her welcome.

Scene four

Which is true. For they may be called to be there nearly
welcome as often.

Act II

Scene one

They may announce one to a dozen three to six or pleasantly.

Scene two

And they will be selfish if triumphant.

Scene one

She will be gentle.

Scene two

With their care

Scene three

As they may care

Scene four

To be careful.

Scene one.

It is by ours that they buy.

Scene one

It is very delicate to be loaned.
Very delicate to be loaned.

Scene one

They will be better welcome.

Scene one

Do not do lightly that which you do do.

Scene one

It was of course that they expressed.
That there were never at all a pleasure
To themselves alone an advantage.
In which they were careful to be able
To thank them one at a time
In every little while.

Scene one

And very well too
To thank them as they will do
For themselves as they like it.
They will be often anxious to risk that amount.

Act I

Oh may they matter to it.

Scene one

As their attachment.

Scene one

She is not

Scene one

So much more than

Scene one

They will.

Scene one

Mean one

Scene one

Which they will

Scene one

Mean one

Scene one

They will be kindness itself or they may like it.

Act II

May be.
Should or it could.

Scene one

If she was cold to him.
Or she was cold to him.

Scene two

Would fulfill.

Scene three

Their doing that.

Scene four

Dislike.

Scene five

Or find.
That they mind.

Scene six

It should be meant as all

Scene seven

That they can if I like.

Scene eight

May be they will be a change

Scene nine

After a time.

Scene ten

It is of no use to be cautious.

Scene eleven

Or should they grow.
To have it kept away at first.

Scene twelve

After every little while.

Act II

She too

Scene one

Was not born to be gone

Scene two

And thorough.

Scene three

For them to like it most.

Scene four

As well as their.

Scene five

Or more than as a chair.

Scene six

She was not then oppressed.
Nor did she give
Nor like it as a loan
Of their indeed
There carefully
Arise in time

Scene one

Coupled by this in time

Scene two

Could it be she meant

Scene three

That they meant

Scene four

It is of no use to have them change and just like it.

Scene five

I meant to be often having been there.

Act III

There is a little bit more of it all.
Which they threw to me

Scene one

But little places have been needed

Scene two

By the calling of none

Scene three

Which is in adding
But which
They mind.

Scene four

Leaving it to know that it has been commenced,

Scene five

Just as whenever they like

Act III

All always went too far to go

Scene one

In there or more their pleasure

Scene two

Very finely

Scene three

It is all but it is not better.

Scene four

I have been disappointed in not having been receiving a christmas card.

Act II

No I do not imagine so.

Scene one

Very soon they did not meet at noon.
But understanding when they would meet again.

Scene one

It was nearly when she understood something

Scene two

Just as early when she felt that it was just as well as one.

Scene two

She might please him

Scene three

With having felt well

Scene three

Him with him.

Scene four

Which means that they were not neglecting her for him

Scene four

Or would they like it if they were not even any more neglecting him for her.

Scene five

She would be very well welcomed to arrive.

Scene five

With every little bit their mistake

Scene five

They will be early every once in a while.

Act II

Scene one

She may be resolute if she was found

Scene two

Nor will they cover this.

Scene three

As anxious.

Scene four

They may be only known as a wedding

Scene four

But which they have a chance.

Scene five

It is always as well.

Scene six

Or how is it to mean
That it is a plainly prepared to marry.

Scene seven

Or they will be exactly.

Scene eight

Should do.
What is the difference between a smile and a change of expression.

Act I

How are ours of waiting.

Scene one

In their despite.

Scene two

Or might they mind it.

Scene three

For them or them
It is too dreadful to have been in that case disappointed.

Scene four

Which they may use and include.

Scene five

As well as

Scene six

Their leaving love out.

Act I

Should it have been arranged just as well.

Scene one

Or not as well

Scene two

Or better than ever

Scene three

In all of it which is in use

Act II

Scene one

Will they mind which they mean

Act III

Or for themselves alone.
Or all alone

Scene one

Name them just as well as they knew how

Scene two

In which they prepare where they go

Scene three

Or if they like it.

Scene four

They could use more than they do they could not use any
more. They could not. Use. Any more.

Scene five

Very likely they could not use any more.

Scene six

As well as they can.

Scene seven

They could use it.

Scene eight.

Which is what I meant.

Scene one

All of it is in the place of their waiting

Scene two

By that time by this time

Act I

She should be ready for any remedy

Act II

I do not like him to be careless.

Scene one

Which made it be that I did not like him any more.

Scene two

Nor made it be that they were careless of me.

Scene three

Just as much and as ever you like.

Act II

They will be prepared to think as well.
They will be more prepared fairly.
They will change it for their part.
And they will like as well as dislike.

Scene one

Which they may be
Or which they may have.

Scene two

In often or often as well.

Scene three

There is with vigilance.
There is no care with pleasure.
There is no time that use
There is nothing that they care about.

Scene four

All of which makes it as talking.
Or should they be made to mean.
That it is what they like.
In every way as well as they like.
In the making of it to be their care.

Scene two

It should be just when
They are wanted.

Scene three.

Or may be they will call it

Scene four

Theirs or arrangements.
Which they told them.

Scene five

All as many as gain.
Or come again.

Finis

A MANOIR

▾ 1932 ◂

AN HISTORICAL PLAY IN WHICH THEY ARE APPROACHED MORE OFTEN

Act I

Scene

The road to a manoir. A manoir is situated. And in the country where it is of course very well known. Here they are independent that is to say they need only go as often to any other way as they like.

Act I

The road to the manoir is not crowded although very often some one is met. When they do they stop or either invite them to say something have they been very often.

Scene I

They were both welcome they brought good weather as well as some one with them.

Scene two

Who were they likely to meet.

They were not likely to meet any one surprising but it is surprising that most any one is confiding. They will tell them how they stepped on a pointed nail and why it should be painful but not visible. They also said that they liked reflecting and if they were offered reasons for reflection they would not be uneasy or rather troubled. In this way they are often grateful not only in expression but in what they thought. This makes it alright.

277

Scene three.

Could all who came be asked to come again instead of waiting. Waiting is easy when they are not there yet.

Act II

Sir Francis Cyril Rose and Carley Mills are to come to visit. They were met before they came to the door.

Scene I

All who know Fontainbleu knowing that this can be far away although no exile is any farther is any farther than what. He was not interested in any kind of Spain as not a king but Fontainbleu is where the roses grow when they are very old and very well oh very well. A king is not a king if he is missing. Every one knows where Finland is when it is not Scotland but we know where Finland is when it is Finland and Scotland is not Finland but Scotland and so if all the hundreds of roses only two were frozen and so we like idleness best which we obtain.

Scene one.

A house in which there is green paper put upon the kitchen shelves prettily which is for them not so many but a few and invention.

The characters who come and go are all here.

Act one Scene one

Everybody felt well who came or did not come often everybody who was not in animosity was not without that in often.

It should change their days.

The characters now commence to mingle and gather.

They will reserve not to leave a door open or rather. I must wait and have a great deal of money in my pocket. Why because I would rather.

And so the characters had better not go. It is very often their choice to come again and may let them. This introduces conversation. She is impatient that they or he arrange it now. Better which they have than they are ready.

Could he look to see another one who is with difficulty deaf to see how it was here. Made in the meantime not for which. They carry.

A scene commences in which a great deal of work is done.

Scene two.

It is not true that they were gainsaid. They were well and they were careful. There are two ways of being satisfied with much or not by themselves.

'With which they were made.
A character feels that they saved well.
One fastens laurels to the same end
Many have plenty of time and furnishes
More think why do they choose
All make theirs strange.

It is more than they knew that they counted. In history anybody remembers names.

My names are he does not like it.

It is a scene in which they are sorry for a dog because he has been well treated and after nobody is blamed they are home again. History takes time.

Scene three.

A manoir is a temporary home.
They are very well placed there.
The object of it is that there is no envy.
All who are around come there.
Could history find a time.
Could it matter that which they may ask
Did they have no one to be sure
Could it be a change once for all.

Scene four

History makes memory.
All historians have their character

Scene five

One man. He has asked me are we pleased with him.

A woman. She was not so awake as she was
A girl. She had a mother and has grown older
A boy. He is not any longer downtrodden.
A little boy. He has not been seen
An older girl. Not the one they knew
A whole family. Those which live there
A bride and groom They had a child before they were married

Scene six.

It is not for nothing that they prefer oxen to a horse.

Scene seven.

Paint my pansies
History is not neglected

Act I

M. Rosset a farmer
When I saw
Or not
I will try all if it is not
Chosen to be welcome
M. Rosset's son is to have gone.
Away for a year
When.
M. Rosset.
Will be pleased to have them
Come to meet his wife.
If no one offers.
Him not to wait.
For him.
A manoir is not a farm nor is it a castle on a hill because a level makes a farm not a hill nor a level until a farm is a manoir not a hill or a level until a manoir is not a farm nor a farm nor a hill.

M. Rosset is a farmer who owns his own land which is still belongs to his father.

And so they are equally able to be ready if it happens.

Act I

A little boy places his hope in gathering as well as finding if it happens. He has lived with a farm and now he knows a small hill is known as well.

He thinks twice about what he says. He calls it not for his mother. But she will not write not only him for his brother. It is very strange but they are very often healthier.

Scene I

A manoir in place of land.

Scene II

Once it was very little known oh yes it was.

All the characters come in and are eventful.

There could be a mistake if you had thought that it was not the one who had one it who had done it and you would have the credit for it only if as it was not as it was. A farmer can be a better known first minister that is to say they may be any day which they had been.

Oh how often are they sure they need to have

More come to them without a cause. They have a certain. They like it best.

Scene II

A manoir could be called a house for a gentleman when they come they will bring a man servant with them.

How often she can say the man. Just when they say she may say the woman.

It is not a way of crediting out loud with remaining in the room not in the sun not out of the noon not out of the sun.

It is coursely grained.

Scene four.

It is remarkable that in two weeks summer has come. And the noon which was yesterday is full of intended measure. She knows that it is as often no mistake.

Oh do be gracious and come too but stay there because after all you will not come by now.

In the country a woman whose mother has been married can have a child.

Scene five

Diana Noon.	Nobody nobody nobody knows how sad I am.
John Dane.	When they see before them trees on a hill that have been one and now are a hill they must choose.
Gwendoline Lane.	For this which they present at present theirs is no return
Arthur Gardener.	May they be close to might they be close to Myron's desire.
Diana Noon and Arthur Gardener.	Have pleasure in hesitating or enjoying the sun. They are close to the more the merrier. It is for them no patience. It could be planned that they would always so so. Which they rejoice. Oh for this because they like that

Diana Noon and Arthur Gardener know no difference. Oh why do you please me. He knows when a door is open and closed and he asked them. Once more he asks them.

Herbert Lane may be very ungrateful.

There is no story in any hurry. But this they know that they are quite as gracious as they carry. Or dear me.

Gwendoline Lane Or does she know that they are just alike. They are not seated separately.

Act I Scene I

Just why do they know that they are here Gwendoline Lane and Godfrey North. They will be partly appeased.

Scene I

Forty more need none.

Scene I

Julius and Claudius are engaged in flattery.

Scene I

Genevieve and Gwendoline Glaine.

They have been in a hurry to see that they count everything after early as late afternoon. Supposing this is this. It is best to see it after one but if they or he sees it before one it is after all after rather early than late and so grass covers the perfume of roses that is to say if he is forbidden to cut them. This makes their way.

John Lane
Bertha Williams
Roderick Fellows
    and
John Blaine.

It is often their occasion that they happen to astonish.

We were so awfully pleased that we were a part.

No one can mistake a spider for an ant and yet perhaps they do or do not do so. As much as they mean.

Scene one

It has come to begun that they feel that they need any one.

Scene one

Scene one is not spacious.

Scene one

Scene one is spacious.

Scene one

They will tell well what they have as instruction.

Scene I

It is lightly that they have a need. It is not always their origin of a desire.

Scene one.

Arthur Carler.	Meaning to be a bee
Henrietta Adams.	Meaning to be better than he or she

May Maiden Hoar.	Which will that they neglect until
Edith Leland.	Until she is better than any one.
May Lidell.	I have a brother who is either or rather pre-paring that they should be safely at a time
Edith Barton.	For which they will wish.
Jenny Bradley.	All who know owe that they will welcome them.

Scene II

He is very excited too.

Scene III

They will remember that others very well for which they will or more than could be needed neither with them or arranged for which they do not care for care.

Arthur Angel.	Shall they be third when no one come
Henry Garfield.	It they like they are tall
Robert Garter.	She may be joined in a garden.
Beatrice Gaunt.	Or which they will fill not only for ought they make a count in tall they do grasp they should solicit may they not be frightened all which they make as in a place of noise or whether peach trees branch.

They need to have peach trees branch.

In this scene they talk as if they knew.

One two three.

It is often obliging to mention my name.

More come just as they did the scene is a manoir where it is not repeated it is extraordinary having been once they come again.

The manoir is not on the side of a mountain how can a manoir be on the side of a mountain in this place not at all or even inexactly often as the bell rings they come like that it is often what she needs she was just as well as wept.

The Manoir is occupied. They know no difference between their staying here each one says how do you do very slowly may they be mine it be mine.

May Lidell.	How heartily they pass what they need oxen need.
James Garfield.	In time for a time for them to like it to be

mine or yes just as soon as they may please it
is often which as soon as wish a considerable
diminution of their extension as they see and
beside.

Henry James.   I made a doubt of the amount.

A manoir may be built of stones and covered with mortar.
Busily done by him when he calls. It is I he call. I am which they
like as pansies. Please do not repeat which they do again.

A manoir in danger of whose stones. She is occupied.

A manoir makes all of us a pleasure.

Act II

Walter.	Leave me to be candidly used to it
Helen.	Or just when will they wish that they need me.
Nelly.	It is for them to like what they do do
Esther.	It is not shameful that they ask them more
Jennie.	Or place them there
Edith.	Or need more than they like
Edgar.	Which they will feel as they mention it
Frank.	Which they knew
Bertram.	In order to change it for an avoidance of their being not so able to be left.
Ferdinand.	Left left left right left
Maurice.	And did I after all leave war to help them too
Paul.	There is no war
Mark.	Not when they wish
Herbert.	It is very well to aid in ploughing and in respecting war.
Marguerite.	But which they say in aid of a name
Beatrice.	Which they like to do.

Scene one

A manoir when they are ready to be satisfied he comes and
says it is done. It is very agreeable to be allowed to do everything.

Scene two

They make it be not only why they like it but which they like.
They remembered that they had been not only certain but very
likely to have that as a choice.

Scene three

Could they know

Scene two

Edith William Carl.   Who should change little birds who can kill big birds for little birds, even one.

May Henry John.   If they think well of waiting they will differ in their account three no doubt maintaining one, for them.

Herbert Minnie Helen Lucy.   For them they finally stand if three or four are mentioned as they will they carry it up very carefully, for which they are interested.

Louis Louise August Finn.   It is just as well not to listen as only not to hear that they accustom a little of all the nightingale for which they are familiar or they must, will it be in disproportion they may amount to it.

Grace Henry Arthur Blaine.   Be rich for us or for us they will mind whom they like or as known for when they call or carry it out may they be free not to be three for them may they.

John Agnes Charles Henry Fane.   Could they be called all may they be met all or may they be just as much met a very little account, of it.

To have known that an apple does not produce wine or birds do not hear him or follow in their train they like no one to be asked for which they have it.

William Bertha Nellie John Blaine.   Could they not be thought to leave them to remain behind and caution which they will them.

August Farm.   She may be happy not only not to have been there but often with them more.

Charles Garth.   Yes we know

James William Bernard Arthur Jane.   Oh yes to know for which they like it as well not only not obliged but by this way in which they hope to leave as they will have it as their medal. Not by which they refuse.

Genevieve Butler.   Will you hear a little more than not it is easy to prepare to say will they.

Gilbert Henry Call.   Just when. May they appoint just when they will please themselves more only not as yet. How do they account for theirs.

Henry Arthur Blaine.   Come to be aware of where.

It is so beautifully all that when they like.

Scene III

A manoir should be such when they have surrounded within reach made inestimably for which they chose

Arthur Griffin Lands.   Nobody may tire since they need them nor may they tire because of their need for them. They have that which is by and by at once and for it hawthorne need not be only fastened and for them not furtively cared for as instantaneous. Should they not ask for venturing in them as they may. If a horse lies down is he careful.

Scene III

Genevieve Land.   Could they deceive her about patience if they wait or not at all in a fright at night which they arrange because of theirs for instance. If they mean all they need not be behindhand with their dahlias too or birds too or seasons too. In this way in case of not being in error and a manoir is a manoir and not easily mistaken to say so. They will divide into two groups. And he has been standing.

Scene IV

Mathilda Grant.   She took it to him to show it to him and she would have confidence in him after she had showed it to him and she would be an advantage in it being the first time because if it were the second time there would be the same confidence in him but there would not

be the same result of the same confidence that
they had with which they would the second
time show him what they brought to him to
show to him. And this is so.

Agnes Blaine.   If which they may be thought an authority
often as they talk they will not manage what
they have this they will all like what they do
for them for which they look where they have
asked no one.

Leonard James.   Of course not just why they should join themselves in not alone not crediting themselves
with often where they went as not only just
for it but also just for it just all the same as
melting.

Arthur Constance.   Could they be granted that they glance this
way because all of them are occupied never-
theless. Why should any one be disappointed
in not being in exchange for which they are
very well very well known. She has lost her
mother not as company but as a fact.

The Manoir is the same yet.

Act II

It is very often very well done

Scene I

By which they relish all at one time a little at a time not when
they make it for which no one adds more than is careless to remind
him has he done it. A manoir is in use.

Act I

Dorothy Belinda Tree.   He hoped that she would remember that
is to say would not object to not forget what
she was about to say.

Gilbert North Lane.   For if she could and he bought wood who
had been first to claim a lake by any name.

Nathan Garfield.   Or rather not to guess which of it is not without their amount.

They will yield a lake or better not at all

It is easy to have a thing if they mention a stairway. For which they will use or if not not a mountain to choose they will all be told not when it is as much as if they can. They have chosen hills or will they say so or as well if they are not by that time for them.

Bernard Blaine.　　Who shall manage the name. The name is they
　　　　　　　　prevail as much as when they can they think
　　　　　　　　well of it all for which then. Come where they
　　　　　　　　come with me.

Mary Horne.　　It is a change from it.

Scene I

Can they be sought to come here

Scene II

Or welcome

Scene III

For very little while.

Scene IV

But which

Scene V

They emigrated

Scene VI

By which they knew

Scene VII

All may be lost

Scene VIII

Which they like

Scene IX

They found.

Scene X

He found the brooch which she had not lost but he found the brooch which she had not lost.

Scene XI

When they do call

Scene XII

It is pleasant to have fifty.

Scene XIII

Fifty white turkeys

Scene XIV

Which they improve

Scene XV

By thinking well of the rain

Scene XVI

Or which they might

Scene XVII

So gently.

Act II

At once she sees four sheep
She also sees vines and rain
She may also see that she uses
Whatever she has

Scene one

Gilbert Marcel and Frederick they come to a halt they examine while they wait and they hope that they will be careful of what they have. Once in a while they come again and they are very welcome it is remarkable that a burning fire in sound resembles rain.

Scene I

Marcel Having been here goes away. Will that be ultimately

Jenny Helen.	May easily bend over and make a sound of pleasant result not only for them but by them as may they mean that there is no difference between what they hear and when they wait oh yes.
Edith Helen.	May she be not annoyed by with them as they go beside she has not waited but she has helped all in a way to be not only not in wishing nor in visiting that they were well
Robert Brown.	May she be called to be better.
Henry Rose.	But come.
Mary Blaine.	For me
Nelly Henry.	Just as they mean.

They all meet where they come up and down it is extraordinary that they do not go further.

If you hear do you think it is a bell that rang.

Scene II

All in one. They hope to reign.
But she may see that they are startling

Scene I

There can be no surprise if roses are green there can be no surprise even when looking closely and the roses are green.

William Barker.	May I see what they mean by here they live part of the winter.
Florence Parker.	If they feel that the winter is colder than the

summer they are aware that they have never met there or been met by any form of restlessness but which they like

Winifred William.
If they feel that they may join or may make plain that they have been thoughtless about wishes for which they will not be well to do they may easily not be under any obligation to remain there

Hubert Draper.
For which they will allow if they cause all who are desired to come to see that now in the future they will be accused will they correct what they mercifully change.

Mary Hewit.
It was not only long but they were anxious they were willing but they were more than ever likely for which they name theirs in seasons all of which they ally themselves as damson roses or wet as pansies or nearly ready or or which they chose come to me and be willing to have more than that made there that they may go and very well as they adapt theirs at one time just when they need not only what they have but once again for them

Godfrey Wilton.
Should they be awakened in time on which account if they look down they see them as if they were waiting to have no one be with them for which they will not only succeed.

James Boyce.
Or should they go

Scene II

It is noteworthy that they looked out and saw below a meadow and lower what they hoped were cows and still lower they had chosen what they need. It is so nearly different.

Scene II

A captain comes in and waits a day or rather which they say that in eight days they will rather gather that any more of which they will not prepare to leave more than yesterday for which they will be inclined to be perverse.

Albert Julian. I believe in perfect likelihood and they please

Bertha Julian. For which I think that I tell it well

Martha Julian. But they will try to cry

James Julian. It is the fashion to think well of him and without doubt

Gilbert Julian. For which they may or may not carry it out

Jenny Julian. She or he are better known than when he or they may be used

Belle Julian. For which they say usefully is no word

Martin Julian. She can be made always really by they can.

Mary Julian. For which it is remarkable.

Howard Julian. They will go or they must go as a band

Herman Julian. Be fairly wise in not which they have gone

Edna Julian. She or he will see.

Guy Julian. If they are met they will be placed well away.

Ernest Julian. It is not only with well but also with what they did well that which concerned them.

Genevieve Julian. Should they bow

Harold Julian. In will they have met with what wishes

Jacob Julian. She will be better perfectly parted by three just as they were or not.

Gustave Julian. May they pay milk for hay and raisins for a dance.

Minnie Julian. It is best not to go away or not to delay to go away or rather more than ever rather that they stay.

A manoir in which they are

Act I

Agnes Fellow. And may I leave it.

Ellen Meredith. But certainly if you wish

Lillian Grant. But may I leave it

Beatrice Blaine. But certainly if you would like to leave it

May Liddle. Should she be estranged by any attempt to have it happen.

Act I

She may be thought not to have returned it which indeed she has not done

Scene I

They may plan that if they return they bring with them their daughter and also plants suitable to the size and situation of their garden which they adore I do not mention here that which may be not an acute but an occasional disturbance but they believe will anything redound to their glory

Scene I

Will she manage to finish
Will they manage to furnish.
Or will they plan what they leave
Or will they arrange what they have
Or will they like what they have
Or will they manage to convey this
To those others who are waiting
And not in vain

Scene I

Ellen Russell sits and thinks of the wind and the cold weather which prevents the development of plant life which in consequence flourishes and they are very content.

Scene I

Quietly placing everything where they hope to see it.

Scene II

Or just at once being very careful

Scene III

They might like to be entertained

Scene IV

By the time they go there.

Act I

They will prepare Act II from Act one.

Act II

One two all out but you

Act II

They are all there and they like it.

Act I

In a manoir in the afternoon she sleeps. And actually to have been where it has been that never has the sky been so blue nor the trees so green. Not only this but also that they are prepared for it

Scene I

Manfred Willow.   Will you call me by my name
Bertie Applegarth.   Or will they never be forgotten

Scene II

She writes excusing herself.
But which may they do.
Oh yes they do.
Bertha Haviland has been held by her arm. Or they may go.
Augusta Blaine for which they are well as they are well if they wish.

Scene III

He believes in enthusiasm.
Or will they call.
Be with them.
Or just.

Scene IV

It is often to be tormented if it has not been or rather already said.

Scene II

Lillie and Nelly.   Will they know that.

Lilly Haynes.   Or will they not know that they are not will-
                       ing to be often making this effort we may be
                       very pleased that they have or which they
                       have not come or inclined may they be either
                       or courteous.
Enid Blaine.   If I hear them come
Jane Blaine.   Or are they called mine.

It is often whether we wonder whether we can wonder what
they look like but not any more. A manoir does not change seats
or love the dew because fairly well they might not without reason.
Be just to them.

Edith Claflin.   Be very well and only promised that they will
                       go.

Act III

A room in a manoir which is in dispute how old is it and
what do they say

Scene I

But which they change.
But of course not which they change.

Scene II

Aloof from conversation

Scene III

But they read or read presently.
Not very slowly

Scene IV

Much of which is appetising

Act I

Just when they knew that the rain was as good if not better
than the sun.

Act one

Scene one

Marion Barley.	Who if who knew that she will add what it could do.
Paul Ronald.	But this we think if we wish wishes. But it does. Please if they may. Or she will be coming.
May Blaine.	For them they leave all of which smells fragrantly.
May Barley.	They can call Bartlett Bartlett as a purpose.

Scene II

This I will in an amount.
I fairly need what they give me
Or should she just as certainly decide
It was not only why they made
Them be here

Scene III

It is very often restful to have flowers cooked in cheese.

Scene IV

Helen Harper.	Will you be free for me
Ellen Gale.	Or she may be not only there where they are called to go.
Agatha Maine.	Should she be all well or all claimed or all of it.
John Gardener.	She may be often wanted to come carefully.
Elizabeth Maine.	It is while they are often there that they are with them.
Henry Blaine.	And so they will be caught both of them to guard them to please.

And so now it is not only why they presume but why they sit here or in a pleasure for them partly pardoning or call call a lily.

Now think why they knew why they never knew which one they could be placed to present to know best.

Cultivate care.

Act II

I care
You care
We care
They care
They come and care
Or they come not to care
Or they will finally care
Or either they will be careful
Or negligent

Scene I

It does not make any difference who succeeded whom as one might say in reference not only with which as preference.

They will carry all or ought.

Scene II

Why will they spell wish
Or why will they have which
They do not prefer not to wish

Scene III

Either Albert or Edith are here

Act II

Do be careful not to like that

Scene I

A swallow or a pair can come in. And has it as a way of knowing that they would like another door open is it not astonishing that they can like this as they like them. It is always a habit. Bartholemew Harbert. Can she like them when she sees us.

Scene II

Henry Bailey.	Or if a moth is careful so that do be careful is what they change when they need most what they leave. It is often rain that lacks and if that it is in their care they do not care.

Scene III

Laurence Rider.	Oh by the way do they prepare whatever they have
Roy Shields.	Of course they do they must add fortunately for which they like.

Scene IV

David Blaine.	Fortunately for which they like.

Scene V

As many as they go away for but neither or should they please not only barely or mostly as if which they do as theirs that matter whether they like it more no one is deceived.

Scene IV

Gabriel Blaine.	Should they happen to be amused as well as pleased by them. No one should describe their hope.

Act II

Martha Infeld.	Will I be well when they are welcome
Alma Corey.	But she will feel what they would like
Pearl Sayen.	Not only why they wish but when they wish.
Hilda Grain.	Or will she wish that they would wish as well as now begin.
Ada Blaine.	For which fortunately for which

Scene I

Two may be too many for one

Act III

It is not why they wish but when they wish that is important. She expected it to rain. They will ask a question.

Scene I

Mary Knight or why she was not only with them
Mary Knight should be soon seen.
They knew that they could happen to have often that they were able to give it all for them.

Mary Cabell.	She was soon to feel that they would account for which of them for which they were chosen.
Henrietta Blaine.	She may be called or this is to blame.
Myron Blaine.	May they be wise and remember where they were able to be about to have it more seen than when they were established.

The life in the Manoir is as tranquil.

Scene I

She will prepare or need it be for them

Helen Lane.	Or would she be and not wish them the same
Helen Blaine.	Or will they like or not prepare it to or for them.
Nathan Blaine.	Of course they name a name

Scene II

Gilbert Horne.	Or should they be in any hurry if they went
Paul Elder.	But which they wish without the wish for which reason which as they often went
Bertram Cairn.	All who have been established dutifully think well of why they went or which they had all which is lost. It makes no difference who liked it.

Scene III

May they be divided alike

Act IV

Muriel Haynes.	Will you think all the better for them because they went there or do allow it.
Maggie William.	But she will leave those to them as much as they can not only why they like it.

Why could they not like the Manoir. They liked the Manoir. Or with them they liked the manoir.

Scene I

They need not say that they disliked Anna.
Nor need not say that they liked Anna.

Scene I

It is often a wonder if they were mistaken did they know that they were unused to it

Act III Scene one

A farmer who has been offered to be at home.
All which they may claim.
Very often in June in the evening they are disturbed by a dog and a ball and also by the annoyance of only they cannot know how to distinguish sunshine from snow as if it were on a mountain.

Scene one

Will you do
Yes not to-day
Nor if they like
Which they may utter as they like
They feel which in meeting
Nor by this time
They can feel
They come
Ours in a chance
Or mine awhile.

Scene III

Would any man be one with always.
Or may be they are not otherwise feeling.
Not more which they can.
They allow themselves always in part.
In a place a person can be with their mother and their father and their grandmother.
Opposite a manoir and on the same side.

Scene five

Should they will or will they be often as much because or ever.
She can be felt to have no known knowledge of when they win rings or wings in quiet places.
Or she can be or as made or as tall.
Which she is on or around.
Often to wonder how much further.
Or indeed how long it will last.

Scene III

She may often be awhile to arrange made in rest of the pleasure they can come from.
Or might they like.
Whatever they had

Scene IV

She may be thought to be a thousand. Or to be thousand.
Or to more.
One of which hope.
Or may they went.
It is rare any one tells anything.
While they wait.
She is rocking in a rocking chair not patiently.

Scene II

It is not more than mean she may be called with which they went with which or without which when they came all the same.

All who pass by are known as anointed or which they wish
to know. It is easy not to know their name but which they had in
no mistake

Scene one

Could they come with as with no reason.
They have been brought to show them since.
They can always have this right that it is better in June that
it is hotter than the month of May

Act I

Could no one dream of which way they went

Scene I

Once when they were not out walking the notary came in he
asked them were they pleased with everything and they were.

The notary was a young man who was being a notary for the
first time and not only that he was able to have children and not
only that he was obliging and very willing to be as sweet and
everything as any one had been who had been

Scene I

Byron.	He called it his name
Basket.	He knew his name
Marguerite.	She did not know the name
William.	Nor which a name and believe them when they do it.

He tried not to divert him
But he did not try not to leave him.
It is often that they are anxious if they are there.

Scene II

Should they call that a color which they know not only because but which they know all that they are alike. It comes to
this that they see this with. It.

Scene III

At one time they are quiet.

Scene IV

Which they knew.

Scene V

John Byron.	Why will no one announce me
John Blaine.	As I am.

Scene I

They often stand not knowing that they stand

Scene I

They should be called will they have been if they come.

Randolph Blaine.	More than they did which they may win once only
Robert Byron.	Not if you like that they did if not at most
Henry Basket.	They will be ready for which
Edith Garner.	They will surprise all for which they call or tell why they did well.
Nero Henry.	Should they be thought thoughtless if they liked it too much.

Scene III

They were either thought to like it or they were thought not to like it.

Act II

Scene III

They should be selfish if they were taught who made them like it either one for them or they will often like it either one for them.

May Richards.	She can be of some account.
Bertie Gilbert.	But they know who they knew when they liked.
Beatrice Hilda.	But she will be
Martin Blaine.	For which they know that not only will they but because they taught him so.
Herbert Rice.	Why often it is not alone not hurried

Scene I

Should they be not frightened by a cloud.
A manoir has remained well placed which they join

Scene I

Hilda Blaine.   Will they be called well do they wish
Edith Hampden.   But they will like it

Scene VIII

It was when Edith and Annie Lyle sat down.

Scene I

She had not met before
But she would leave it as before

Scene II

If they could be there not in beside the door
There not as yet

Scene III

Should it not be
An insistence

Scene IV

They may be asked not explicit but only for the name

Scene V

Just when they liked to mind
And when they will for which they knew
Always once in a while.

Scene VI

Not only known to leave as well as love flowers.

Act VIII

She may state that if she did not she could not only not come to hate if not or not to not to date act eight.

Scene

It is very difficult to follow an ant sidewise.

Scene I

Peter can be known differently as Agnes and he can come as if be not come to have been if only they did not care but is it not only kindly which they know almost not once at all for them as a care

Scene II

They meet regularly in the afternoon

Scene III

It is made by which that they seem to mean

Scene IV

Should or would she be not only ready as if to be here when it is not a possibility that they could be not only where they went.

Scene V

I should just join

Act IX

Better than which it is better than which that he should have that

Scene I

William Genevrey Henry Marine and Ida Williams come fairly well to-day after all.

Scene II

Or should it be why not.

Scene III

They make a plan.

Scene IV

Why not if not not now

Scene V

May they like them

Scene VI

In one at a place

Scene VII

It is fortunately not.

Act X

James is vacant when parks are full.
Or Jane is present when a lake may be a hill
Or not if James is present when they will
They Jane is vacant when if they will
Would they go

Scene I

Arthur and little Arthur are very well and happy having been well enough alone and they will.

Scene II

Annie Lyell. Who comes through
Gilbert Wells. I do
Janet Pearl. Which they may
Bertie Blaine. Any day
    All of them ask who came in

Scene III

William Henry Taylor. I do not get it it eludes me
Maybelle Edith Grosvenor. Will they be weeding well with add-
               ing which they tell.
James Hope.   It is of no use.
Henry Blaine.   For they will add meaning that it is add to
               add and not the same as the sense of shame.

Scene IV

May Rhone.   For which they could ask any across.
   Will they
Anna Blaine.   Of course not will they
Guy Foster.   But which yes which will they like.
May Hilda.   May Hilda like what they like.
    A manoir is habitable.
    I will never listen to one
    Tell about a manoir being habitable
    But this is the result
    Of it all
    That they will inevitably
    Be not only softened but refused
    To be admonished.
    Why can no one not please bees
    If you please
    A scene in a manoir is often not a disturbance.

Scene I

    I could just join it with it.
Henry Moon.   What will they think of him
Henry Blaine.   That no one is to blame
Bertie Lamb.   For which they come
Guy Lane.   But which will they do
Charles Hilder.   Whatever they like
Dan Sloane.   Not which they want or may
Abel Stone.   Not at all

Scene II

Everybody as well as anybody too.

A manoir.

Which is inhabited in the summer but not in the winter and has a garden.

Scene I

It is indeed just how they liked it.

Scene I

They may be asked to make at which they like.

Godfrey Fisher.	What is it.
Abel Nobel.	Nothing but what they do.
Godfrey Fish.	Add or do add it to.
Abel Noble.	That which they will it will for you.
Godfrey Fish.	After it they like
Abel Noble.	But after which they do like what is it that they wish.

Home in a manoir.

Not often may they but which indeed which they will

Scene II

It is not why they like.

Godfrey Blaine.	Make it or do be make it.
Abel Blaine.	I will leave it alone.

Scene II

Not which they think it is not any or a mistake.

Adam Forsythe. What do they think of a garden which they have when they look wherever they may place one two or three balls.

Balls may be black or red larger smaller or medium sized and of no return.

Abel William. She may be often very careless because of which amount.

Myra Henderson. Though only not for which they meant to pay Should they could they couple it with him.

No one asks would they or would they not relieve it not only as they will but as if they will.

Now think plainly of a manoir.
She meant with or not without her consent.

Part one Act I

It could be sent that if they went they could not be sent without their consent one at a time. And how many cherries make a tree. Or if not how many pears have no consent.
And if not he was successful.
And if not will they grow
And if not by that time not to have been mistaken
Nor if not will they not go.

Act I

Scene I

Any one which one will be one who is one of such a special blessing as they knew.
And so they ate no orange which had not grown or been taken away.
This makes a manoir in the north and if after or before July a temperate climate

Scene I

When she sees that she is seated they will leave the room alone they wonder will they change their mind or if they wonder do they not more naturally appear to mind.
A manoir is not related.
They think all of it as they think well of them.
How many rooms in a manoir.
How many houses in a place.
How many buildings of which they have not any
Or else would it not be difficult to erase.
What they should like to do or not.
They would not care to give an account of it.
Nor might they be neglected even if not.

Inside of the manoir.

When they are not seated what do they do.
Or if they are not seated what do they do

Scene I

By nearly a manoir by nearly by nearly.

Scene II

Mark Byron.   What shall I do
Henry Horn.   But which they like
Martin Blaine.   All which are occupied
Beatrice Blaine.   For which they do

Scene III

The upper land is below where they cut hay

Scene IV

But when they were relegated and they waited.
Paul Morrow and Richard Blaine.

         For which they remember just the same that
         they were in a hurry when they came and
         this will not do for them

Paul Morrow is not kind he is in a pleasant flurry
Richard Blaine is fortunately yet not yet better and very well
as yet

They could not be thought either to be in a hurry or to be
well-to-do.

And so they managed not to finish what they had been waiting
to do which was just as well as they were welcome.

Paul Morrow knew that it would not do
Humphrey Blaine came very early to blame him
Janet Sayen was very well in indifference when they were
taken they were not taken oh no they were not taken away and
they leave they leave all of it as if they were better not known.
Of course they were known they were very well known and pleasant to all. It is certainly very indifferent and accustomed to it.

No one knows with what fancy they dispose of themselves.
Paul Morrow.   It is a great comfort
Humphrey and Richard Blaine.

         But which they do. When they are impatient.

Scene II

Birds are more necessary even than trees.
Oh are they
Yes for these.

Scene III

Much as they like it.
Or will they eight
For which they like.
They will not remove trees.
Because eight are made anxious
Once again as to or about birds and trees.
Now the thing that is very likely is.
That they will not disturb either
Her or him.
Just as much as they touch
Because they have been left as much
As they need them

A Manoir

Anything that is and it is a dish
Is amusing.
She will love like is the word
Anything Spanish.

A Manoir

Once in the morning it was after
They looked after them.
A manoir is exceedingly rich.
And not fortified
And not a pleasure
And either or
Their own surprise
As they try
To believe why

Scene I

After one they came one

Just Henry Byron.	Who had led him here
Ernest Fisher.	But which they willed
Bertha Basket.	But will they love William
Edith Arnold.	She is my delight.

After any minute they went around.

Bertha Basket.	It is very well to assume that a jacket
Edith Arnold.	Is what they prefer to lose.
William Fisher.	But which they please
Henry Byron.	To lose

Oh why will they wail
Oh yes or why will they wail
She could not deny or destroy a veil
Or in plenty of time escape
Or end in an end
Or better not
Or for which they will reply

Scene I

They feel that they will end one
One and one.
Henry Basket is all on edge

Edith Byron.	Is very well open to delay
Bertha Byron.	Shall share no one with no one
Edith Winter.	Full of when she and they plan.

Or not as a rest

Scene I

Henry Arthur Byron is not restless one and one or in in a celebrity because of a garden which is green why is a garden green when roses are red and pansies too or not.

Arthur Henry Byron is lonesome at once
Edith Angel Basket is very well on suffrance
Minnie Herbert Johns is plainly for them alone
Bertha Martin Fisher is meant when they met
And all of it they will like

A manoir

She had said

Scene one

One to four

Scene two

After that two

Scene III

In which they may
Or can they do to say
I mean which when they can
She said if a god is or can
Not to be said to be only
Not only when they can
For which they may account too much

Scene IV

Hilda Hildebrand and Lucious Land
                    And when they met they knew that the
                    ground would need leaves and sand because
                    it is very well known
John Ferguson and Henry Winters
                    They were surprised
Jenny and John John Blaine
                    For which they will tell their name
    Oh think well.
Bertie Maine.   Can it be made to be muddy
                       Beside.
                       Mud is or has been dried
                       And so she feels
May Maine.   Why will they please
                       But often refuse trees.
                       Trees are meant to be bought.
                       Or which they blame it if they are bought
Hilda Hildebrand.   But may be they like it
Edith Blaine.   Why will.
                       She be well.

Scene V

A company needs two.
Or three days.
The two dogs too
Need two
Or three days.

Scene VI

Fasten it.
Herbert Maine sees how well they like it.
It is fortunate that a manoir wishes
To be delivered across
Which a cross stitch
And she would be pleased
To do as she wishes.
Anthony Blaine.   And so they mean this just the same

Act II not followed by act two.

Act II

One one is a cloud
One one one is out loud
Three one one one is not tried
But she is not why beside.
It comes to this.
At the foot of the hill not at the foot but very near the hill
the beginning of the hill there is nothing to compare with this.

Act III

Should she have been in a manoir too if she knew just how
often they had left it to them or to her. This is how they think of
everything.

Once in a while it makes no difference how they went and
once in a while it makes no difference when they went.

This they may do.

Scene II

Bertie Robertson felt well when they felt well
Jenny Blaine was not only made anxious on occasion.
Hilda Knowles was not with them fortunately
James Garfield planned what he planned.
Marguerite Halstead was famous for her name
Edith James not only felt well but meant to do well.
So then they came altogether.
Only they did not come just when they did not come.
There can be manoirs in many countries.

Scene III

In each country the guests as well as the owners are different.
In their manners in their habits and in the change of address
and also in their return to their place or wherever it is no effort
either to go or not go. And so as nothing changes why not come
again.

Or if not to not be either in the place of when they went
they will be always not only welcome but will they come or not
or not at all once.

Thank you for a cool summer and much rain and many wishes.

SHORT SENTENCES

1 1932 1

The scene is one in which nicely they go.

Madame Bucher.	Will you come
Nathalie.	Oh yes will you come
Amelia.	But I know you will come
Barbette.	I ask you to come
Eugene.	Will you
Joseph.	I have been able to come
Edmund.	Is he better because you bring what you bring when you do come

Chorus

And so they are all not alike.

Alvara.	Should my
Belle.	Should they by and by
Robert.	Should it be my turn
Henry.	Should they
Mrs. Andre Paquet.	Should they be
Helen.	With them
John.	Just more than then
Ferdinand.	As well as able
Mildred Aldrich.	Why they beware
A Chorus.	Should she be joined.
James Bellingham.	Not to-day.
Winfield Scott.	By which they hope.
Henry.	For which they like.
Jerry Holmes.	All of which.
Marguerite Lamb.	They may be included
William H.	For which they like
Arthur Balfour.	Please play best.
Joseph Hone.	By which they count.
Martha.	As well as they like.
Chorus.	It was why they mean.

317

Sir Robert Albi.	May chooses soon
Mildred.	With which
Meraud Guevara.	Just why they if.
Henry Melun.	Not for this
John Surgeon.	Just why they will
Edith.	But which if
Janet Blaine.	More have been here even
Arthur Chadbourne.	Just when they will
Edith.	If they mind
Martha.	It cannot be thought.
William Rufus.	May you be pleased.
Chorus.	They shall exchange.
Henry Winter.	It is most.
James Ferguson.	Which is for them.
Arthur Prentiss.	All of which is for them
Jane Heap.	All of which
John Randolph.	Is for them
Nelly Mitchell.	But which she will
Arthur Grafton.	But all of which
Janet Tanner.	May they be thought
Neith Hapgood.	It should be bought
Elsa Abrams.	They will be violent
Neith Boyce.	When they have
Chorus.	All of which is to blame.
May Hatteras.	Could I think of it
Jenny Fletcher.	With which they come
Edith Archer.	Or just the place
Frederick Wendel.	Made by their blessing
Roy Clair.	Surely be generous
Laura Armour.	Come to be granted
John Sigfried.	With which they dash
Ben Hodge.	Just why and not
Arthur Balfour.	In no reunion
Winifred Stanhope.	Should they be there
Laura William.	They must soon excuse
John Goat.	Or should they rejoin
Walter Arthur.	This for them
Chorus.	It is well neither of which.
May Welch.	She could be treasured.
Arthur Bird.	With me in politeness

Albert Lincoln.	Should much
Edith Lorer.	As very likely
Mabel Earle.	Just why they rose.
Abel Melcher.	Just if they thought
Ruth Winfield.	Just why they left.
Edith Henry.	Making it be right
May Janes.	Which whenever they doubt
Mark Williams.	It is because of gratitude
Arthur Nobel.	Just why they may
Edith Adler.	It is in a way a choice
Chorus.	She may be seen needless to say.
John Nichols.	But which they start
Bertha Reynolds.	But not with them in part
Wilton Friend.	She may be mine as a choice
Jeffrey Sands.	But which they call
Ellen Knoll.	Could it be heartily
Reynold Nice.	By me in so far as it does
Ernest Johns.	She may be bought to call
Neith Johns.	In middle cases
Edna Mills.	Why should she see
Lincoln Johns.	We can be better known
Andrew Orden.	Should which they choose
Martha Winters.	But not left immediately
Chorus.	She must be just.
Ivan May.	Could these for hers
Barnard Noll.	Which made it come
Nellie Wendell.	She for which they were satisfied
Edna Aldrich.	Could it be turned to be blue
Neil Bartholomew.	She for which they were finished.
Milton Eisner.	Or just as much as plainly left.
Arthur Belton.	Should it be curious.
May Glass.	Could they be cautious because of this.
Janet Painleve.	Because why ought they ordinarily
Edith Melrose.	By me or why by me
Arthur Lamb.	Just which as much
Bertha Winter.	All for it to close
Bertie Applegarth.	It is my hope
Chorus.	With why they were wading or wailing.
Maria Martel.	To think of it is a pleasure
John Moses.	But which they will point out presently

Mabel Eastman.	She needs me for herself.
Arnold James.	Could she be truthful
Bernard Alden.	She could meddle in despair
Nelly Winfield.	Much of it.
Allen Ingram.	Might whoever came
Arthur Lane.	Just why they will
Nathan Within.	Could it be known dexterously
Mildred Maine.	May they be careful
Egbert Eustace.	All kinds at all
Martin Johns.	It could be on account
Edith Burns.	All known
Chorus.	They may claim.
Martha Mint.	When will all be sent
May Coleman.	Just by them without reason
Nelly Marks.	Joined as it is best not
Mary Coburn.	For which they add relief
Norman Blaine.	By which they mean belief
Arthur Johns.	Just by their nearly choice.
Henry Winters.	Leave all to them adjoined
Jacqueline Christian.	Should made the door
Arnold William.	But which hour are meant
Edith Sinclair.	Just which it is as kind
Leonard Bartholomew.	Would five stay in place
Bartholomew Franklin.	She is my kind
Chorus.	But she is very willing to be let alone.
John Burton.	It is always a part.
Bernard Jackson.	With it a prayer for theirs
Gardiner Harrison.	All birds are held by halves.
Muriel Williamson.	As which they feel the name
Minnie Parker.	Best known for an instance in which.
Nelly James.	I knew all are called delight.
Barbara Knowles.	She should be just the same.
Warren Winship.	For which it is as mine
Barnes Oliver.	Very likely they like me
Arthur Barker.	It has been mine for the time
Elihu Neith.	She may be paid for me
Daniel Sonne.	We often hear her names
Bert Johns.	By which. They express.
Chorus.	It is not just as well that they waited.
Maggie Prentiss.	For them or which as precious.

Jonathan Calder.	Because below in using them.
Benjamin Duncan.	This is at least not all
Dorothy Johnson.	By guessing as a pressure
Robert Woods.	Should they be obliged
Martha Ingram.	Like when they shall be please.
Norman Taylor.	It is more than increasing
Barbara Edith.	In which it is a cause
Paul William.	He met two neither of which they bless.
John Burt.	It is why they know most.
Eric Blunt.	She will call all who know it at all
Arthur East.	He could be here to flourish
May Harriman.	Why can they and do guess
Chorus.	It is their meaning.
Philip Arnold.	Who may be placed in preparation
Nicholas Farmington	All of which they are not appalled.
Malcolm Winship.	But which not nearly fairly
Benjamin Winters.	By which they say
Martha Eustace.	But it is clearly
Edith Alding.	They look for all
Jennie Baker.	But which they may
Neith Brackett.	While I like alike
Jonas William.	It is a pleasure a test
Barbara Earle.	It is as well to be mistaken
Louise Florence.	She could be all well presently
May Lidell.	It is a mistake to know
Bernard Carter.	All will have been here
Minnie Sherman.	It is in the main not in them
Chorus.	She may be gently furnished theirs old.
Frank Paul.	Who may with it in a likeness
James Bell.	Or which is it that they know
Martin Tucker.	But which is kindly
Charles Brillmore.	But which they plan
Andrew Foller.	For it as a portion
Janet Stone.	She may call to see
Henry Surgis.	With it as indignation
Robert Strange.	For it as owned at all
Albert Watts.	She should be met always
Conrad Pleasant.	For which they will carry all
Guy Paulding.	This is their estrangement
Henry Fuller.	By which they arrange a stream

May Knowlton.	For it they have meant instinctively
Edna Bowles.	Should for a certainty.
Chorus.	It is all bought.
Oswald Parker.	She shall all call her first.
Arthur Lane.	Is it as a part of a requital.
Gustave Blaine.	She should be caught as much
Belinda Court.	For which they exact their satisfaction
May Sinclair.	Be nearly acquainted with there impatiently.
Nathan Andrews.	For them fortunately they have not taken it away
Marguerite Howland.	Just why should there be an authority.
Mortimer Arthur.	It was painstaking to prepare the name
Gladys Ewland.	May she in practice be coming
Henry Winthrop.	It was just suggested as steadily
Allan Arthur Griggs.	Four hours of outside it.
Agnes Shelden.	But just in which they joined
Martin Kings.	But which they knew as well.
Benjamin Hall.	It was thoughtful of no one at all
Henry Casket.	Might be is well satisfied for her
Marjorie Anton.	It was of no use to ask
Edith Acton.	It is not strange to mind
Guy Forest.	But which with well
Chorus.	It could not be separated.
Ada May.	What kind of care has she
Florence William.	But which they will not be met
Christine Barker.	For which they will neglect no one
Beatrice Grand.	For which they know
Ernest Carl.	Why should they search
Grace Fane.	By which they declare
Edith Rose.	It is by no means pleasant
Hilda Bloom.	For which they make it do
Arthur Grace.	It is for this that they are likely to be known
Andrew Place.	May they be much with them
Joseph Blunt.	For which they make no extra signs
John Colbert.	Please may they cross
Gilbert William.	It is nearly not tender.
May Cross.	Which they declare
Constance Beaver.	She may call more own

Angela Gardener.	Be often gracious.
Evelyn Barker.	By their occasionally
Chorus.	It is not noticeable
Emanuel Dearborn.	Who will be like that
John Angel.	Ways of after guessing
Mary Martin.	Leave more than they allow
Ferdinand Prince.	She judges best
James Coventry.	It is all bold as stated
Mary Glove.	But they can still better.
Arnold Felt.	They can change better for paper
Winifred North.	It is all which they color
Bertha Eusted.	It will be called ordered excellently
Margaret Garnet.	But well whether the other
Jonathan Carpet.	It is ours if they ask
Martin Jonas.	Who will they hold in respect
Hilda Argus.	She may be welcomed well
Agnes Elliot.	It is often all sold
Barbara English.	Who will tell what to do.
Marion Talbot.	Which they will tell
Harry Allen.	It is too to trust
Marmion Plane.	For which they welcome
Gustave John.	Which they commence
Chorus.	It is not likely.
Adam Beach.	For which it is not neglected.
James Lynn.	But this is nearly an outlet
Charles Blaine.	For which they think well of them
Ulric Arden.	May they not neglect
Fred Winship.	It is taught best more.
Archie Reynold.	Coming when they came
Edith Winslow.	Just when the chance came
Agatha Rumbold.	Now joined fairly
Theresa English.	She may liken it to a shell
Bertha Faine.	It is not as precious
Winifred Halsted.	She may be anxious to be duly there
Egbert Hamilton.	She may be strangely
Herbert Gibb.	May she be called well enough
Andrew Garden.	She may be kindly obliged.
Howard Bliss.	Who will fail them as well
Bernard Hammond	For which they cry
Emanuel Winter.	It is just not arranged

Chorus.	Fearing it felt as well.
Etta Atlas.	She may be called cautious
Edith Granville.	For they mean more than their share
Fredigond Hazard.	She may join mine with time
Gladys Deacon.	Whichever they will they may more because
Hervert Maine.	It is of no matter if they are cautious
Arthur Gardener.	Whichever they like unlike
Hugh Andrews.	They may be calm in with peril.
Nathan Lane.	For which they will
Harold Mathew.	Which is it that they like
Maria Christine.	It is often meant otherwise
John Cook.	It is fastened by their meaning
Amalie Winter.	For which they will not be differently courteous.
Amelia Richards.	Or always more all alike
Janet Ediths.	So they may call for them who have been
Olga Nawsen.	When they like they will not be felt as theirs
Richard Maine.	Once when they came they were well-known
Dorothea Hilda.	It is as if ought should be then seen
Theodore May.	She may or he may be often with them
Theodora Garden.	Or will they may if it could.
Elisabeth Church.	She will come too
Eleanor Richards.	With them
Chorus.	It is very often abandoned.
Mabel Almond.	Who will she know for her
Belinda Ruth.	Just as well as anxious.
Grace Church.	May she be corrected as yet
Margaret Hubbard.	May Edith go away
Lena Gardner.	Which will she place
Beatrice May.	She may join mine by mine
Henry Englewood.	For which they know
Sylvia Hawthorne.	Shall they join miles and miles.
Evelyn Roberts.	Which can they say if they may
Bertram Fields.	For which they thank if they can
Leopold Means.	Well very well if they caught.
Leonard Faulkner.	But which they call
Eli Gardener.	It is not often that they meant well

Hilda Williams.	She may be generously at one time
Enid Holden.	For which they will not change as they are selfish
John Blaine.	May they be often thoughtful
Ezra Hildegarde.	Should they be just changed I cherish
Arthur Manners.	For which they name
John Arnold.	It is mine at one time
Peter Olds.	May we think well
Chorus.	Does which they meet.
Egbert Winthrop.	It may be united unexpectedly.
Nathaniel Hubbard.	In which case they will not ease them
Bertha Hampstead.	May they not crowd with them in vain
Bridget Mabel.	As it is just as well that they are involved
Anne Nicholson.	Could they be pursued by their way
Edith Blaine.	Ours on account of methods
Helen Virginia.	It is often their hope to see easily
Olga May.	She should have been won in between
Abraham Hope.	It is kindly made with it
May Freedman.	Should those who know be meant then
Agatha Carley.	It is mine with mine
Fred Susan.	She may always just as she may know
Yvonne Marbel.	He can by his determination see for them
Bessie Edith.	It is not known gradually
Minnie Wintrop.	Could they see which it is that they like
Arthur Blaine.	She may be often thought cautious has been
Arnold Hermann.	Which they will not abuse at any time
Henry Edith.	She will have been met by him
James Israels.	Could it be by him that she has bought.
Martha Olds.	With which could they not abandon
Bernard Blaine.	May they come with delight
Francis Mary.	Just when could they come
Maurice Fitzhugh.	Just while they like
Robert Caesar.	It is often their way to be there
Chorus.	It is not only this.
Julia Lessing.	Who may be bought at the close
John William.	May she be first as well as better.
Herbert Andrews.	She may be just as well as that
Laura Hat.	She could be best as well anxiously
Nathan Bertram.	Should it be just a choice either chosen

Martha Narbon.   Should they better leave it as advice
Mabel Cunningham.   For which they may in their case
Gustave Mine.   She shall be told boldly
Beatrice Fletcher.   For which they tried
Marguerite Eustace.   It is often of the interruption which she
                         minded

Arnold Baine.   For which they cause
Jonathan Synes.   It is taught as an address
Bartholomew James.   For which do they add for which to which
James Basket.   He will be need presently
Agatha Holden.   They will call not only there but for them
Conrad Holds.   She may be only troubled
Gladys Wells.   Please be a choice for choosing
Genevieve Gold.   She may be appointed to be welcome
Jenny Baine.   May she be told for which they went
Arthur William.   There is no cause for uneasiness
Godwin Heart.   But just as well
    Chorus.   For they establish.
Dora Fortune.   For whom will whom bend
Dorothy Fisher.   Because she will wish it well
Donald Baine.   She may be often just as serious
Daniel Edith.   May she be called bad
Duncan May.   It is often very well that they are carried
David Eustace.   She may be sent for just as she is
Ethel May.   It is often if they wish that they are
                        anxious

Robert Sweet.   Who shall she be if she knows it better
Rebecca Andrews.   They will not better pretend for whom
                        they are anxious

Roland May.   Just as often as when they were there
Nathan Burn.   She will be singularly softened by the
                        sound

Frank Houston.   She will be because of it with him
Ferdinand Marcelle.   They will be as likely
Paul May.   She will often be polite again
Peter Hope.   It is without her that they will be jealous
Beatrice Blaine.   She may not choose this
William Basket.   When they come they are not careless
Arnold Margan.   In which cause they will be polite
May Greene.   May she be tall and not seen

Martha Steve.   Of which they were in welcome
May Nathan.   It is in a way extraordinary
    Chorus.   They will not blame.
Louis Lamb.   By which this means
Leonard Blaine.   May they excuse them
Louise Beatrice.   She may be justly chosen
Lillie Fans.   It is with out it presently
Conrad Wilson.   Makes it be selfish
Lilac Blunt.   May be in their way they know
Lena May.   She may be used to weeding at this time
Angelo Winters.   For it it is a pleasure for it
George Garfield.   May they follow
Janet Grace.   It is.
Mary Maine.   In which they go away
Nelly Lane.   It is a pleasure to practice where they
                        went

Harold Lyon.   May be they will be soon as precious
James West.   For this which they choose as flourish
John Grant.   To call it down
Gladys Reath.   It can be as well left to them
Will Cato.   Shall she mind just when
Gustave Wynn.   It is more than a pain
Martin Black.   We will call for them
Nat Wingield.   She will be found there
Neith Heathcote.   It will be no advantage
    May *   Just when they like
    Chorus.   Hours or ours at one time.
Barbara Coates.   Who should be named for him
Benedict Neith.   It is mine that they count
Henry Allen.   For which they are not lost
Grace Bennett.   They may insist that they change
Jane Lane.   May be they will not be known
Edwin Fortescue.   It is because of ought that they will know
Egbert Change.   She needed their decision
May Blaine.   For which it is brought as well
Margaret Finland.   Once when they come
Bertha Call.   She may be might they be there

---

* First names are missing
  in the manuscript.

Edith Farmley.	It is by this way that they mean me
Gustave Richards.	It is brought more than that
Genevieve Garland.	It is by the time that they like it
Arnold Bliss.	It is bought carefully one by one
William Ewing.	Could they be too nearly there
Grace Blaine.	It is mostly just a chance
Oscar Hone.	Could they be bought to be very well
Nathan Blaine.	She may not be the cause finally
Isadore Hubert.	For which they fortunately are all
Hugh Walker.	Could they think well of neither
Henry Blaine.	It is by this that they are selfish
William *	She kindly knew their own
Arthur Soame.	Could it be at rest alone
May Thunder.	With which it more known
Grace Pleasance.	She could not account for it.
Chorus.	Just why they knew best.
Jenny Heather.	For which a mind is more inclined
Elbert Smith.	Could they be caught by which they tell
Neith Winship.	For which they can be spared
Ada Comstock.	Glorious is certainly robust
Marguerite William.	She will have hope that they are lost
Nathan Gilbert.	For them or will alike.
Hubert Angel.	She may be utterly unprepared for their wish
Manuel Blaine.	They might cause them to be nervous
Agatha Winship.	It is not only that they bought
Guy Heath.	For this which to them is a pleasure
Ida Hall.	Can they call me and let them see this
Irving Brewster.	Could she know what they brought
Archibald Hunter.	Can if it is in no place where they met
Frank Eustace.	It shall be pleased
Martin Paul.	Come be in best of wishes all for me
Anne Brice.	Could it be kept as fortunately as that
Carol Count.	Own or they will but which they mean to plan
Gustave Frederick.	It was often that they knew that they counted
John Frame.	Tell what they like as often as they please
Arthur Blaine.	It chooses mostly more than by that time
Godfrey Winter.	Should they in their account be known

Edward Martha.	Hope to enjoy finally means that
Hubert Garfield.	I know why I do not feel more of it.
Edna Whitehead.	Believing in return
Jeanette Stone.	May they have not been known for it.
Arthur Blaine.	They will be best for it
Chorus.	She shall be changed for a day.
Vincent Garland.	Or why may they be well
Virginia William.	It is very well thought of.
May Blaine.	May they be cautious
Valentine Jane.	They may be settled as much as they understand
John Harden.	It is by this that they may miss this.
Ferdinand Glover.	It is not strangely by their name
Lionel Blaine.	It is for that that they make it be believed
Frederick Bernard.	For this they may without doubt fly
Grace Garfield.	It is within the blame that they may choose
Ada Barber.	Which is it that they like the best
Edith Gardener.	She may be thought she may be sought further
Harold Simpson.	In which case may they go
Arthur Paling.	Do they believe it better to have held it
Frederika Holding.	She may be certainly stern
Marguerite Line.	No one who has been told can go
Madge Cotton.	She will believe that they announce
William Mander.	Not only will they try
Herbert Blaine.	She may change what she likes
Hubert Mann.	It will not be more than just this
Arthur Wills.	She who had been seen well was there
Gustave Ferguson.	May they be well known for that instance
Virginia Pastor.	It is well to think well of their time
Violet Princeton.	She may be thought often with as well
May Agatha.	Shall we be there without being seen
Martha Strange.	She may be thought to be with them yet
Winifred William	Should it matter just when they came
Charles Arthur.	Why will they wish more of it
Andrew Lovell.	It is often met with as often
Chorus.	She shall be well
Louis Here.	When they were well attended.
Charles Bird.	For which they feel a flower.

George Fred.	Might they have thought that they declined
Edith Frederick.	It was all lost or presently.
May Firth.	Will beauty be for most.
Hilda Strong.	It is at best as well
Frieda Mars.	Should she be met yet
Lorna Blaine.	It is fortunately not that they bewilder
Brenda Custom.	By this which they decline
Gustave George.	Once in a while they play
Barbara Sweet.	Or just when they are made prettily
Violet Holt.	Should they make more than join
Ada Clark.	Just when they like they may mean
Agnes Sickle.	It is often all who felt very well spoken
Manfred Shawl.	With which they are welcome to attack.
Magnus Gaylord.	Will they be bought as peace
Fred Chapman.	Think in which way well known is clouded
John Gay.	It is by this that they can hear.
John Basket.	It is very likely in the country that any sound can be heard.
Wilfred Humbert.	Or should they mean that they will join
Francis Home.	He meant to know his brother
Robert Stone.	He was his brother
Diana William.	She knew two who were incomparable
May Blaine.	Which they mean for them as well
Fergus Blaine.	They think well certainly
Chorus.	Should they be right.
Pierre May.	Did he leave it or not close it often
Hugo Blaine.	Not which it is in which it is encouraged
Charles Ferguson.	It is attached by them with which they blame
Maggie Lane.	They may recommend all of which they do.
Edith Jones.	How do they place day light
Frank Rudder.	It is all of which there is there
Bernard William.	She may be thought to be appointed
John Lathrop.	Think more than they have with their wishes
Guy John.	It is a thought which they enjoy
Bertie Garfield.	Do you choose who they know.

Mildred Trust.	Finds out how many are heard
Jane May.	It is often out of it that they like
*	Feel well they chose who do
James Royal.	She will think as well as sing
Andrew Hilda.	Do and did make it kindly
Gilbert Husted.	To be quite right
Marcel Johns.	It was part of the time in winter
Myra Blaine.	For which they had their use
Louise Garfield.	All which are known are called my own
Peter Williams.	She may be liked as well as known
George Mansfield.	Why do they call out occasionally
Arthur Blaise.	It was a task that they used all
Richard Bliss.	May they be mine for which.
Abraham Blaine.	Like it or not as well
May Basket.	What did they believe they change
Paul Arthur.	It was theirs which was a mistake
Chorus.	Will they held.
Christopher Jenny.	How are they divided for many
Isabel Friend.	She may be very likely nine.
Therese Fold.	May she be taught as well
David Join.	She could be dearly a wonder
Rene Herbert.	For which it is as seen
May Gardener.	Might it not be a weight
Bartholomew Laws.	Could who be a hood
Barbara Neith.	Why should they leave with their name
Any Harp.	Could she be taught well by the truth
Dinah William.	Which may many of them touch
Agatha Pearl.	They may think lightly of their ought
Agnes Carew.	Could it be worth their delight
Dorothy Elf.	It was all they needed
Donald Edder.	Could they carry salt.
Daniel Hubert.	A cartridge is used as a well
Bertie Blaine.	She may be thought curious
Beatrice Howard.	Nor may she wish her well
Genevieve May.	It is not without delight
George Blaine.	Should she be thought.
Mary Blaine.	But which they knew

---

*The name is missing in
  the manuscript

Merton Blaine.	It is by their aid that they wish well
Manfred May.	For this is what is now added
Israel North.	Could there be a wonder
Bertha Gaylord.	She may think well
Winifred Dwight.	It is not known
Chorus.	In no time.
Muriel Head.	She may be thought.
May Shipman.	It is more than idle
Hiram Flood.	They may be caught close
Hilda Lamb.	Or which they think
Henry Martin.	Could they be relieved by them
Marius William.	It is often that they call it alike
Barbara Blaine.	Should she miss use and treasure
Ferdinard Wills.	It is always best to be taught.
Jenny Sheridan.	Think more than they will will
Grace Fellows.	It is not why they ask
Martin Lane.	All which they have they can
Guy Mann.	It is often by themselves thoughtful
Herbert Blaine.	All which they come to have
Mary Care.	It is ours to have ours known
Howard Blaine.	All which they think
Hector Strings.	Might it be well on the chance
Edith Rown.	It is more likely in time
Denis Round.	She will be nearly in their way
Margaret Elk.	Should she leave the door open
Bernard May.	If she could easily be influenced
May Blaine.	Or for themselves
Minnie Blaine.	Or may they be always alike
Dora Fisher.	Which it is lost
Donald Rolls.	May they be left as courteous
David Grace.	She may be thought as well
Louis Blake.	Will she be told
Louise Thorn.	Not if without their hold
Nellie Blaine.	Should it be nicely now
May Helen.	If it likes
Chorus.	By them.

Finis

BYRON A PLAY

◂ 1933 ◂

But Which They Say Byron A Play

Act I

Byron
Yes Byron

Act II

Will she need me if they go too.

Act I and II

I think so.
Byron came himself to ask if he were not satisfied but believe
me.

Act I

Byron is a queen

Act II

Indeed but two

Act III

It may do well not to be tall at all if not at most and so in
Byron there are no changes which makes it do and now a theatre
is a place. It arranges itself as a purse at most or a rest. At rest.

Act I

Byron may be as soon begun.
And nobody knows a name.

Act I

Should Byron be any one and which rich.

Act I

Byron being refused nourishment. He may not be angry not
sorrowful and not pale.
They neither seize one.

Act I

I wish I was fish with a great big tail a lobster or a whale.
They know there is no need of names.
Byron is cautious when he sees three.

Act I

Better Byron

Scene I

I have lost Byron in a play of worms. Or would he be just as
he liked. I never think why they welcome dogs nor does Byron in
soliloquy. I should just or rather prefer.
Suppose you think in plays or suppose you do not.
Suppose you do not at all think in plays.
But if why they went.
Oh yes if not.

Act I

No one not any one not if any one knew any one which is the
same thing or not but which in weighing made five pounds more
not less or they or not any one or may be not if they guess yes.
And so Byron vanishes. Not at all. It is not meant which they
imply or find why.

Act I

Byron John Byron or John or Henry or Irving or General or
William Byron was much at last he knew what he said. If any one
alone made it say here I am when I am not led away. Byron believe

not believe what is made just as well as not in time repeat not in repeat in time. They watch me as they watch this.

There we are as they watch this.

Act I

He came again to have been run run is not ran or rain or not begun which is why they mount in amount. They can be thought always to be ready with either of which they refuse wish for relish.

Act I

Be which.

This is how he sees any or which one.

I knew I did not like it as they grew particularly not only which is which for or by you. Not made a name a claim a made a be a claim a need of a needle of a name. How do hats grow.

Act I

Remember Byron.

Act I

He was busy at first and for more shelter in place of it as they were well in a way. How can you refuse a play. We forbade him not to.

Act I

Who cost who lost Byron.

Act II

There is no hope of not being there to remind them that if they like it is always not behind them. If once in a while they mean to place between them just whatever they do when any one of two makes no difference why they find or do not find them. This makes a play lugubrious but not long. She would not be satisfied if she heard them do what they do. This which I think is a play is a play.

Act II

Which she will. Will which he will watching. They might not

like that he had while he did not wait without it this makes a distance not only not but a play and so to say like that.

I wish I were
To wish two were
Or wish not what I wish
Two wish to were.
Byron a play he got it away.

Act I

I could be one with one of two
But it may do to do what one can do
For not for you to do but it is not gone where
Make it be mine.
Byron can be anxious not to wait he does not wait too.
He is occupied
He is not veritably concrete
For which they may be shown
Of not as well as sown
As he begins again
Byron a play to call Byron a play to call it Byron or to call it Byron.
Byron come here.
Nobody called Byron come here if you can come Byron come here.
I do not have to wish to know that it is to say so.
A play is when there is not only so but also.
A play may not be removed.
We have just been with him seen.
Byron a play

Act I

It is the first time that Byron has dug not dug because he is not persistent but dug as is his history. He has been all called a color and silver which is not only not at all I cry out not with not at all.

May you think so.
Now a play oh a day by the day in a play
A play is this. They manage to stage this.
Stage this or just or join.

Anything will do for them or through. A play is made to date her or create her.

But it is Byron who had given up earth for wood.

Oh yes it is Byron who has given up earth for wood. He has not given up earth because of the grass and he has not chosen wood because of where he found it. I have often not thought of where he found it as I meditated upon a play. And now I know where he found it.

If it is as beautiful as it is if it is. As beautiful as it is a play is not but a play is.

I think I have steadily said yes.

This is a play

Yes I guess.

Byron a play.

No need to imagine a share in a play.

No not even to mean whatever they care to to have a play

Not even which if they care to to have a play

Just which way to they care to to have a play.

A play is this.

If a play is this does it make any difference if the air is there. Or not.

A play does not depend upon what not

It depends upon the way a day is made to stay.

Oh yes you know you do.

And so which they have for their reason to care

This play is here

That play is there

Their play is where.

I wish I knew a play to run away

This play is to stay naturally.

> Byron a play.
> Anyway to-day.

I have remembered by observation that it is not peculiar to him to have that.

> Byron a play.
> Byron at play
> Byron they play
> Byron may play
> A play so they say
> Byron a play

I wish to say that I sit to a play
I also wish to say that a play is this.
Not will you say only.
Not only will you say this.
Because a play is this which makes it a play to play this.
                    Byron a play.
It happened that when they were here they liked it.

Act I

How many reasons are there for playing a play

Act I

A hill if it will
Oh yes a hill or if a hill will.
That makes the scenery as well as the sky or if I or if I a sky.
So much sooner.

Act I

Anything can be a play if they stand or sit to-day

Act I

It is very strange but anyway there is a difference between act
one.

Act I

Is not undertaken not to be begun
For instance act one.
                    Byron a play

Act I

If you know how to say pansy.
Say pansies.
If you also know how to say pears.
Say pears
If you also know how to say well
Say well.
Byron was busily one.

Act I

I could know that if the sun shone
The birds would not sing.
Neither would Byron nestle
Neither would a play content itself.
Because to say to-day is not a play to-day.

Act I

Byron may be well if he is he will tell.
Byron one.
If they may take which they may make
Or rather if.
And so Byron will come along
Let Bryon think of this

Act I

Bryon was happy when he was there.
He was happy when he was here
He was just as happy when he was here
And he was just as happy when he went there
And so in a minute there was no relief.
I have forgotten what I thought of plays
Because in a minute I was filled with anguish
Lost not at once if they went there
They would happen to think
That this was of no importance.

Act I

I love to love not wind but summer for the sake of Byron.
Or may he be for my sake all his for the name of Byron.
Byron is a play but when he wishes that they were there makes
this as an enterprise.
How will Byron live.

Act I

I wish to say everything I know about a play a play can
proceed not to widen.

An hour in a play is not to-day.

I have thought of a play.

The difference between a play and not a play is this a play states that if they like they will come and leave a day. This which is a rejoinder. In a play there is no rejoinder because in a play they never tried. And so they may.

What is a play to-day.

A play can be revealed by placing if in being higher they look again or if being not higher they do look again. This is often their thought necessary. On which accounting.

A play they know a play.

But not if they dovetail a play.

Five ducks leaning all make six.

This is a play. Byron is a play.

When will they come in is a play.

Imagine is a play.

A play is used to eat used it.

How can hours be a play but naturally it is

A Play Byron a play

Act I

Byron was brought when he came he drooped.

Act I

When he remained he felt well and remained to place where it chooses.

Scene I

He could Bryon could.

Bryon and called Byron

Byron will you come.

Of course he could not know a name but of course.

Just when they like Byron just when they like

And now a play is no play.

Act I

He should not have minded how many went when he sent coming again to say.

Byron

It is not often that they choose
Which if they like which if they lose
What is the difference here between there and here
May be they may choose to lose
What they will with each whether they choose.
In this way Byron is ceaseless.
Byron may be understood to understand
Not only which they reach but when they leave
All might Byron might Byron repeat
Byron will leave it alone.
Oh yes Byron will leave it alone.
When next you say Bryon anyway may
Be Byron.
It is pleasing with him to be with him.
Byron who could or might Byron.
Byron early ease or is it may be cease
To be not only with him.
This may be as easily early with him.
Byron was his name which they will name
As next to name a name.
I could avoid which when.
It is often that it may be soothing
To be all made and be as much.
He felt it more Byron felt it more
When he tore from door to door
And Byron.
Can a play be a name to say
All which is yes to say
Or Byron
What is a play when they have come
Or or none.

Byron Act I

What is a play. If you look do you see a play or a door.
Or not any more.
In this way a play loses or excuses.
But a play may be in a way

A play.
A play may even be called Byron.
Byron a play.
This is what there is to say about a play.
A play should not be seated
Nor need they be nervous or go
Nor need they be with or without speech
Or at least do it again.
In a play they must do it again
As much as yet and yes.
What is a play
Not to guess yes.

Act I

Byron may not be anxious or not if he is if not he is not a memory if remembered or if not if not he is not if not he is not if not remembered.

Oh may they be gracious to Bryon.

But this is not so if they make a play.

Act I

A play is a day or not to say so I wish to make a play not a day or even not what happened but only not what is seen.

This is a play.

There can certainly be heard or said that it is never seen or heard of led they may be rejoined.

There is no reason why they should be refused.

Here and there is no play.

Or happily any day.

For which they remain to play

That they will which they may

May believe it to or may.

This which they say.

An act is a play.

In this way one act is not one play.

Two may be two acts or acts as they complete or not if not add once to a play.

Act I

Byron has run home.
Scene one
He has remained upstairs where he belongs if not allowed to
descend in the meantime they will wish for the wish or half of it
as if they were open to a frown for which they may like a denial
of a memory more than they could which will in amount but which
they share more than if most at most they will not bother to
believe me.

Byron will be very often simply attached or left more than they
wish this may be a play or which

Act I

Byron may be in union.

Scene I

May Byron be one one of one of one.
Or may Byron be one.
Thank you for pansies and thank you for thanking you for
roses.

Scene I

To wish to be wished to add which to forget made Byron.
Or which rather which which to add which to add wish to
add forget or not forget to be not be but Byron this may be made
into a mistake which if they wish or do wish to mistake.
What can be added to no play or well rather a play.
If not if they continue.
A play need not be made nor if not if they continue which
they do not if not.
Add a place to continue.
A play is this they lose interest in moonlight if they look again
also a play is this a place is this may they be which moreover they
may add benefit to neglect.
What is the play or a play not in the meantime.
Or can they rather guess.

A play is this Bryon if he wishes is no play

Nor either is Bryon a play if in their play there is this with no wishes.

Admire or administer that there are made of which no wishes.

In this way they return to no play

A play is may be this

A Play

In this sense Byron is no play nor any more not by their time What is a play or not.

He quietly attends to wishes.

In a way they blind or are blind in a day to play, or to a play not necessarily.

A play is this Bryon may not do so as he means or by no means or as a means if they are Byron.

But despair is despair or care is care.

They need or a benefit or fairly more not even yet to need Byron.

This cannot better plan a play.

What is a play or Byron

Scene I

Byron by this time had not met one.

One and one is not Byron

Nor may they relish

But better made as relish

For fairly well tell which

Which whenever they used

But made it be at once

Theirs or there where they mean as won

Byron.

Byron may not need a play.

There is this to be understood if disturbed a play is not a play.

Scene I

Byron is not not only readily but added readily to as made in a way and so two people pleases but not only not pleases Byron and so not a play not even not a play but Byron which when they withstand.

This which I wish to know I do know

Scene I

I can clearly understand now what a play is.

Act I

They may proceed to winning.

They do not come in but being in and within they may be made to be in and within.

And so Byron challenges but not changes.

A play may be in speed indeed.

Which may not be why they like Byron.

It is easy to be well-known.

Act I

Let alone a play.

Scene I

It is not known as is it not curious she manages that without a place to mean that if they call.

Two makes a scene.

And when they prefer one

There may be in if in when in resolution.

How can you call it a play if they like however they like it together.

It is not a play if he rests.

They may more than they know.

Each in a little while in a little play but they they if they may do which if they may alike receive and regret not only which that much.

A play is made.

There can be never more than two to play exactly for which they might in their amount.

Not only why they like.

There can never be more than two to play.

One for one.

And it is might it be as with their opportunity as a chance.

Why can they not go farther with a play.

This is a reason which they like you either look or act if you are looking and acting and minding and as if not then resisting beside which they may rather go.

For which with which.

As much as with much

As much as it is.

Scene I

They may not been reminded of any one.

In one way one can act alone.

This may be due to pleasure or if they like it may be due to a pleasure.

Scene I

They will like what they like as they may prepare to deny that it is useless to try.

After all each one waits here.

Scene I

Byron will you come here or will you wait here or either then be with or without which is an addition to liveliness.

Of course which if they do.

Scene I

Byron.

By run

They may

It is

One.

By and by it is one

Bryon

Scene I

Not while they like which is not really as the same why they like.

Byron

Scene I

Little Bryon.
As for the rest.
Little Byron may very well be
For the rest.
He is very lively when he is active.
Which makes a play

Act I

How did Byron like what he did.
He did not make any mistake in a swift movement.
Nor might they continue to believe it of them.
And this how this makes a play.

Scene I

If Byron made a change.
Or if it made no difference
Or rather if there was no help for it.
Or if indeed interest in it diminished.
Or if indeed rather
And if they met and waited
This is what it may not have as help
Very often in rocking Bryon was or is nervous.
How can a play have it happen

Act I

A play is spelled spacious
It may have a waterfall
It had better have it alone.
What is a play a play is more than if they did.
What is a play a play is pause or loss.
They need repeat a play to stay
But they will anxiously ask less.

Scene I

A play is mastered by which they arrange this.

Scene 1

They come to differ at a distance
The impression differs that is to say
If they see them near
Or rather have they nearly left them.
In this way no opportunity is arranged for
But most is first and at last

Scene I

I wish now to say what the relation is of a play.
            To words
            Or not to words
Does he understand words
Or if he does not add to words
Does he if he should win delight
So that if all he might.
He should not call courage at once.
In this way I finally wish I wishes.
A play then may be a day without words
Or indeed if they call at all they may call it a word with which
they wish words were thirds.
    It is best to come once at a time.
    What I wish to say is that if he is not interested in speaking
perhaps he is not interested in hearing not at all he is interested in
either or a play.
    This makes Byron a play say.
    Now the other one thinks everything one because he thinks
therefor no play thinks thinks.
    This is why he fits and falls readily.
    Now suppose either two make a play.
    Bryon a play.
    They are not alike for which they look alike
    Bryon a play.

Act I

What I wish to say
Byron does not hear a play
If you look and look away

Byron will stay
A play.

Scene I

I could I would I did.
There is a difference between.
For which they meant why they meant.
Believe it in I mean.
Byron comes in looking for an apple not looking for an apple
because he has it.
No one has lost it he at least not at least at all.

Scene I

He has changed an apple for a pear and a pear for a stone
not that he has changed one for one nor abandoned one or one
it is not rather that not when it is in arrange arrange they will not
add we to strange arrange he will be weeding soon oh yes not
weeding soon. Who has been said that he has not spoken.
What is a play.
As he lies there he may.
They add a play a play.

Scene II

There may be many who add yet to yes.
If they feel as yet
If they feel oh yes.
They may add this to is it.
Also they may be well considered.
I often ask do they believe that he sees what he feels.

Scene III

A play may be of grass.
A play may not be as neither one of two.
Or just why all they like.
Or may a play be three or at play
What is a play.
Bryon a play.
Byron may not feel that it is as likely Byron.

Scene IV

Why should Byron not be left to know be left to know.

Scene V

To have been arranged to change four is to may they go.
Byron is not speaking.

Scene VI

Why should they may they be in a pleasure next.
I have abandoned no one.
But indeed they claim to change.
But indeed they need not be a plan to stage.
We have decided not in giving away but in going away.

Act II

May Byron be thought carefully to think as well of two.

Act I

Byron cannot commence with difficulty.

Scene I

I feel I know now what a play is there are many kinds of
them.

Scene I

A play is this if born or not born whether with this.
This is a play that they stay if they may before or rather in
their way. This makes a play without which they stay.
What is a play.
I like which they may.
If he lies there and watches as he gazes his attention is easily
distracted.
Then after then he comes back again.

Act II

Byron come back again

Scene I

He comes back bringing something. Of course he comes back and of course bringing something. Neither one of two. And therefore having left that behind he remains not to share to care or rather yes as he uses. Of course nothing need be used even at this distance.

Act I

Byron remains.
And not easily seems anxious.
Nor should he be distressed by wood.
Or not if not he could.

Act I

What is a play. As they may like and rises.
Byron could watch if he could.

Scene I

It is not by this he feels as if he left.
What is a play. There is no nearer yesterday in a play.

Scene I

Byron chose in chooses one.
This may mean one or none.

Scene I

Could he look and see. In this is the essential of a play.

Scene II

They could they should and choose this makes no play.

Scene III

To return to a play.

Scene IV

Will they tell will they reach it. He reach it. Of course he will reach it. He has it.

Scene V

They may rather which they mind.
They follow too easily.

Scene VI

Beware of which they held.

Act I

What is a play as they could leave it here.
Clothed in white makes one play.
Clothed in black and outlined in tan makes another play each one equally serious. I should feel daily an obligation.

Scene I

Why will Bryon more.
Will he need length and strength as well. This is no play.
I know very well what is a play. I will not even presume to like hours alike.

Scene I

A play may called for which they stay.
Byron a play

Act I

A garden with a wall grapes growing on the wall of the house. Byron gazing not at the grapes but at a stone and other things beneath the grape-vine. He leaves them. At the same moment no one hears though any one easily manages to be ready to be here.

By the time that they have looked at one another even though he
might be ceases to be restless.

Scene I

It is not very easy to leave him then.
Nor might they be obliged to feel that there.
Is made no happening of leaving there.
They will contend
In often resting one in blue.
And one in black and tan.
And all in white.
He is not here to share.
No moments of remaining where.
The one in blue is resting on the ground.
After the church.
The one in black and tan is on the wall.
After the wood and stone.
After the wood and stone.
They will be seen as well
When we all look.

Scene II

Why should Byron be well named.

Act II

Byron.

Scene I

It makes easily be known that delicately is not with difficulty.

Scene I

Leave or let Byron lie in the sun on the stone.
Even if it is not a stone but only as if it were a stone which
however it is it is a stone and Byron can lie in the sun on the
stone as if the sun were setting but not set yet
Byron never dreams.
Has this to do with a play or has it not.

If in dreams. But excitement readily denies dreams and wondering and wandering mean sleep is awake and so they think that they mean that they will not cherish but cherish which is well of which.

Byron a play.

If in weakness can there be a play.
It is doubtful if in weakness there can be a play.
And so undoubtedly in weakness there is not a play.

Byron a play.
Not to-day
Byron a play.

Scene I

Byron does not speak but hears
Having forgotten whether it is better to know more than that if there were loss of more than none.
Would which they choose
Often there is no choice.
There is no help to which to lose.
May they come which they choose.
May they wish which they choose
Byron sleeping upon a stone hears no one.

Scene I

Byron sleeping upon a stone a little hears some one.
If not by rain then by water will one hope to wish that now they wish.
Byron has fled but will return and sleep again upon the stone.
He has not been interrupted but disturbed in which way he will.
A shadow of Byron falls upon the wall. He needs no one to defend him from the sun or the wall nor to disturb him.

Scene I

Do not walk away Byron.
Do not leave there to come here.
Do not refuse the sun for the shade
Or the shade for the sun

Do not run
If Byron if you run
Do not run.

Scene II

May you be surely Byron
Not only which you name
But welcome to the claim
That Byron won.
One and the name is Byron
May it be that which they name one.
Byron

Act I

Byron a play.
Not only may they be heard to be a play.

Scene I

There is no one and one.

Scene II

I have no doubt that he has gone away
Which they might have
Which they might do.
Or rather not to do
I have forgotten that in a play they do not do that as you.

Act I

What is a play when as they change the place they do not
change the name of Byron.

Scene I

He has left yesterday for to-day

Scene II

That is to say

Scene III

That yesterday be followed all the day

Scene IV

And to-day

Scene V

He was not as ready as he had been

Scene VI

Not to go away.

Act I

He prepares something and not for some one.
He has been known to be when they went.
In view of that he does not play and stay
Nor does he play and remain away
Nor does he leave to add a way.
Not in any way is there an added way to stay
Byron
Come and stay.

Scene I

Byron has wished well of everything.
He has followed when he has been and has called.
Not easily to be added where
He was.

Act II

Byron now comes to be in the midst of ought.
They could learn could they will they.
They could learn
Will they not.
They also might reason
Which is lost is cost.
They could always succeed well.

This does not make a play.
            Byron a play.
Byron has a wealth of wishes.
He wishes he were well.

Act I

Which he is in appetite and three white as a butterfly. Three
butterflies make four if they are white and Byron has no hope of
any such attention he plans to add it then when resting.
Might they not know that noon has passed.

Act I

Venture to know a play.

Scene I

Why should they add.
A play not yet to-day.

Scene I

They must be weighted or wait.

Act I

There was once upon a time a place where they went from
time to time.
I think better of this than of that
Of course you ask why had you no ball
Of course you ask at once or not at all
Byron

Act I

And now a little change
May make a day
But not a play.
Oh no or yes
Not a play
If any day
There is not either or

Or just a play.
Why did you if you do
Forget at all.
Why may they
Which if they may
Exactly as exactly
Yet a play.
Byron a play
It makes it hesitate before a play
Or to be a play.
Once in a while
Oh once in a while.
Oh do or dear as dear
As once in a while.

                    Byron a play

Act I

I will not cease a play
Just when a play
Is not a play
To-day.
To-morrow we will see Basket.

                    Byron a play

Act I

Byron oh little soul.
When you are where you are
Nobody stole.
Byron Byron who could and told
When it is not at all
That they could hold
Byron
I imagine a play.
He is not playing to-day
Bryon.

Act II

He will come again
If he can come again.

Thursday he can come again
And be one of one
And then the play will come again
To be a play of come again Byron.

Scene I

May I know if I go.
Of course you may know if you go.
But may I know if I go
Of course you may as well know
If you go.
But if I go may I know
Not if you go
If you go you may know
But not if you go.
Byron may not know if he is to go.

Scene I

After waiting awhile he will not go.
It is often not only why they go.
It is better so
Remember not to go.
But not to go oh no
Byron will not welcome it to be so
Not now not when
To go.
                    Byron a play
                    Which is a day.
We will wait until Thursday
And imagine what is happening to-day
We hope nothing which is not only this.
Be sure Byron of a kiss,
                    Byron.

Scene I

I would like Byron to be here
Oh yes I would like Byron to be here

Scene II

If Byron were here
It would be a pleasure
To have him here
Byron.

Scene III

Not only would he be here
But it would be a pleasure
That he could be here
Byron.

Scene IV

Once well of Byron
Byron will be well
Not only Byron Byron well
But well Byron
A well Byron.
Byron which it is well to have Byron
Here

Scene V

They may a play of Byron

Act II

No one can change
Not no one can change
Hair for hair
Or rather please or care
Which when they may
Have better than
The time to-day
He came away
Byron
By and by Byron

Scene one

How often often have I thought
Which would I rather know
Would I rather know that a Basket can be bought
Or if at once I Byron or be thought
Be rather thought than old
Or caught or can be sold
Byron among the thieves
Not thieving thieves but which
When generally thieves
May be joined thief to thief
Or chief to chief
For which they called they said
For which they called they said
Not only why Byron
Not only if led.
Byron can be frightened but not said
To be Byron

Scene I

It happened to come that he went away among more than
he knew.
He would not he knew be welcome
But which once more made no one doubt.
That he knew
Two from one.
Byron
Come here Byron
But by and by Byron
Busily if emptily with two with one
Byron.

Scene I

It is acceptable that a scene is better than anything.
And now I have lost two in one.
Byron.

Scene I

Once upon a time a visitor came and he said that he was welcome
He wished to be angry and he was.
The occasion was one
By no means one and one.
By the time all were here they were welcome.
They may be thought to be welcome.

Scene I

If no one knew his name was Byron.

Scene I

Are you sure his name was Byron
George Byron.
He was not angry when his name was
George Byron.
Not at all angry when his name was.
George Byron.
No one named George is angry
When his name is named
George Byron.
If not.
I wish I knew why they wished it to be so.
Now I know.

Scene II

Byron is settled down and if loving to sun.

Scene III

Byron may be enclosed by a passage.

Scene I

While Byron was wondering if at once one and one.

Act I

Once in a while they like it as well as if they did they were not without this use.

Byron

Would he come if he were called and not afraid.

Would he mean to love tube-roses if he loved wood more.

They know Byron can know the difference between a tree wood and woods. Oh my why do they go away and try to be well aware of their fate

Byron may make no mistake.

Act I

After one he felt that one was one after one.

Byron

A play may be acted by having left them for him.

Byron standing alone runs away and is afraid to pass some one. If there are two he is afraid to pass two and to pass one of two of them.

Then he comes on a run

Byron.

Act II

This makes no one for you.

Byron

Scene I

What is a play to any one

Scene I

Byron

Act II

Best of all which it is

You may not know the reason

Read if you cannot run

Under which change
Need it less than at first
Oh not if you need or instead of under
This is my mistake.
But which they will welcome now
Yet or yesterday and why they will
Raised as much as if they changed the place
Ours are not without a change
Not for which they like

Byron

Scene I

Byron I request you not to be fastidious in coming again fortunately.

It is very fortunate that you have found such a happy home.

Byron a play two months later

Act I

She might be thought to think again that she had not mentioned to him that he had done it again.

Scene I

She found excuses for him that is to say not to say but to do and not only not to do but to feel and not only not to feel but to caress and not only not to caress but to hold and not only not to hold but as well.

Byron does not answer not only angrily but as often as disturbed.

If disturbed they will attack less that is if he snarls and much as they may do if I do if he snarls. Should a distant nearly found as not as distance when they mean to like alike.

By which they will if all they need is care.

Let us think often of a name.

Byron May be called Byby.

May he not be angry.

Not only may he be angry but very angry.

Or rather had he not thought

Not only why he wished but if.

May they if they should mix delight.
They may gather or rather.
May they color stare with share.
She may be thought very welcome
As she came every once in a while.
No one will fill a basket
Not only will but daffodil
She may be thought that Byron choose
He likes to climb and sleep.
Or however should a tower not distress
Which if he is held with tenderness.
Not only that like alike
But may they shatter they as much
As they can.
Not only without their amount
They will not call me.
Oh no they will not call me
They come whether they can come.
Has Byron chosen his name
No I think not.

Act I Scene I

In the room she is sitting by a new lamp reading a book and holding Byron.

He is not holding a basket he is sitting beside a table writing and if he sneezes he covers his shoulders with a shawl knitted for him as a new years present by a dear friend.

When all this has happened it has been all very fairly begun. And no one has been not only not famished but indeed durably have determined not only more which but not at all that without an obligation to an error. Think lightly while they meet.

Byron cannot be punished for the sins of commission and omission because partly and happily he earns nothing for any one. He can by contact impart so it would seem or would they mean that they like what they ate or eat.

Should they prepare.

Act I Scene II

Not only when but when they are through

Act I Scene III

Should they mind if they thought as well as they thought about it.

Byron runs and comes.
Byron says that which he knows is anger
And why should Byron be angry.
Because he is disturbed and awakened.

Act I Scene IV

It may be fortunate that the scene changes

Scene V

Those which they like they like not only when they reach out for it but when they feel that they will finish quickly.

And they end so that they may begin
What is a height
A height is where they are put
And so Byron waits or is helped down or descends
Differently here from there.

Act II

He resembled so many animals a deer a cat a fox a hound.
The little boy said a kangaroo.
The little girl said see the two of them one along side of the other.

Not any more than two.
A great deal of water came through.
One of the two.

Act I Scene I

Byron left at home was not saddened by this circumstance alone if he cried, crying can be a song and singing may not be bereft of left.

Byron not being left was not left to be alone.
And so he was not followed.
By which they plan
That they will be

For him rashly
Seen as where
Up there
Higher
Much which
They could include
Not only now as food.
Byron could contentedly sit.
If he climbed
For which at once
They could allow.
That excellence is most.
Might Byron be a baronet.
Or better yet
As better
Met.

Scene II

Byron is often alone in a scene but not in a place it may be said that he is practically never alone in a place and it is more often as well to be at once and foremost which they mean by an avowal.

That he came when he ran
Fear can be in three places
Fear of yes
Fear of not yet
Fear of felt it as fear.
And so he came here
Not of his own volition
But once here
Accustomed to being here
With much enjoyment
To himself as well
This does not make Byron cautious with restraint.

Scene II

May I like to know when Byron's birthday is but it is not known.

Scene III

I like Byron he likes me
Byron will or will not be
With me.
Think of Byron.
She appreciates Bryon
Not foolishly but as if foolishly.
Byron is settled as a settlement will
Byron
Come here Byron.

Scene III

It was not a surprise that he cries
Nor indeed that he tries.
Which he does very well.

Scene IV

Why should Byron resemble him
Which he did.
Nor why should Byron cast shadows of himself
Which he does.
And interferes with the light
Which he does
But does not destroy
Nor even damage
So adroitly as he comes to and fro
Which is not an amusement nor an amazement
But suddenly to understand.
Gnawing at it instead of adroitly squeezing past it.
Oh why should Byron be so gracious
If he is badly spoiled.

Scene V

Byron may mistake himself for himself all the time.

Scene VI

And so poor Byron is suffering

As besides he is ill.
And must eat bread alone
And must eat bread alone.
Not the kind of bread he has eaten.

Scene VII

All of which has not been decided to-day.

Act III

A great deal of frightening may divide Byron

Scene I

Should they be anxious to please be everything.
And having left to come
And having left a place
To leave it here.
Not only not startling
But not annoying
And not displeasing
Now some decision has been taken.

Scene II

Who uses Byron or one two.
In this act Byron has been put in to his place.
And what is his place
What is the place of Byron.

Scene III

Richly believe that he is will he be.
Renewed and put where he is or will he be.
                    Byron.

Scene IV

One two three when they call Byron.

Scene V

No they will not.

Scene VI

In this long scene Byron soliloquizes.
No one can say that a soliloquy is addressed to the world.
And of course it is.
Much less of course it is.

Scene VI

Byron could be careful to drink milk.
Any Byron could be careful to drink milk without salt.
Oh yes with tears or without tears any Byron could drink milk.
                         Byron.
Why do or does Byron drink milk without tears.
Why does Byron drink milk without salt.
Why does he turn angrily.
Because he has been left with it.

Scene VII

Byron Byron Byron.

Scene VIII

I could if I felt like it stay here.

Act III

As much Byron as she liked.
Byron was born Byron.
He calls as if he came.
And so without any doubt he may.

Scene I

Byron never sits and thinks he neither sits nor thinks. Byron.
If he rests he warms himself not by reflection but by need.
Warmth is a pleasure and a necessity to Byron.
He listens and waits while he waits
And never leaving never rests.
Sleep does not rest Byron because he does not wait to sleep.

They may be said Byron they may be said to need what they
need. Byron.

That is very strange I heard her say quiet.

Scene I

Byron was waiting to run.

Byron was not waiting for the morning.

The morning having come.

Oh Byron come. The morning and the evening for waiting has
not come for Byron.

Better than not at all after all.

Scene II

Byron how do you do Byron.

Scene III

She knew she meant Byron when she called him Byron.

She knew she meant more when she knew that Byron would
come.

He knew her when he came.

Scene IV

They may make a mistake in mistaking Lord Byron for Lord
Byron.

They may also make a mistake in fondling Byron.

If he is defeated he is accepted but he is not defeated and
accepted.

Byron has no choice in falling.

He falls when another rises.

This happens naturally.

As being dependent upon being seated

If the one seated rises Byron falls.

Scene V

There is but there has not been an illusion of Byron.

Act IV

We widen was it.
Byron.

Scene I

Byron. I love not cold nor freezing.
I love not following when a sound is coming
I do not love whether I love or whether paper is moving
I love and do not gather crumbs for birds which have been
Birds which have not been there
Once more I hear paper moving.
But whether which have more Byron.
Byron hears me hear Byron.
Byron asks for may be not be higher.
Than they name hanging.
If a anything hangs in front of him
It is disconcerting.

Scene II

Byron by and by Bryon.

Scene II

By by Byron.

Scene IV

Or be Byron.

Scene V

Not Byron

Scene I

Byron has may be not made a name
But a name has been given to him.
The name given to him has been Byron
Or whether a name which is Byron is given.
He does not ask give me the name Byron.
He only says if you call Byron I am coming

Scene II

More than which may be they do which.
Byron.

Act V

Byron, when Byron droops he droops because he has been not
only not invited but compelled to face the cold. He droops.
Sometimes he compels her to carry him.
Oh yes
Sometimes he compels her to carry him.

Scene I

Byron for which he loses their have there.
Byron would not avoid this if he were there.
Byron.
Once when they dragged him.
Byron.

Scene II

He could do what he could refuse to do.
Byron

Scene III

A garden is a garden of paths and garden.
Byron.

Scene IV

Byron. At a street.
Byron. By a wall
Byron.

Scene V

May they make they make
Byron.

Scene VI

Byron may they make Byron.

Scene VII

Act as if Byron were to be meeting.
He could be angry with a child.
As if a child were a victim winning.
Or whether they should be called rather
Beside in age a change.
He would wait backing.
Oh yes Byron.

Act VI

If she knew how old Byron was she knows how old Byron is.

Scene I

Part of the time in which Bryon rests although he trembles he is not restless.

Scene II

If moreover Byron is placed where he is to be rested he may not protest because he inquires but not enough.

Scene III

If in waiting he does not pray to wait this is because of their place there where they have placed him.

Scene IV

But which of which does he know.

Scene V

They must be as much stranger.
Oh Byron will you come.
Come Byron come.
There is need that you come.

If not this may be for my sake
So as to avoid that I stoop.
Not to you but to it.
Oh Byron. Come Byron.

Scene VI

Once more come Byron.
How often Byron
How often must you come Byron
Wherever Byron.
Come Byron.

Scene VII

Byron or may they be by and by Byron.

Scene VIII

Come now Byron

Act VII

If he loves food he did not always love it.

Scene I

Byron. If he loves food.
Byron. He did not always love it.
Byron. Now he will take it.
Byron Even when it is not given to him.
Byron. He will take it.
Byron He moves quickly.
Byron In taking it.
Byron Oh yes.
Byron And he is punished for it.
Byron As much as ever as quickly.
Byron And fiercely.
Byron And back well back.
Byron And pleasing.
Byron.

Scene II

Byron. As much as if they knew.
Byron That they were not through.
Byron For which in pleasing.
Byron After suffering exercising
Byron. They will hide
Byron With care
Byron Under this chair.

Scene III

May be I will but I doubt it.

Scene IV

Byron with which they are gaily alike.

Scene V

Byron which with not as an exception.

Scene VI

Byron. May they be reached by Byron.

Scene VII

All which is told when thirteen is eleven.

Scene VIII

Byron.

Act VIII

She did not ask for Byron. Byron was waiting although waiting is not possible for any one.

Byron think which is the same as a varied speech but not for which they thought.

Bryon they may or they may not be mistaken but Byron is not mistaken Byron is not mistaken for any other one nor need he be mistaking anything for anything or any other one and so Byron.

Scene I

Byron. May we be left to any one.
Byron. Or waiting with no misgiving.
Byron Or Byron with Byron waiting.
Byron And waiting for any one.
Byron is not angry when he is waiting
Although he seems so when he is waiting.
Byron is not angry when he is leaving.
Byron is angry when he is looking.
Byron is not angry but with him when he is to leave a place
not a person but a place. Not a person but a place.

Scene II

For which they will smile or yet once in a while.

Scene III

For a while Byron for a while.
Some one can carry the burden of Byron.
For awhile
But some one relieves them of something.
Byron may be they will but I doubt it.
Byron.

Scene IV

Byron. How many days are days with Byron.
Byron. But which do you wish do you wish for him or for
Byron.
Byron do you wish for Byron.
Byron or Byron do you wish for a wish for Byron.

Scene V

She may be leading Byron

Scene VI

Or if she may be leading Byron.

Scene VII

Byron. To relieve Byron.

Scene VIII

Which they relate but not to Byron

Scene IX

Could Byron be with a kind and not sing.
Not.

Scene I

If he could not.

Scene II

Byron is within.

Scene II

Byron with which within.

Scene III

Byron may be Byron was a twin.

Scene IV

Or may be may be again.

Scene V

May they seem which they may be thin.

Scene VI

May be a king or twin.
May be Byron.
May be Mario
May be Pia
May be anything.

Will he go with him
Will he go with her
Will he go with them.
Yes if they carry him.
Byron or in within.
Byron is a king or twin.
Not often or so Byron.

Scene VII

Forget him or within a Byron or in.
Forget in within or Byron.

Scene VIII

She often said that if she could change as much it would be
frightening.

Scene IX

But I said everything or not a king.
Byron.

Scene X

Byron ruined a horse
Or was it Mario.

Scene XI

Not interesting.
Because of nothing.
And glass
Even colored blue.
Is if it is not interesting
And has been noticed often.
Is not absent or alone nothing.
Leave well enough alone.

Act X

Act as if he ran.
Oh do oh yes do act as if he ran.

He ran and snarled.

This is not only true of Byron because he ran to follow and stop.

Byron. After all whom.

Byron.

Believe me Byron.

Byron, believe me Byron.

And again.

And again

Byron Byron

Or if believe me Byron.

Excuse they snarled.

Believe me Byron.

Scene I

Believe me Byron

Scene II

Which follows better for which Byron.

Scene III

Have been Byron.

Scene IV

Next to having been.

Scene V

Byron.

Scene VI

May be they like Byron

Act XI

Why should they change Byron's name to Mabel.

Scene I

Byron has been bought and taught as Byron.

Oh yes Byron.
Byron has indeed been neither bought nor taught.

Scene II

Oh yes Byron.

Scene III

Byron could be longing but he never longs long.

Scene IV

No Byron.

Scene V

Whichever name they like.

Scene VI

No Byron.

Scene VII

Not if they like.
And in exchange.

Scene VIII

No and yes Byron

Scene IX

I like what I do.

Scene X

No Byron.

Scene XI

As well as I like what I have to do.

Scene XII

No or not no Byron.

Scene XIII

As much as ever Byron

Scene XIV

Of course not for Byron.

Scene XV

No Byron.

Act XII

Byron Byron could he be sick with cold and full to be of not eating.
Byron.

Scene I

Why is she fondest of Byron. She says she is not but she acts so and this perhaps is because he is it is Byron.

Scene II

Byron. I am warming and waiting
Byron Warming and waiting
Byron Warming and warming and waiting.
Byron.

Scene II

Once which they may.
Byron.

Scene III

Byron Or which or one
Byron.
May be they may need Byron.

Byron. Which one is Byron.
Byron. One of which one.
Byron. Said I am not sleeping.
Byron. But he slept.
Byron. After warming.

Scene I

Not to have seen Byron all evening.

Scene II

Because of Byron.

Scene III

Byron may be overlooked but not forgotten.

Scene IV

Byron may be jealous of Byron.

Scene V

Which makes a wedding an intention.

Scene VI

Byron. Because of Byron.
Byron. By which Byron.
Byron. May Byron.
Byron Lay Byron down
Byron Escaping Byron.
Byron Byron makes no attempt to escape.
Byron. If it may be Byron
Then Byron Because Byron.
Byron. By which Byron.
Byron If Byron.

Scene VII

One two three four five six seven.
All good children go to heaven

Some are good and some are bad
One two three four five six seven.

Scene VIII

Byron can date his hate
But cannot remember his hate.
Because his hate is without fate
But from the scent and sight.
Byron.

Scene IX

Byron.

Act XIII

Brush Byron.

Scene I

But which brush.
For Byron.

Scene II

But may be which brush for Byron.

Scene III

Or brush and comb.
Or Byron.

Scene IV

To be often satisfied for Byron.

Act IV

Why should Byron have been where.
When he never had been there.

Scene I

Italy and Italian a wife cooking and a husband cleaning.
This may make it as seeming.
That Byron was lying leaning.
And a foot had that attention
From which not only which to mention.
That they will ask after they answer
No in no way if they look well
Do they see that he could dwell
Except in seeking warmth and heating
Which they can call
Which they can manage
Better manage can call.
Byron.
And he comes
And he comes appealing.
And she is meaning
To have feeling.
Which she does.

Scene II

Byron. May be we are Byron.

Scene III

May be we have Byron

Scene IV

May be we do

Scene V

But may be you

Scene VI

Know Byron by Byron.

Scene VII

Byron and clothing

Scene VIII

Byron and carrying.

Scene IX

Baby and Byron

Finis

LISTEN TO ME

⟨ 1936 ⟩

A PLAY

There are three characters.

The first one says. No noun is remown
The second one says. Forget the air
The first one says. But you need the air
The third one says. For has nothing to do with get.

They giggle

And then they are not through with three.
And then they are solemn and they know that the world will.
If they know that the world will.
It is not used that they need where.

Three characters.

There are always more than three characters because air is
where.

Now I ask you if you listen to me do you say as air is there.
And so no longer three characters but all who are there say this.

Listen to me

A soliloquy

There is any day not what they say there is a man there and it
is well done. If he likes it or not it is well done. They like to know
that it is well done. That is what a man is they like to know that it
is well done. What is it that a man is a man is that they like to
know that it is well done. If it is not well done he is dead and they
like to know that he is dead if it is well done. That is the one thing
that there is that there is now that he is dead and that it is well
done.

If three characters are in the play is it in the way.

No more than four characters ever go away.

A chorus of three characters and then a chorus of four characters but the characters that are the three characters are not the
same characters as the characters that are four characters.

Four characters now come together and think apart. They do not think therefore they think apart.

The four characters.

First character.   Since there are no men in existence anywhere except here on this earth being men is not an easy thing to happen.

Second character.   Listen to me and they do.

It is natural that there are many
It is natural that there are few
A city says how do you do
Or only one or two.

The third character has a french poem.   Un ecrivain a un ecrivain
une amie a un ami
Les années fait des années.
Si non oui.

The fourth character.   After all they enjoyed themselves
And if they did not after all they enjoyed themselves.

After four characters have thought apart and been together they always have to say it to each other.

And so now they do.

Listen to me

Now they do.

And so they do

Listen to that.

A motto

Why should alas be near to nothing.

Any one not looking on would say

Anything is a careful story of how they enjoyed themselves if they do.

Curtain.

There are never five characters in listen to me. Why is that.

Sweet William had his genius and so he did not look for it. He did look for Lillian and then he had Lillian.

That shows that five characters are not that.

Three four seven characters yes because seven is seven.

How sweet of seven to be seven.

The last of seven speaks first.

What does it speak about. It speaks about the great difficulty of what anything is about.

Is about. He says. Is about.

About what. He says. And what is about.

Well what is about.

What is it about puts in another word and it is as best yes.

There are seven characters and the last spoken.

Now the next to the last will speak.

All that was inside him inside dear Sweet William was shown not to be in him but to be held up so any one looking could see them. Dear sweet William.

The third from the last now speaks which is not the same as is now speaking. But is it.

He says. I am forty now it is funny isn't it. I am forty now and that is funny.

The fourth from the last one has no reason not to have any feeling. He remembers all the time that he has not had it before.

Well well who is a genius he said and she said well well. He the fourth one from the end one would that make the third one well the fourth one did not say well well who is the genius.

The fifth one from the end one said. What is a genius she said and he said what is a genius, and they both answered at once who is a genius. When they both answered at once they answered well well what is a genius.

Then then the second from the front one spoke more slowly and he said.

It is always well to tell what it is that is done.

And the first one the first one of the seven of them said in meditation. What is a word of one syllable is it easier to understand than one of several. I wonder, anyway anything is the story of anybody's life. No story is interesting although I always listen to it and they have to make up the ending and if it does not make you cry and nothing makes them cry because no one can try to make them cry and so there is no ending. That is what makes stories what they are and now I will tell one. That is what the first of the seven is saying, and just then they have to do as they are told.

And so all together they say, I wish words of one syllable were as bold as old. I will tell in words of one syllable anything there is to tell not very well but just well.

And so there was no curtain.

Curtain is a word of two syllables.

Guess again.

And just then nobody disturbed them and so they could listen and they listened to this.

Now Sweet William had his genius and so he could tell a careful story of how they enjoyed themselves. But he did not have his Lillian, he looked for Lillian and so he could not tell a careful story of how they enjoyed themselves.

Curtain.

Then Sweet William forgot nothing. To forget is not to remember but to remember is not to forget.

Act I

Sweet William and Lillian

And so Sweet William was nervous as is his habit.

And Sweet William said because Sweet William was saying.

It is always well to tell what it is that is done.

And then Sweet William saw his Lillian and they said.

He had his birthday on his birthday.

And he said

All that was inside him inside dear Sweet William was shown not to be in him but to be held up so anyone looking could see them

Dear Sweet William.

There is no sighing.

Lillian

Need is not more cared for then needles.

Dear Sweet William

But weed to weed is not more cared for than nettles.

Dear Sweet William

Whatever we see is not whenever we do what.

Lillian

What.

And she lay down on a sofa.

All five characters rushed up.

But there are not five

Not even not alive.

Sweet William stopped at any time and at any way.

Lillian Lillian is not as easily remained or remaining as Sweet William.

Now imagine a scene which is on this earth and as many come about as are and are not there. They are so careless with their luggage and luggage gradually gets reduced, at least they find there was a place where more could be put and so there was less in any other place.

This is what Lillian had as her blessing.

And Sweet William, sweet William had Lillian.

So then as often as any one all the characters are talking.

To talk is very pleasant when it looks like writing.

That is what three said when they were five.

But there are never five.

No one literally no one must remember anything.

They must be old with thought and they must not remember anything.

All of which very gradually if it is slow is slowly.

Oh can you be left with me.

Sweet William.

He arouses Sweet William.

Curtain.

Every one is saying there is no Lillian for Sweet William.

And Sweet William

Sweet William is saying there is no Sweet William for Sweet William.

All of it has changed.

There is no Sweet William.

All of it has changed

There is Lillian.

And then the edge of dresses all seven place dresses where dresses were.

Sweet William. It is no anxiety to be Sweet William.

And now all the world is full of people that means it is all covered over with them, and nobody knows who anybody looks like and that is no trouble to any Sweet William.

Sweet William says enough is enough but he does not mean it. If he did would Lillian would Lillian.

If he did would Lillian.

And so the world is all covered with Sweet William not Sweet William.

The world is all covered with Lillian all with Lillian.

And why could there be any world if there is sweet William.
Nobody answers enough.

There is a description of the world covered with Sweet William.

Curtain.

Very likely no one needs to remember any time.

Dear Sweet William.

They came to see to say to say dear dear Sweet William.

They did not leave to have to be Lillian.

And so at a last means nothing to dear William.

Because if the world is all in covering then it is nothing that there is not any more Sweet William.

But there is dear Sweet William

Sweet William had his genius and he looked for Lillian.

He had his Lillian.

Now might the world be covered over by what it is.

It might.

And if it were were were.

It is.

Were

It is.

And if it is.

Were.

Well if it is.

Were if it is.

Now you all know.

Five

Three

Eight

You all know

Have you forgotten that is was three four and seven.

Well I would smile if smiling suited sweet sweet William **and** his Lillian.

And so the world is covered with Sweet William.

And his Lillian.

With Lillian.

With Sweet William and with Lillian.

And so it makes no difference

Which had better remember to remember.

And which had better forget to forget

It makes no difference
Listen to me
Dear Sweet William and Lillian
Curtain.

Act II

The three characters and sometimes two come together and without sitting down they frown.

First character.   Why do you do what you do.

Second Character.   If the earth is not covered with water what is water.

Third Character.   If the air is not filled with air how can they dare.

Two together say, that they will finish with everything.

Three and two do not make five because five is a number that they do not use therefore three and two make six.

First character.   First character is not lonesome when chess is changed to checkers.

But said the other one no one can use these words because these words can change.

Oh said the other one can words change.

Yes said the other one words cannot change but anybody can put anything away.

Where said the other one can they put anything away.

Why not if they do.

Is said by not more than one at a time.

This prepares everything so well that very soon and very shortly they are not able to cherish what they would like.

The first character.   What would they like.

All of them.

Now does not that sound like Sweet William.

What would they like.

Sweet William has not been missing.

Nobody is bolder and so sweet William is never nervous.

All who are old are older.

Five Characters.   Remember that these are never.

Is there any matter that there are no five characters when so many nations are dutiful.

Sweet William has never recognized nations.

And Lillian,

Lillian has never divided anything from anything and in this way the earth is the earth and the earth which is the earth is the earth which is, there is a hesitation not within but without, which is, there is no hesitation within without, which is, do not like what there is not to like, within, very quietly five enter.

In no time at all there is no time.

After all what had the two and the three done, and what had the four and the six done. Some can count to eight but had they ever tried.

Sweet William said that they had not.

Curtain.

It is very charming that the whole earth is covered with people and everybody counting no one can count five. they can count two and three and four and six and seven but they cannot count five and eight not really five not really eight.

And after all make it daily.

First character.   Some count eight daily.

Second character.   Nobody denies that the earth is covered with people and since there are no people except on this earth people are people.

Third character.   And how about counting.

All the characters. What do we do when we do not do what we do.

Neither Sweet William nor Lillian are lost.

All together.   How can they be lost when the earth is all covered with people.

Sweet William and Lillian.   With people.

All together all the characters all together.   All the earth is covered with people and so no one is lost because as the whole earth is covered with people people are people.

Suddenly in the midst of all this silence somebody begins talking.

Sweet William has heard nothing.

The first character.   Please be patient because I am going away.

Second Character.   Where

Third Character.   Where where I am going.

Fourth Character.   And have you been there

Fifth Character.   I am there.

Oh yes said the first character I have been there.

The second character likes everything that happens.

Once in a while nothing happens.

Third Character.   What is the difference between what is al-
                    lowed.

The second character is nervous.

Sweet William was but he is not so any longer.

Not all this having happened it is time to look about, none of
the characters say this neither does anybody else have to say this
but nevertheless this is what happens, this is what happens all the
time just as often more nearly is everything prepared than it was.

And Sweet William is very happy he would be now that he is
no longer nervous and very often just as likely he is no longer
nervous. If he is then he is and he is no longer nervous.

So then although no one does say so what is it that does happen.

It does happen nobody says so but it is so it does happen.

There is no curtain because it does happen.

Very well it does happen but very well is a hesitation and
as there is a hesitation they say very well.

So then they do say something.

All together they say

Very well.

Does anybody know for certain how many characters are they.
That is a question.

And as the earth is all covered with people this is not a question because listen to me does anybody know for certain how
many characters there are.

First character.   I can count them.
Second character.   Count them.
Third character.   I count them
Fourth character.   There is no use counting them
Fifth character.   What you need to do is to count them
                            Curtain.

It is very wonderful but everybody can tell the first character
apart.

First character.   I know I am
Second character.   Who told you
Third character.   What did they tell you
Fourth character.   If they told you did you know or did you only
know that they told you so.
Fifth character.   The best thing to do is to know the first char-
acter by looking.

All together.　　　　Which is the first character.
All together.　　　　The first character.

After a little silence the first character says, After all does it matter.

After that the first character says.

But after all it does matter.

The first character.　　I have never thought of telling.
The first character.　　No I have never thought of telling
The first character.　　I have never thought of telling anything.
The first character.　　No I have never thought of telling anything.

Curtain.

It is very easy not to be very lively in the morning as the earth is all completely covered by people.

Curtain.

Any curtain is a curtain but no curtain for a curtain as a curtain may a curtain try.

A curtain is very old if a bed is said to be in there and suddenly no one knows why curtain have gone away.

First character.　　　There is no place where tables are since the earth is made of gold.

Second character.　　Since the earth is made of gold there is no happiness as old.

Third character.　　　Never listen to another

Fourth character.　　No mother to another

Fifth character.　　　If the earth is covered with people and it is and they come to cover which they do the earth altogether which it is then neither one nor another has any bother never to be left to one another where they are.

Remember there is no fifth character anywhere.

Chorus of characters.　　Remember

Chorus of characters.　　That there is no fifth character anywhere.

By and by believing that there are as many people.

No where except on this earth are there so many any people and nowhere except on this earth are there any Sweet William who had his genius and then he looked for his Lillian.

First character.　　　If you were going to look for anything on this earth what would you do.

Sweet William.　　　Begin counting.

Lillian.　　　　　　　How many would you count.

First character.   Any million.
Second character. If you counted a million would it make a trillion.
Third character.   Not necessary if there are never any less than six or two.
Fourth character.   No five or eight
Fifth character.   No five is ever alive.
Sixth character.   Counting does not letting counting count.
Seventh character. And so every count is counted.
Eighth character.   No by me.
All the characters together.   There is no eighth character.
      And so Sweet William sighs.
      Sighing is not only natural but never natural to Sweet William.
      Sweet William never means Sweet William he just means that the earth is all covered over with the people on it and all of it is as Sweet William says, Sweet William does Sweet William is Sweet William.
      Sweet William
      It is not necessary that Sweet William says that all the earth is covered with Sweet William but he knows Sweet William knows he knows he knows he knows Sweet William is Sweet William.
      And so everybody begins to delight in a fight.
      What is a fight.
First character.   What is what is light
Second character. Which is which is might.
Third character.   Did I hear something about words of one syllable.
Fourth character.   Well yes perhaps you did
Fifth character.   Perhaps if there are words of one syllable there is a fifth character.
All the characters. There is no fifth character.
The sixth character. I can change words of one syllable into words of two
Seventh character. And he did
Eighth character.   He did not
All the characters. There is a ninth character.
Ninth character.   It is well that he did.
      Sweet William is not hearing he is only listening.
      He listens and as he listens they all are ready to cover the earth completely and the earth nobody knows about it but there is

lots of water on the earth, nobody knows about it it is just the same as if nobody knows about it and Lillian, Lillian makes it all be very well as much water as there is.

Sweet William not no Sweet William not.

This sounds like a confusion but confusion is more than two syllables.

Anybody can count anything they can count syllables and people and each is each but Sweet William is never Sweet William and Lillian is Lillian even Lillian.

The third character interrupts the earth and the earth is all covered with people.

Anybody can be careful of what they do.

So says Sweet William and Lillian.

And if they are not what do they do.

What do they do says Sweet William and says Lillian.

Curtain.

Fifteen characters cough altogether.

What have they seen.

They have seen what they said

What have they said

They have said what they have seen.

That is what has happened to all fifteen.

And after a while.

There is no after a while for fifteen.

And for forty-six.

There is no after a while for forty-six.

And so counting is lugubrious.

Character.	And everybody counts.
Second character.	What is a count
Third character.	A count is a gentleman who has a name
Fourth character.	And what is his name
Fifth character.	His name is count.
All the characters.	In this case is there a fifth character.
Fifth character.	Yes because he can count.

Curtain.

Act III

The world is all covered over with people.

As the people cover the world all over the world is all covered over with people.

And nobody can believe what they hear.

They do not hear that the world is all covered over with people but it is. And everybody can count and they do.

First character.   I wish Sweet William and his Lillian could count.

Everybody follows the first character around and he never gets lost. When he gets lost he has been bewildered because Sweet William has been nervous. Sweet William is nervous and so is Lillian but Lillian is not nervous not at all nervous and so is Sweet William.

In this way the first character gets lost.

When the first character gets lost he finds the second character and as soon as he finds the second character they lose the second character and all the time how can they if the world is all covered over with people and it is how can they lose the second character.

Listen to me

How can they lose the second character.

Which character have they lost.

They have lost the second character.

Curtain.

As soon as they know they lost the second character there is no curtain and they know that they cannot lose the second character because the earth is covered all over with people.

The second character. There is a second character

The third character.   There is a third character

The fourth character.   There is a fifth character

The fifth character.   There is no fifth character

Curtain.

Sweet William prepared verdure.

Sweet William prepared pools.

Verdure two syllables

Pools one

Sweet William prepared what he had.

Had one syllable

He one syllable

What one syllable

Prepared. Three Syllables

Sweet William prepared verdure and fountains and he admired what he did.

Sweet William continued to prepare verdure and fountains and continued to admire what he did.

Sweet William had his genius.

Sweet William had his syllables

Sweet William had water and had no water in his pools sweet William had water in his water falls

Water-fall Three syllables made up a two syllables and one syllable

And so Sweet William came to be about.

About two syllables

Came one syllable

to one syllable

be one syllable

Now there is no opposition to anything being together.

Sweet William had his genius and he looked for his Lillian.

Did Lillian know that the earth is all covered over with people which it is

Lillian had no connection with syllables. Syllables are not so

And now there is action.

Action is two syllables

Curtain.

Action just as so which is so

Curtain.

Any one counting to-day does not count once a day. This is what Lillian would say if Sweet William were not in the way.

Sweet William cannot go away. How can Sweet William stay if they are or are not counting to-day.

In no way is every day a part of speech

Curtain.

Sweet William remarkably can not go away.

Curtain.

Sweet William is not surrounded by anything the earth is that which is covered over with people and Sweet William has a fountain.

He had his genius but now he has his fountain and he is looking has been has been one syllable has been is having his Lillian Two syllables

So now be ready to prepare to come in and out. Out and about.

Come one syllable

In one syllable

and one syllable

Out one syllable
about two syllables.
And everything startling.
Three syllables.
You see why Sweet William is often. Very often.
Everybody sees it all coming.

Curtain.

Sweet William occasionally on account.
They all three stare.

If you say that the earth and the air is all covered everywhere then there is nothing to do but to do it too. And that is what they do.

Sweet William if he had his genius and he had that is what he had to do. He had to look for Lillian too.

The scene is the earth all covered over with people and the air and beside that there is not anywhere.

Naturally not since there is the air and the earth and all filled with everybody everywhere.

So then what can they do they cannot come back to earth too.

First character.	Not to do
Second character.	What they have to do.
Third character.	Because they have not it to do.
Fourth character.	Because it is done.
Fifth character.	What is done
Sixth character.	The earth and the air.
All together.	Dear me the earth and the air and I thought it was everywhere.
Seventh character.	Well is it not everywhere
Eighth character.	No indeed because there are people everywhere

All together the characters. Like it or not they are there there everywhere on the earth and in the air.

Ninth character.	Everybody has ceased to consider water.
All together.	Nobody is altogether anywhere And so there is no place to stare.
Sweet William.	And what is a genius
Dear Sweet William.	Where is a genius
Dear Sweet William.	Why is a genius
Dear Sweet William.	When is a genius

Dear Sweet William.   Sweet William had his genius and he looked
for his Lillian.

First Scene in the third act is now finished and the second
scene is begun, in the second scene there is no question that
there is nothing to do.

Scene II

The moon

First character.	No dog barks at the moon.
Second character.	The moon shines and no dog barks
Third character.	No not anywhere on this earth.
Fourth character.	Because everywhere anywhere there are

lights many lights and so no dog knows that the moon is there

Fifth character.	And so no dog barks at the moon now no not anywhere.
First character.	And the moon makes no one crazy no not now anywhere.
Second character.	Because there are so many lights anywhere.
Third character.	That the light the moon makes is no matter.
Fourth character.	And so no one is crazy now anywhere.
Fifth character.	Because there are so many lights anywhere.
First character.	And so then there it does not matter
Second character.	The sun yes the sun yes does matter
Third character.	But the moon the moon does not matter
Fourth character.	Because there are so many lights everywhere

that any dog knows that lights any night are anywhere.

Fifth character.	And so no dog bays at the moon anywhere.
All the characters together.	This is so
	This we know
	Because we wondered why,
	Why did the dogs not bay at the moon.
	They did not but why
	But of course why
	Because there are lights everywhere anywhere.
	And that is what they meant by never yesterday.

Scene III

After a little while all the characters take part.
How many characters are there.
As many as there are
And how do they know there is no moon.
They know there is a moon but there are so many lights that
are bigger
And so the moon is there.
But not any dog can care
About that
And they do not.

Scene IV

Now very earnestly all the characters do not come together.
First character.   But how could they when the earth is covered
all over with everybody.
Second character. And what would they do if they did
Third character.   It is never better to have any character come
further as the earth is covered all over and any light is bigger
than the moon.
Fourth character. Oh yes bigger and brighter
Fifth character.   Than the moon.

Scene V

What happened when the earth was covered all over which
it is
This happened that there was never any yesterday before to-
day and no to-morrow after yesterday.
First character.   And everybody said yes yes
Second character. And everybody said nevertheless
Third character.   And they said
Fourth character. That there is no question and answer.
As you see the fifth character does not exist and this is natural
oh so natural when the earth is covered all over with everybody.
So now this scene is to take place it does not take place no
scene takes place but it is to take place all over.
If it is all over it does not take place.
Any dog knows that about the moon now.

And now this time there are going to be five dogs who do not bay at the moon and the fifth one does not matter neither does any other one of the four of them for that matter.

All the dogs.   It is very necessary that they do not bark at the moon and it has come to be that the moon does not matter because all the other lights are so much better.

And so any dog can know that luna now any longer has nothing to do with lunatic.

In this scene the earth is to be covered over all over and the dogs are not to bay at the moon.

Scene V

There is no scene V.

Scene VI

As soon as everything that happens does not matter anybody eats better and so in this scene there will be cooking.

There will be the making of apple and banana fritters and Butter Scotch ice box cookies, and as soon as nothing is happening everybody eats better.

Eating has nothing to do with yesterday or to-morrow or the earth being covered with people all over or the dogs not baying at the moon because all the other lights are so much brighter and the word lunatic having nothing to do with the moon shining ever after.

Scene seven.

A cooking.

First character.   Butter
Second character.   Eggs
Third character.   Chicken
Fourth character.   Meat
Fifth character.   Anything else that can matter

And now all the characters prepare to eat.

This is not necessary if anything is to happen after but oh so necessary if nothing is to happen after and as nothing is to happen after all the characters are preparing to eat.

Fourth character.   Eating is to eat

Second character.	There is no after
Third character.	There is no butter
Fourth character.	No butter
Fifth character.	To eat.
Sixth character.	There is butter
Seventh character.	To eat
Eighth character.	And there is nothing.
Ninth character.	To happen after.
Any character.	The world is covered by people all over
All the characters.	Yes Yes

Curtain.

Sweet William
Dear Sweet William
There are no characters where there is Sweet William
Sweet William says
What each one can do
Words of one syllable
What each one does
Words of one syllable although it does not sound like it
What each one can do
There are no characters where there is Sweet William
Sweet William is never all alone
Therefore there are no characters where there is Sweet William

Sweet William.   Suddenly there is a war
               Suddenly is a word of three syllables
               There is a war
               Words of one syllable

Sweet William.   Suddenly there is a war.
Sweet William.   What is suddenly there is a war.
Sweet William.   The earth is all covered over with people when this is so then it is not so that suddenly there is a war.
               Because suddenly if the earth is all covered over with people then sudden is not any more.
Sweet William.   Suddenly there is a war
Sweet William.   If the earth is which the earth is covered over all over with people then there is no sudden no sudden any more.

Sweet William never weeps and never expresses himself
Sweet William never weeps
Sweet William never expresses himself.
Suddenly there is a war.

If the earth which it is is covered over with everybody which they are then never any more is there any sudden any more.

So then where are we

Words of one syllable

Sweet William.   Where we are.

Sweet William had his genius and he looked for his Lillian.

Sweet William.

Curtain.

Sweet William had his genius and he looked for his Lillian.

There is not any sudden any more.

Sweet William

Sweet William had his genius and he looked for his Lillian.

There were people here and there everywhere.

Sweet William.   There are people there and here everywhere.

Lillian.   There are people here and there everywhere.

All at once Sweet William had his genius and he looked for his Lillian.

Curtain.

All of a sudden there is no all of a sudden.

There are people everywhere.

Sweet William.   Where

Lillian.   Everywhere.

Sweet William.   But do I like it.

Lillian.   You do not like it.

Sweet William.   Everywhere.

Curtain.

And so there.

There are people on the earth everywhere.

Sudden is not sudden anywhere.

Sweet William.   Do I like sudden if there is no sudden anywhere.

Sweet William.   Do I like everywhere if there are people on the earth everywhere.

Sweet William.   Everywhere

Lillian.   Anywhere.

Sweet William.   No war is begun again because war is sudden and there is no sudden anywhere because there are people on the earth everywhere.

Sweet William.   Did I say it as I was saying.

Sweet William.   Saying something.

Sweet William. Saying if I was saying
Sweet William. Saying something.
Sweet William. Was I saying something.
 Sweet William had his genius and he looked for his Lillian.
Sweet William. Saying that it was just as well not to see what to say.
Sweet William. There.
 All at once there was and there had not been a war
 All words of one syllable.
 All at once
 Words of one syllable
 All at once.
 More often
 Not words of one syllable
 All at once
 Words of one syllable.
 Sweet William was never troubled never troubled by words of one syllable or more more syllables.
 Sweet William was never troubled by a war.
Sweet William. Was I troubled.
Sweet William. Not any more
 Any is a small word but made up of two syllables.
 Small words made up of two syllables
 Any.
Sweet William. Not troubled any more.
 After the earth was covered all over with people which it is.
Sweet William. Not after
Sweet William. Not ever after
Sweet William. Ever after
 Small words two syllables.
 Any ever after.
 There is never any ever after in a war so there is no war.
 Not ever after any more.
 Sweet William had his genius and his Lillian.
 Sweet William had his genius
 Sweet William had his Lillian
 Sweet William
 Had his genius
 Sweet William
 Had his Lillian.

Sweet William never said I because I has not any syllables not even one.

Can one letter be a word of one syllable.

Sweet William did not ask every one.

How can any one ask every one when the earth is covered all over with every one.

Sweet William did ask any one.

Sweet William.

Dear Sweet William

Curtain and end of Third Act.

Act IV

First character.   Some more
Second character.   If you say it again say it again
Third character.   Say it again
Fourth character.   No say it again
Fifth character.   Listen to me say it again
Sixth character.   Say it say it some more
Seventh character.   Say it more and more
Eighth character.   Say what you say

All these words of one syllable.

Yet and again

All the characters.

They chose say as the word to say because to say it is what they say.

Sweet William was not present he never was neither was Lillian

Curtain.

It is Sunday afternoon and birds are singing some in small cages for sale.

First character.   They made a joke of the first character
Second character.   It is easy to make a joke of the second character
Third character.   One at a time it is easy to be one at a time.
Fourth character.   As everybody knows what everybody knows.
Fifth character.   Monuments are often placed where they can be seen

Sixth character.   It is unfortunate that the sixth character comes after the fifth character.

All the characters. Sweet William had his genius and he looked for his Lillian, we hope we hope we know that he has found his Lillian and that Sweet William has his genius.

All the characters. If it were Sunday afternoon Sunday would come before Monday.

Sweet William.   Sunday is Sunday afternoon but it does not come after Saturday or before Monday.

Lillian.   Sweet William has found his Lillian.

Curtain.

The earth is all covered over with people and they do not care about it any more.

All the characters who are there say that they had not been there before.

First character.	Before
Second character.	Nobody knows before.
	Words of more than one syllable.
Third character.	Begin at the other end
Fourth character.	The other end has begun before.
Fifth character.	How can there be another end when the earth is round.

All the characters in tears. If the earth is round and there are people on it everywhere.

After a moment's quiet nobody cries.

After another moment's quiet nobody tries.

Then all together they sit down.

The earth is all covered over with people and they all are seated down.

First character.	More arrangements are made
Second character.	For getting up
Third character.	No for sitting down.
Fourth character.	Sitting down has so many syllables
Fifth character.	Not at all
Sixth character.	The fifth character never knows about syllables.
Seventh character.	Not at all
Eighth character.	It has happened so often that everybody is dead.
Ninth character.	Not at all

All the characters.   The earth is all covered over with people.
All the characters.   Not at all
Sweet William.   All ready
Lillian.   I never change my mind.
Sweet William.   Already.
All the characters.   Dear Sweet William
All the characters.   And Lillian
All the characters.   Not at all

 After a quiet moment there is no quiet moment there is no quiet moment after or before.

All the characters.   Why not
      One syllable
All the characters.   Because there is no after or before
 Two syllables.
 Sweet William
 And so gradually there this this understanding about syllables.

 Anything that is not is more than one syllable two or more. After and before.

 After that there is no silence.
 Silence. Two syllables.
 Two Syllables Silence
 Everybody knows better than that syllables knows better than that.

Sweet William.   Syllables have to be
 There is no argument that makes anything better that is the reason that they laugh.

Fourth character.   First Syllable
      One Syllable
      That they laugh.

Second character.   That is what arrangements are.

 They all the people all over the earth and there are people all over the earth all sit down.

 That is what arrangements are
 Three syllables in arrangements.
 And that makes it never be ready.
 Oh yes I see
 That you see me
 And when you see
 That I see you
 You do then see

That you see me
Which you do do.
This makes a crisis in the life of Sweet William.
Curtain

Lillian together Lillian.
There is no reason why any Sweet William.
A dark day where side walks are unknown.
There can never be too much of nothing.
Sweet William never said anything.

Sweet William.   Said why do you not come.
Sweet William.   Said why
Sweet William said why do you not come when you do come.
Sweet William was adding.
He added Sweet William.
It was not a dark day and there were side-walks.

Sweet William.   Very much it was very much better.
Sweet William.   When was it very much better
Sweet William.   It was not very much better.
Sweet William had nothing to do with its being a dark day and no side-walks and a brighter day without any side-walk.

He was very much interested in side-walks although he never managed to believe that pools pools where there was or was not water was really not alone but of much more importance.

By this time it was not once again.

He had forgotten about it being the earth and all covered over with people but forgotten forgotten was never a memory to him.

At once he had a bright thought.

He thought that if he did not have water in a pool and of course he did as well as he did not of course he would be would make nothing more likely and yet if was likely not at all that there was the earth if not why not and why only people everywhere on it. He never had thought of that better not.

Sweet William was often hopeful.

What is the earth. Sweet William asked that but he meant not.

Sweet William.   What is the earth
Sweet William.   I like not to know.
Sweet William.   I like not to know where there is no difference.
Difference has so many syllables.
Sweet William is never discouraged.
Like the earth he can have it be that it is never again.

Sweet William.   But he is never encouraged
Sweet William.   Would hope that he would like that they would
have that they must never all the people be there.
Sweet William.   There is no one because I like it.
Sweet William.   Because I like it there is no one there is no
earth and there are not people everywhere on it.
Lillian.   There is a wish
Lillian.   There is a horse
Lillian.   There is a head
Lillian.   There is an eye
Lillian.   There is a kneel
Lillian.   There is a wish when I kneel on the eye of the
horse and wish it.
     Sweet William was not there.
                    Curtain.

Act V

     All the characters are in act Five.
     It is interesting if it is true that all the characters are in act five.
     But there never is a five.
First Character.   Never
Second Character.   Never a five
Third Character.   Any one can choose anything that there never
is.
Fourth Character.   Choosing
Fifth Character very fifth Character.   There is no choosing.
Sixth Character.   There is no fifth Act and there is a fifth Charac-
ter.
Seventh Character.   Left alone means everything.
Eighth Character.   Once in a while they think that they wish they
were well.
Ninth Character.   Very well
Tenth Character.   Very very well
                    Curtain.
     If the earth is everywhere covered all over with people nobody
sees them all.
First Character.   And if anybody does why not.
All the characters. After all that is what it is after all.

All the characters.   After all never happens again.

All the Characters.   Does it.

All the Characters.   Perhaps Character is four syllables.

All the Characters.   Perhaps

All the Characters.   And so it is important

All the Characters.   Perhaps

All the Characters.   That there is the earth and that there are people everywhere on it.

All the Characters.   Perhaps.

All the Characters.   Why is there no Sweet William who has his genius and looks for his Lillian in Act Five.

All the Characters.   Why not.

All the Characters.   Because not.

All the Characters.   Why is there no Act Five

All the Characters.   Of course not

All the Characters.   Of course of course not.

All the Characters.   No Act Five

All the Characters.   No never.

All the Characters.   Of course not.

All the Characters.   Any number could be like that.

All the Characters.   Of course not.

All the Characters.   Of course any number could be like that

All the Characters.   Like that

All the Characters.   Of course

All the Characters.   Not of course not.

All the Characters.   And so it is perfectly true that through and through any number could be not true.

All the Characters.   Happily arrange not to have the number five. And they count like that.

All the Characters.   When they and we

All the Characters.   The earth is all covered over with people everywhere and nobody counts five.

All the Characters.   Nobody

All the Characters.   Counts five

Curtain

Act Six

Sweet William has just met.
Curtain.

All the Acts together.   Any act rather

                What is a game.

First Act.   What is a game.

First Act.   A game is where they do it again.

First Act.   Oh yes no doubt a game

First Act.   Oh yes no doubt a game is where they do it again.

First Act very harshly.   Oh yes a game no doubt a game is where they do it again.

Second Act.   What is the earth

Second Act.   The earth is altogether with or without water.

Second Act.   With or without thunder

Second Act.   No with or without water.

Second Act.   That is what the earth is with or without water.

Third Act.   And what are people.

Third Act.   People are all over

Third Act.   Do you mean all over

Third Act.   No I do not mean all over.

Third Act.   Do you not do you not mean all over.

Third Act not necessarily sad.   No I do not mean all over the earth and even if I did I would not even if I did have it all over.

Third Act.   Why not

Third Act.   Because not

Third Act.   Because if the people are all over the earth which they are it is not all over.

Third Act.   Not all over

                Please kindly notice that over is two syllables and that makes all the trouble. Trouble has two syllables too.

Fourth Act.   And what is the air.

Fourth Act.   The air is there.

Fourth Act.   The air is there which is where it is.

                Kindly notice that is all one syllable and therefore useful. It makes no feeling, it has a promise, it is a delight, it needs no encouragement, it is full.

Fourth Act.   The air is full

Fourth Act.   Of course the air is full

Fourth Act.   Full of what

Fourth Act.   Full of it.

Fourth Act.   The air is full of it

Fourth Act.   Of course the air is full of it.

Fourth Act.   Of course
Fourth Act.   The air
Fourth Act.   Is full
Fourth Act.   Of it.
Fifth Act.   And Sweet William
Fifth Act.   And his Lillian
Fifth Act.   Tell me
Fifth Act.   Did dear Sweet William
Fifth Act.   Find his Lillian.
Sixth Act.   Sweet William had his genius
Sixth Act.   And he looked for his Lillian
Sixth Act.   Dear Sweet William he has his genius.
Sixth Act.   And he looked for his Lillian
Sixth Act.   The past has nothing ever nothing to do with
Sweet William
Sixth Act.   Because
Sixth Act.   There can never be too much of nothing.
Sixth Act.   Not for dear Sweet William
Sixth Act.   Not for looking for his Lillian
Sixth Act.   Sweet William dear Sweet William
    And then the Sixth Act was forgetting.
Sixth Act.   It is not easy to remember what one is for-
getting.
Sixth Act.   Not ever for Sweet William.
Sixth Act.   Sweet William has never to remember for-
getting.
Sixth Act.   Dear Sweet William
Sixth Act.   And his Lillian
                   Curtain.
All the Acts together commence to read out loud, they have
not learned what they know and they have not heard what they
hear but every little once in a while they read out loud together and
finally once in a while they hear what they say.
    So now listen while all the Acts together hear what they say.
    They hear now.
    All the acts together.
                   A Soliloquy.
For whether or not
Suppose whether or not
Syllables change

Babies arrange
Any exchange
Whether or not.
As anybody looks they see that it is so.
Think of syllables
That it is so
That is what Acts altogether are.
Acts
One syllable
All
One syllable
To
One syllable
But gather or gather never never one syllable.
And so the Acts altogether know
They know as if they tell it so.
That to gather together
Is not one syllable.

Acts altogether.	And so
Acts altogether.	The earth
Acts altogether.	Are all covered over with everybody
	And so
	One syllable
	And so
	One syllable
	It is so
	One syllable

The Acts altogether do not say so altogether although they know altogether that it is so.

The Acts Altogether.	It has come
	That the earth
	Is there
First Act.	Yes
Second Act.	Yes
Acts altogether.	It has come
	Not to go
	But to go
	And to come
Third Act.	All one syllables are not ways

Third Act.   It is why I have said that it is not well to be
found in and out.
Fourth Act.   Determination
Fifth Act.   Some say that they look as they do they do
not look to see what they saw they look to add two to one.
Fifth Act.   Two to one makes five.
Acts Altogether.   A great triumph for Act V
Act one.   If I do
Act two.   But you do
Act three.   What do I do
Act four.   What you do do

Act V

I had a triumph to have a triumph there must be more than
one syllable.

Act V

Triumph

Act IV

I had a triumph
Acts Altogether.   They all say
                      Go go away.
Triumph and away are two syllables.
Fifth Act.   I like what I have
Acts altogether.   Five all one syllable
                      And then they do not sadly say
                      Act V can never go away.
                      Because it never has been there.
                      Act five dear Act five
                      Caught alive.
While all this is anxiously progressing, Sweet William has been
forgotten. He likes having it known that it is not a meadow if the
road is cut in he likes it not to be known that it is as often made
again.
Dear Sweet William   Could we know how we have it.
Dear Sweet William   Remember looking alike has nothing to do

with it they do not change they do not care, they have no need to follow any one about because says dear Sweet William what is their better way.

Sweet William is always careful of their feelings even if he knows that he is very sorry. He is very sorry he is always careful of their feelings even if he knows he is very sorry.

That is what Sweet William is he is very careful of their feelings he is very sorry he is very sorry he is careful of their feelings that is what Sweet William is he is very sorry.

That is what Sweet William is.

It is not a pity that William is two syllables not at all a pity.

Sweet William is careful not to say that Acts are altogether he is very careful to say that he is not very sorry he is very careful to say that he is not very careful of their feelings he is very careful of their feelings he is very sorry he does say that Acts are not altogether. That is what Sweet William is he is careful to say that Acts are not altogether.

All the Acts together   All the acts are never together nothing is ever together there is no act one no act two no act three no act four no act six there is act five.

Act V

No act five

Act five

Act five

Act five

Yes act five

After a while Sweet William is answering.

Yes I am here.

Very well then.

Who is there.

Who is there

I am here.

Sweet William is answering he is very careful not to hurt anybody's feelings and he is sorry.

First Character.   Sweet William has his genius and he looked for his Lillian

Act V

There is no strain in being act five

Curtain.

The play now ends in detection, they look alike and they look for one another and they find it.

First Character. If I am the First Character how do they know I am not the Second Character.

Second Character. Who is.

Second Character. Not as loudly. Who is.

Third Character. If I meet a stranger how do I know he is a stranger.

Fourth Character. Who is

Second Character. Quite as loudly. Who is.

Third Character. If I look like the Ninth Character how do I look

First Character. Who can look

All the Characters. We can look

The Ninth Character. If I look

Eighth Character. If you look

Fifth Character. What do you see when you look.

Fourth Character. The only one I know is not the one to know.

Third Character. No

Fourth Character. Oh no.

First Character. There is no no in no.

All the characters who have been looking about see Sweet William he is nowhere to be seen. They count eight he is to be seen, they count five he is nowhere to be seen they count one he is nowhere to be seen.

Sweet William is nowhere to be seen.

They count five one at a time he is nowhere to be seen.

Curtain.

The first Character seems to like it.

The second Character after he stops to think seems to like it.

The third Character finally says that he is not likely to be added

The fourth Character does not want to know added to what but is there any trouble about it.

The fifth Character makes every one leave every one alone

The sixth Character finds it very happily that as any one comes in was it the one he saw.

The seventh Character says alright.

All the Characters together. After all there is or is not one who comes in and recommends another one although at no time is there not more than one.

So then all the Characters wish that they were detecting.

So then Character one.

It does not make any difference who is the other one because no one,

The second Character.   Because no one

The third Character.   Which is which

The fourth Character.   Neither any one.

The fifth Character.   But if they came

The sixth Character.   But they do come

The seventh Character.   Well nobody nobody nobody

The eighth Character.   Yes indeed I saw them

And so all this time what is all this time.

Well well even if we had not met we would have met.

Even if we had not met.

Yes met

Even if we had

Not met.

And so even if we had not met.

Fourth Character.   We did

Second Character.   Meet

Third Character.   Not met

Fourth Character.   Any yet.

Fifth Character.   Not met

Sixth Character.   Not met yet.

All the characters.   And so that is what happens. What happens is this none of the characters have met they have not met yet if they have not met yet none of the characters have met none of the Acts have met none of the Characters and Acts have met yet they have not met none of the Characters have met none of the Acts have met and if they have not met they have not met yet.

And Sweet William

Sweet William has not met

Sweet William has met yet

Dear Sweet William has not not met yet. Dear Sweet William he has not not met yet and Lillian well Lillian Lillian has met. Has Lillian met yes Lillian has met yet Sweet William dear Sweet William and Lillian only Lillian and the Characters each one has not met yet and all the Acts have all of them not yet not met yet.

And the Curtain. The Curtain has met not met yet and the Curtain has met.

The Curtain has met.

Curtain.

After the curtain.

I like a curtain because a curtain has always a curtain to see. If you see the curtain then anybody can see that after it it is not one two three.

A curtain is two syllables and as such it is a curtain.

One syllable.

How I would like that it could be that it could be said that it is true that one is too and two is three and three is four and five is two and one is one and a curtain can come and come, the only word here in two syllables is curtain, the only word in two syllables is William the only word in two syllables is Lillian the only word in three syllables is Characters and the only word in one syllable is Acts.

Acts

Curtain

Characters

Characters

Curtain

Acts

There is no one and one

Nobody has met any one

Curtain Can Come.

Curtain

A PLAY CALLED NOT AND NOW

◂ 1936 ▸

Characters

A man who looks like Dashiell Hammett
A man who looks like Picasso
A man who looks like Charlie Chaplin
A man who looks like Lord Berners
and a man who looks like David Green.

Women

A woman who looks like Anita Loos
A woman who looks like Gertrude Atherton
A woman who looks like Lady Diana Grey
A woman who looks like Katharine Cornell
A woman who looks like Daisy Fellowes
A woman who looks like Mrs. Andrew Greene

These are the characters and this is what they do.

A man who looks like Doctor Gidon and some one who looks like each one of the other characters.

The play will now begin.

The difference between not and now. That is what makes any one look like some one. All the characters are there and the one that looks like Doctor Gidon is the one that says what has just been said only it is not what Doctor Gidon would say but is said by the one that is like him.

The characters are now all in order.

They move and speak.

They first meet as each one is just about to go away.

Hullo they say and the do each go away. Not that that makes any difference, as the real one is not there but just the one that is just like him.

This is what they all say, that anybody can get impatient with an aurora borealis.

One has a bad temper and the other is irritable, the one like Picasso meets the one who looks like David Greene.

And then they all come around and say that they are not going
away.

All who look like anyone of them do stay.

Act I

The ones who look like Dashiell Hammett Picasso Charlie
Chaplin and Lord Berners stand around.

They hesitate about making witty remarks to each other but
they do do it just the same.

This is what they say.

The one who looks like Dashiell Hammett looks at the one
that looks like Picasso and both together look at the one that looks
like Charlie Chaplin and the three of them then look at the one
that looks like Lord Berners, and then they all say, we do not look
like any other one and they did not and do not. And they say they
say all together we will look at the women and then each one of
them says each one as he sees each one another one, at which one.
They all answer as they look as if they did look like them.

Yes they say one says yes. Then one says if you say yes and I
do not say yes will he say yes.

The one that looked like Dashiell Hammett said he was saying
yes. The one that looked like Picasso said yes he did say he had
been to say yes and the one who looked like Charlie Chaplin said
if not no one had not said not yes and the one who looked like
Lord Berners said yes, yes he said yes. And then they all looked at
the women. None of them who looked like Anita Loos or Gertrude
Atherton or Lady Diana Grey or Katharine Cornell or Daisy
Fellowes said yes.

That is it.

And so they all began again to look like another one.

The one that looked like Dashiell Hammett said.

If I look at you you will not look like me.

The one that looked like Picasso said, I said I did not look at
two and three.

The one that looked like Charlie Chaplin said.

Charlie Chaplin looked like me.

The one that looked like Lord Berners said.

I do not look at me.

And all of them then came to be nearly ready to stay where

they were as they stayed where they were they came one by one to look at the women the one who looked like Anita Loos the one who looked like Gertrude Atherton the one who looked like Lady Diana Grey and the one who looked like Katharine Cornell and the one who looked like Daisy Fellowes.

While all this was happening the one who looked like Doctor Gidon came in. They all looked at him but nobody began speaking.

Dr. Gidon said where is the man who looks like David Greene.

The one who looked like Dashiell Hammett did not answer but he looked as if he saw the one who looked like Mrs. Andrew Green. When he did he was not interested. The one who was like Picasso was but he did not say so. The one who looked like Charlie Chaplin did not look. The one who looked like Lord Berners was not looking that way.

The one who looked like Doctor Gidon said. There is plenty of time.

Each one then looked like the one he looked like and said is there. Dr. Gidon said yes there is, there is plenty of time, and the one that looked like Dashiell Hammett did not come again, he was there but he did not come again, the one that looked like Picasso was not there but he did come again, the one that looked like Charlie Chaplin was there, the one that looked like Lord Berners was there and he came again. They all looked around for the women so that they might look at them but they were not there the one who looked like Anita Loos was not there the one who looked like Gertrude Atherton was not there the one who looked like Lady Diana Grey was there the one who looked like Katharine Cornell was there the one who looked like Daisy Fellowes was there too. They all all of them who looked like them looked around and as they looked around they saw everybody who was there and so now they were all there and they were all looking around them. That is the way it began.

Doctor Gidon the one who was like him came in and when he saw that every one was there because the one who looked like Anita Loos had come in and the one that looked like Gertrude Atherton was there so he said What is it. And nobody answered him. The woman who looked like Mrs. Andrew Green came and stood beside him and the man who looked like David Green came and stood beside her.

Every one was looking it might have been exciting, they each one looked around them and saw that there they were which of course they were.

So everything began.

They were not at all next to each other none of them were and they were there, which made them see each other without looking.

The one that looked like Dashiell Hammett began to go away. The one that looked like Picasso looked as if he was interested in the one that looked like Dashiell Hammett going away but he said he was not. The one that looked like Dashiell Hammett did not hear him but he did not go away he went nearer him, the one that looked like Charlie Chaplin was gone but nobody had been looking and the one that looked like Lord Berners looked again. The women said the one that looked like Charlie Chaplin have come in again.

The one that looked like Dr. Gidon said that the one that looked like Charlie Chaplin was gone. All the others agreed with him. The one that looked like Lord Berners said I saw him come again. The one that looked like Picasso was not looking at the one that looked like Doctor Gidon he was looking at the one that looked like Charlie Chaplin looking at the women.

Nobody said anything.

The one that looked like Anita Loos did not say anything the one that looked like Dashiell Hammett did not say anything to her. The one that looked like Gertrude Atherton said something, the one that looked like Picasso did not say anything to her. The one that looked like Lady Diana Grey said a great deal. One after the other then said they were ready to stay. The one that looked like Dashiell Hammett did not say that he was ready to stay. The one that looked like Katharine Cornell said that she was talking to the one that looked like him. The one that looked like Picasso did not say what he said but he did say that he was looking. The one that looked like Lord Berners very pleasantly went up to the one that looked like Gertrude Atherton and asked her if she had seen the one that looked like David Greene. The one that looked like Daisy Fellowes said that she had seen two of them the one that looked like David Greene and the one that looked like Doctor Gidon. The one that looked like Mrs. Andrew Greene did not come in when she did come in she did not say anything.

Little by little each one of them looked at each other and

were not going on doing so. They knew that money was a bother. The one that looked like Dashiell Hammett did not look to see if he had any money, he knew he had nevertheless he did not look to see. The one that looked like Picasso looked to see if he had any money and as he looked to see he looked around but did not see any one. He looked where the women were and when he said where they were he looked to see the one that looked like Dashiell Hammett. When the one who looked like Picasso saw the one who looked like Dashiell Hammett he went on looking at him. The one who looked like Picasso knew that if he had money he had it with him and he had. The one that looked like Charlie Chaplin looked as if he had money with him and as if he did not look for any one. The one who looked like Lord Berners looked at the one who looked like Picasso and he saw that the one that looked like Picasso had all his money with him.

The one that looked like Anita Loos did not look around she did not look to see if they had money with them she did not look alone and she did not look with any one. The one that looked like Gertrude Atherton looked like Gertrude Atherton and she did not look at any one or if any one had all their money with them. The one that looked like Lady Diana Grey did not stop looking, she looked as if she did not see anyone have any money with them any one that looked as if they looked like that one, the one that looked like Katharine Cornell did not look at any one, as she was not looking at any one she did not see that any one looked like that one. The one that looked like Daisy Fellowes looked while she was looking.

The one that looked like Doctor Gidon came in very hastily, did anybody who looked like any one love anything. No one answered him as no one looked like any one and so nobody looked around to see any one.

The one who looked like David Green said not very much better.

The one who looked like Mrs. Andrew Green was not present when they were looking for water.

In the midst of all this there was an interruption the one that looked like Dashiell Hammett said he had seen it see that the one that looked like Picasso looked like Picasso.

It was an interruption and no one was astonished when the one who was like Dashiell Hammett was interrupted. He was interrupted by the one who was like Picasso. The one who was like Picasso suddenly noticed the one who was like Charlie Chaplin and said he had seen him. The one who was like Charlie Chaplin did not interrupt anything. The one who was like Lord Berners did not interrupt the one who was like Charlie Chaplin. He did however say that he saw when he was looking that the one that looked like Anita Loos was looking at the one that looked like Charlie Chaplin. After that the one who looked like Gertrude Atherton said something. And after that the one who looked like Lady Diana Grey looked again and she saw what she was looking at and the one who looked like Katharine Cornell saw it again saw that the one who looked like Gertrude Atherton was looking at something and the one who looked like Daisy looked like Daisy Fellowes.

The one who looked like Doctor Gidon did not disturb anything because he said to disturb any one is to interrupt them.

The one who was like David Green finished as he was beginning and the one who was like Mrs. Andrew Green came and went and meant to be interrupting. After that they all went away but soon they were not there. They came to see where they had been and so they met and there they looked at each one. Very much.

Nobody looked like each one which was not at all surprising. Each one looked like the one he looked like. Each one looked like the one she looked like. And as each one looked like that one there was one who looked like Dashiell Hammett one who looked like Picasso one who looked like Charlie Chaplin and one who looked like Lord Berners. Help them to look like the one they looked like.

There was one who looked like Anita Loos one who looked like Gertrude Atherton one who looked like Lady Diana Grey and Katharine Cornell and Daisy Fellowes they could not help looking like the one they looked like not one of them could help looking like that one.

What did they say when they looked like the one they looked like and they always looked like the one they looked like. What did they say when they looked like the one they looked like. What did they say. They said everything.

What is there to say when you look like the one you look like. The one who looked like Picasso said that he did not look alike. The one who looked like Dashiell Hammett how well the one who looked like Dashiell Hammett looked like Dashiell Hammett and he looked at the one who looked like Picasso when he said that he did not look alike. The one who looked like Charlie Chaplin looked like Charlie Chaplin and he was ready to be looking at the one who looked like Lord Berners and who said everything. The one who looked like Charlie Chaplin did not say what did he say, he did look at each one and the one he looked at was not the one who looked like Picasso and not the one who looked like Dashiell Hammett. The one who looked like Lord Berners had that to say and he looked at the one who looked like Dashiell Hammett he had looked at the one who looked like Charlie Chaplin and he knew what to say when he looked at the one who looked like Picasso and he said it then. They all turned around and they saw the ones that looked like Anita Loos Gertrude Atherton Lady Diana Grey Katharine Cornell Daisy Fellowes Mrs. Andrew Greene, and then as they looked the curtain fell not between but so that no one could see any of them.

Curtain.

Act II

Now comes the time when they come in one by one, they are not alone as they come in one by one because there is never any other one.

The one who was like Dashiell Hammett came in alone but he did not stay although if he had been coming in alone he would not have gone away when he saw the one who was like Picasso had come in to stay and he did. The one who was like the one who was like Charlie Chaplin that would make two and there was only one came in as he came in that is he was all alone as he came in. The one that was like Lord Berners was like Lord Berners and he came and went in. So each one of them was alone and the women all came in and came up and as they came up they came in. Who is with them asked each one the one that was like Anita Loos asked who is with them the one who was like Gertrude Atherton looked at them to see if any one was with anyone of them the one who was like Lady Diana Grey looked around at each one and said no one is with any of them and the one who looked like Katharine Cornell did not look to see if there was any one with any one of them and the one who looked like Daisy Fellowes looked around with them and the one who looked like Mrs. Andrew Green looked to see if any one looked like Doctor Gidon and the one who looked like David Greene said everything, he was never silent at any one time.

They never did sigh. It was not likely that they could.

The one who was like Dashiell Hammett had never had to sigh. The one who was like Picasso left the one who like Charlie Chaplin had something to say about some one having had to come and the one who was like Lord Berners did sigh.

As no one did not sigh they saw that the one who looked like Anita Loos did sigh. The one who looked like Gertrude Atherton did not with that the one who looked like Anita Loos did sigh.

The one who looked like David Greene smiled when he sighed. The one who looked like Mrs. Andrew Greene, looked as if when she sighed she died. She did not die and she did not sigh.

The one who looked like Lady Diana Grey did not look to see anybody die. The one who looked like Katharine Cornell did not smile and sigh. The one who looked like Daisy Fellowes did cry and she did sigh and she did die.

And so as the one who looked like Dr. Gidon came in the one who looked like Dashiell Hammett came in. The one who looked like Picasso was not there. The one who looked like Charlie Chaplin did and was there. The one who looked like Lord Berners was there.

And so they all smiled and looked as if they met. The one who looked like Dashiell Hammett smiled as if he met. The one who looked like Picasso was not there to smile, the one who looked like Charlie Chaplin looked like Charlie Chaplin and he smiled like Charlie Chaplin and he sighed like Charlie Chaplin and he did not die.

The one who looked like Lord Berners did not sigh and die he did not smile and he did not look as Lord Berners did when he did not sigh.

All the others sighed. All the others who liked the others sighed.

The one who looked like Dashiell Hammett looked as if he had seen the sun as it set and the little moon. The one that looked like Picasso did not let the one that looked like Charles Chaplin look to see the sun set but he did not see him not see the little moon. The one who looked like Lord Berners looked to see if it was a little moon or not a little moon and he did not see he did not look to see if when the sun set there was a little moon but the one

who looked like Dashiell Hammett looked to see the one who
looked like Picasso look at the little moon. The one who looked like
Doctor Gidon did not see the little moon the one who looked like
David Green did see the setting sun and the little moon and the
one who looked like Anita Loos and the one who looked like
Gertrude Atherton and the one who looked like Lady Diana Grey
and the one who looked like Katharine Cornell and the one who
looked like Daisy Fellowes did not see the sun setting and did not
see the little moon. The one who looked like Mrs. Andrew Greene
did not see the sun setting and did not see the little moon.

Act III

A mysterious assemblage of women.

Three boys who look like men.

The mysterious assemblage of women did not look like Gertrude Atherton and Anita Loos Lady Diana Grey Katharine Cornell
and Daisy Fellowes, they did not look at all like them not at all,
they did not look like a mysterious assemblage of women, they
were a mysterious assemblage of women and they all were in their
ordinary clothes and sitting down in chairs under a shelter in the
Luxembourg Gardens, there were no men or children with them
and what were they doing, they were talking not much but some.
They were not at all like Anita Loos and Lady Diana Grey and
Gertrude Atherton and Katharine Cornell and Daisy Fellowes not
any of them were like any one of them but they were a mysterious
assemblage of women.

Three boys who looked like men.

The three boys who looked like men did not look like Charlie
Chaplin or like Picasso or like Lord Berners or like Dashiell Hammett they did not look like any one of them the three boys who
looked like men nor like all of them.

Scene I

The three boys who looked like men were not very near the
mysterious assemblage of women.

Scene II

The one who looked like Doctor Gidon was not there either nor

was the one who looked like David Greene nor the one who looked
like Mrs. Andrew Greene.

Scene III

The ones who looked like Dashiell Hammett and Charlie
Chaplin and Picasso and Lord Berners were always being there
where not any one did see them. They might have but if they
would have then the ones who were like Dashiell Hammett and
Charlie Chaplin and Picasso and Lord Berners would have been
always being seen. And they were but nobody saw them. Nobody
does not include the one who was like Doctor Gidon and the one
who was like David Green and the one who was like Mrs. Andrew
Greene. The three boys who looked like men never saw them never
saw any of them nor the mysterious assemblage of women they
never saw any of them but then they were not looking and the
three boys who looked like men were not looking. They were not
looking around them.

The ones who were like Anita Loos and Gertrude Atherton and
Katharine Cornell and Lady Diana Grey and Daisy Fellowes were
not seen by any of them but then the ones that were like Dashiell
Hammett and Charlie Chaplin and Picasso and Lord Berners
were looking toward them, they were looking at the women, they
did not look at the mysterious assemblage of women they did not
know where to look at them and if they had they would have gone
on looking at the ones that looked like Anita Loos and Gertrude
Atherton and Lady Diana Grey and Katharine Cornell and Daisy
Fellowes. The one who looked like Mrs. Andrew Greene might
have been one at whom any one of them might have been looking
but she was not anywhere just then.

Scene IV

The one who looked like Mrs. Andrew Greene.
But she had a piece of what she had.
And she said she ate it if she did.
And if she did she ate it with her mouth
And with it she was welcome here at once.
The one who was like Dr. Gidon.
There is no use in saying money is not so.
It is.

The only difference between man and monkey
Is what money makes.
If there is no money then like anything
They eat what they have.
But money is not so.
It is kept.
That is what it is.
And nothing is kept except what money is.
So you see money is so.
That is what the one who is like Dr. Gidon has to say.
And the one who is like Dashiell Hammett what has he to say about money.
He says money I have money
He says money when I have no money.
He says when I have no money
He says money yes money
And what is the one who is like Picasso what is he to do when he sees money all the way through.
He is to do what he does.
Hold it hoe it
Hold it and hold it.
Have it and not have it.
But he knows where money goes
And so also as money goes
He does not go oh no.
Where is money to go
Money can not go and say so.
Therefor money is always best
And best is better than butter
And without money there is no butter.
And so there always is money.
The one who looks like Charlie Chaplin arranges neatly that he is not there. Where is he. He is not there. And where is money. Money is there.
The one who is like Lord Berners never arranges that money is money. Why not because of course why not.
And so they all think, each one who looks like any one that money is money.
The ones that look like Anita Loos and Gertrude Atherton and

Lady Diana Grey and Katharine Cornell and Daisy Fellowes they do not know oh no because of know and no.

So as they are looked at they are.

No money is not so and so.

As each one who looks like that one turns around no one is seen.

It is easy to see what is seen.

Money is not seen ohno.

And so.

There is no no in seen.

There is no in money.

There is so in seen.

There is no so in money.

And so the ones that look like Gertrude Atherton and Anita Loos and Lady Diana Grey and Katharine Cornell and Daisy Fellowes are seen so.

The ones who looked like Picasso and Dashiell Hammett and Lord Berners and Charlie Chaplin were not seen they were seen to see them.

Scene V

Nobody is late, nobody who looks like anybody is late oh no they can not be left and they can not be late oh no.

The one that was like Picasso was not late, the one that was like Dashiell Hammett was not late the one that was like Charlie Chaplin no he was not late and the one who was like Lord Berners was not late.

As they were not late nobody had left, the one who was like Doctor Gidon had not left the one who was like David Greene had not left the one who was like Mrs. Andrew Greene had not come.

The one who was like Gertrude Atherton was not late the one who was like Anita Loos had not left the one who was like Lady Diana Grey had not left and the one who was like Katharine Cornell had not left and the one who was like Daisy Fellowes had not left. If no one might have left and they all might have come and any one might not have been late and they all returned one by one and they all turned and they were more of them not one who did not look like the one they looked like then not any one of them was one who had not come, no not any one of any one of them. Not one.

It is not temporary to look like that one not temporary at all.

The one who looked like Picasso did he look like Picasso looked now or did he look as Picasso looked when he had looked like him. In the middle of looking like him he went on looking like him that is what the one did who looked like him. That is what the one did who looked like Charlie Chaplin he looked just like him and he always had looked like him just like him. The one who looked like Dashiell Hammett looked like him he could and did look like him and in looking like him had looked like him. Oh yes he had. And the one looking like Lord Berners looked like him just looked like him and as he looked like him he was looking like him. He did look like Lord Berners he looked like him.

The one who looked like Anita Loos was looking like Anita Loos at any time and this made that one look like Anita Loos as she looked at any time. The one who looked like Gertrude Atherton kept on looking like Gertrude Atherton just kept on looking like Gertrude Atherton and the one who looked like Lady Diana Grey and who had looked like Lady Diana would look like Lady Diana Grey and the one who looked like Katharine Cornell looked like Katharine Cornell and the one who looked like Daisy Fellowes could look like Daisy Fellowes could look like Daisy Fellowes, and so each one of them who looked like the one she looked like saw that she looked like the one she looked like and that the other ones who looked like the ones they looked like did look like them as the could and did look like them which they did they did look like them.

The one who looked like Picasso looked like him one Sunday morning. The one who looked like Dashiell Hammett looked like him one Sunday and he looked like him as he looked like him every Sunday. The one who looked like Charles Chaplin looked like him every Sunday afternoon and the one who looked like Lord Berners looked like him Sunday morning afternoon and evening.

The ones who looked like Gertrude Atherton Anita Loos and Katharine Cornell Daisy Fellowes and Lady Diana Grey saw that they looked like them Saturday and Sunday and every week day and just then quite as often they saw that the ones that looked like Lord Berners and Picasso and Dashiell Hammett looked like them Sunday morning and they all together looked at everything

Sunday and Sunday morning and Sunday afternoon. After that they looked like them and they looked at one another all of them looked at any of them Sunday evening. Just then a noise was heard.

Scene VII

There is no leaving when a noise is heard.

Scene VI.

This is a short scene and the moonlight. None of them who look like any one of them are interested in the moon-light not even excepting the one who looked like Dr. Gidon or the one who looked like Mrs. Andrew Greene nor the one who looked like David Greene not even that one.

Act III

Pronounce their name. If they look like them they do not pronounce their name, the one who looked like Picasso did not pronounce that name, the one who looked like Charlie Chaplin did not pronounce either the one or the other part of that name the one who looked like Dashiell Hammett did not pronounce that name the one who looked like Lord Berners had not pronounced that name. Pronounced that name who had pronounced that name not the one who looked like Lord Berners not the one who looked like Picasso not the one who looked like Dashiell Hammett not the one who looked like Charlie Chaplin, not any of them had pronounced that name and so not any one of them had pronounced that name.

The one that looked like Doctor Gidon could have pronounced that name but he had not pronounced that name. The one who looked like David Greene could have pronounced the name to pronounce a name but all the same he did not pronounce that name. The one who looked like Mrs. Andrew Greene could not pronounce that name.

The one who looked like Anita Loos could not pronounce that name that is a question and the one who looked like Gertrude Atherton could pronounce that name that is not another question and the one who looked like Lady Diana Grey could not pronounce that name and the one who looked like Katherine Cornell

could or could not pronounce that name and the one who looked
like Daisy Fellowes could not pronounce that name.

So then each one who looked like that one did not pronounce
that name.

Scene I

They did not shake hands with any one not any one of them
who looked like the one they looked like, of course not of course
they did not shake hands with each other or with any other one
of course not.

Yes the one who looked like Picasso, after all did shake hands
when the one who looked like Doctor Gidon shook hands with
him and the one who looked like Charlie Chaplin did shake hands
when the one who looked like Anita Loos and the one who looked
like Gertrude Atherton and the one who looked like Lady Diana
Grey shook hands with him and the one who looked like Dashiell
Hammett did shake hands when the one who looked like Mrs.
Andrew Greene shook hands with him and the one who looked
like Lord Berners did shake hands with each one of them who
shook hands with him and the one who looked like David Greene
did shake hands with the one who looked like Katharine Cornell
and the one who looked like Daisy Fellowes and each one of
them who looked like the one they looked like did not shake hands
with any one.

Not any one of them who looked like any one of them could
see what they saw. The one that looked like Picasso did not see
what he saw the one who looked like Dashiell Hammett did not
see what he saw the one who looked like Charlie Chaplin did not
see what he saw the one that looked like Lord Berners did not
he did not see what he saw.

Scene II

If it rains every day there will not be a flood.

Scene II

The one who looked like Picasso looked to see what he saw
and if he could see the difference between pale green and white.
And as he was looking and looking as if he were seeing the dif-

ference between very pale green and white the one who looked like Dashiell Hammett did not look as if he were looking at the difference between pale green and white and he was not looking as if he were looking at the one who looked like Charlie Chaplin but then he was never looking at any one who looked like any one of them not at the one who looked like Charlie Chaplin not at the one who looked like Picasso not at the one who looked like Picasso. He was looking at the one who looked like Mrs. Andrew Greene and she was looking as if she were looking at the difference between pale green and white.

The one who was looking like Lord Berners was not looking at the difference between pale green and white, he was looking at the one who was looking like David Greene and who was looking as if he was looking at something that was pale green and not white.

The one who looked like Doctor Gidon never looked at anything that was pale green and white. The one who looked like Anita Loos was looking at any one looking at what was pale green and white. The one who looked like Gertrude Atherton was not looking, the one who looked like Lady Diana Grey was looking at Lord Berners who was not looking at anything that was white but was looking at anybody looking at something that was pale green and not white. The one who was looking like Katharine Cornell was looking at all of them who were looking at anything that was pale green and not white and the one who was looking like Daisy Fellowes was looking at something that was pale green that was pale green in not being pale green that was white.

And nobody that is not one of them who was looking like the one that one was looking like looked at anything that was pale green when they were looking at anything that was white.

And when they did this what were they seeing. Could anybody who looked like anyone see pale green when they were looking at white.

The one who was looking like Doctor Gidon had gone away.

The one who had been looking like David Greene went away, the one who had been looking like Mrs. Andrew Greene went away.

The one who looked like Picasso had come to stay. The one who looked like Dashiell Hammett did not go away. The one who looked like Charlie Chaplin looked the other way. The one who looked like Lord Berners did not look to go away. The one who looked like Gertrude Atherton did not have to go away the one who looked like Anita Loos did not have to stay the one who looked like Lady Diana Grey looked away the one who looked like Katharine Cornell looked as it was to look away the one who looked like Daisy Fellowes did not look away, and so they met for which they had a fan. A fan is never used any more.

Scene III

Picasso he does not know that he does look like Picasso, and Charlie Chaplin he does not know that it is so that the one who looks like Picasso does not know that he does look like Picasso and the one that looks like Charlie Chaplin he does look like Charlie Chaplin even if he does know that the one who looks like Picasso does look like Picasso. The one who looks like Dashiell Hammett does not mean anything when he is saying anything and that thing because he never says anything does mean to say that day after day any day before any day which is what he does not say he does not know that he looks like Dashiell Hammett and there is of course no one to tell him so because no one can know that there is one who looks like him that is to say he does look like him he looks like Dashiell Hammett as everybody looks at him but nobody looks at him and so nobody sees him he looking as he is looking which is that he looks like him he is the one who looks like Dashiell Hammett and that is so and nobody could say no if they were looking at him but they are not looking at him nobody is looking at any one who looks like any one and somebody does look like that one looks like Dashiell Hammett and he is that one. So then there is one and he looks like Charlie Chaplin and there is one and he looks like Dashiell Hammett and there is one and he looks like Lord Berners and there is one and he looks like each one not the same each one but each one as is the one which is that one.

And so then what are they doing they are looking at the women not each one of them but all of them.

And who are the women at which they are looking, they are looking at the one that looks like Gertrude Atherton not all of them but all of them not each one of them but all of them are looking at the women and one of them is the one that looks like Gertrude Atherton. And there is one that looks like Mrs. Andrew

Greene and each one of them are not looking at that one but they are all of them looking at the women and one of them is the one that looks like Anita Loos and another one is one that looks like Lady Diana Grey and each one of them the one who looks like Doctor Gidon and the one who looks like Picasso and the one who looks like Lord Berners were looking at them and one of them at whom they were looking was one who looked like Katharine Cornell and the one who looked like Dashiell Hammett was one of them who were looking at them one one of them at whom they were looking was one who looked like Daisy Fellowes and one of them who was looking at all of them who was one of all of them who were looking at them was one who was like David Greene and he was one who was one of them who were all of them who looked like Picasso and who looked like Charlie Chaplin and who looked like Dashiell Hammett and who looked like Lord Berners and who was one of all of them who together with all of them was looking at them who were ones looking like Daisy Fellowes and Anita Loos and Gertrude Atherton and Lady Diana Grey and Katharine Cornell and Mrs. Andrew Greene and as all of them were like each one of them and each one of them was like the one that one was like and as they all looked at them none of the women looked at any of them who were like Picasso and Lord Berners and Charlie Chaplin and Dashiell Hammett and Doctor Gidon and David Greene and the ones who did look like them did look all of them not each of them but all of them at the women and there were ones who did look like Anita Loos and Mrs. Andrew Greene and Gertrude Atherton and Katharine Cornell and Lady Diana Grey and Daisy Fellowes and as all of them were seen by all them who were looking at them they were not any of them looking at any one of them because all of them who looked like Picasso and who looked like Lord Berners and who looked like Charlie Chaplin and who looked like Dashiell Hammett and who looked like Doctor Gidon and who looked like David Greene looked at them looked at the women who looked like the ones they looked like but each one of them was not seen by the men looking nor was any one of the men looking looking at them but all of them all the men who looked like the ones they looked like were looking at the women who were looking like the women the ones the women did look like and that was what was happening.

Curtain.

FOUR SAINTS IN THREE ACTS

⚘ 1927 ⚘

AN OPERA TO BE SUNG

To know to know to love her so.
Four saints prepare for saints.
It makes it well fish.
Four saints it makes it well fish.
Four saints prepare for saints it makes it well well fish it makes it well fish prepare for saints.
In narrative prepare for saints.
Prepare for saints.
Two saints.
Four saints.
Two saints prepare for saints it two saints prepare for saints in prepare for saints.
A narrative of prepare for saints in narrative prepare for saints.
Remain to narrate to prepare two saints for saints.
At least.
In finally.
Very well if not to have and miner.
A saint is one to be for two when three and you make five and two and cover.
A at most.
Saint saint a saint.
Forgotten saint.
What happened to-day, a narrative.
We had intended if it were a pleasant day to go to the country it was a very beautiful day and we carried out our intention. We went to places that we had been when we were equally pleased and we found very nearly what we could find and returning saw and heard that after all they were rewarded and likewise This makes it necessary to go again.

He came and said he was hurrying hurrying and hurrying to remain he said he said finally to be and claim it he said he said feeling very nearly everything as it had been as if he could be precious be precious to like like it as it had been that if he was used it would always do it good and now this time that it was as if it had been just the same as longer when as before it made it be left to be more and soft softly then can be changed to theirs and speck a speck of it makes blue be often sooner which is shared when theirs is in polite and reply that in their be the same with diminish always in respect to not at all and farther farther might be known as counted with it gain to be in retain which it is not be because of most. This is how they do not like it.

Why while while in that way was it after this that to be seen made left it.

He could be hurt at that.

It is very easy to be land.

Imagine four benches separately.

One in the sun.

Two in the sun.

Three in the sun.

One not in the sun.

Not one not in the sun.

Not one.

Four benches used four benches used separately.

Four benches used separately.

That makes it be not be makes it not be at the time.

The time that it is as well as it could be leave it when when it was to be that it was to be when it was went away.

Four benches with leave it.

Might have as would be as would be as within within nearly as out. It is very close close and closed. Closed closed to let letting closed close close close chose in justice in join in joining. This is where to be at at water at snow snow show show one one sun and sun snow show and no water no water unless unless why unless. Why unless why unless they were loaning it here loaning intentionally. Believe two three. What could be sad beside beside very attentively intentionally and bright.

Begin suddenly not with sisters.

If a great many people were deceived who would be by the way.

To mount it up.
Up hill.
Four saints are never three.
Three saints are never four.
Four saints are never left altogether.
Three saints are never idle.
Four saints are leave it to me.
Three saints when this you see.
Begin three saints.
Begin four saints.
Two and two saints.
One and three saints.
In place.
One should it.
Easily saints.
Very well saints.
Have saints.
Said saints.
As said saints.
And not annoy.
Annoint.
Choice.
Four saints two at a time have to have to have to have to.
Have to have have to have to.
Two saints four at a time a time.
Have to have to at a time.
The difference between saints forget me nots and mountains
have to have to have to at a time.

It is very easy in winter to remember winter spring and
summer it is very easy in winter to remember spring and winter
and summer it is very easy in winter to remember summer spring
and winter it is very easy in winter to remember spring and
summer and winter.

Does it show as if it could be that very successful that very
successful that he was very successful that he was with them with
them with them as it was not better than at worst that he could
follow him to be taking it away away that way a way a way to go.

Some say some say some say so.

Why should every one be at home why should every one be
at home why should every one be at home.

Why should every one be at home.

In idle acts.

Why should everybody be at home.

In idle acts.

He made very much more than he did he did make very much
of it he did not only add to his part of it but and with it he was
at and in a plight.

There is no parti parti-color in a house there is no parti parti
parti color in a house. Reflections by the time that they were given
the package that had been sent. Very much what they could would
do as a decision.

Supposing she said that he had chosen all the miseries that he
had observed in fifty of his years what had that to do with hats.
They had made hats for her. Not really.

As she was.

Imagine imagine it imagine it in it. When she returned there
was considerable rain.

In some on some evening it would be asked was there anything
especial.

By and by plain plainly in making acutely a corner not at
right angle but in individual in individual is it.

How can it have been have been held.

A narrative who do who does.

A narrative to plan an opera.

Four saints in three acts.

A croquet scene and when they made their habits. Habits not
hourly habits habits not hourly at the time that they made their
habits not hourly they made their habits.

When they made their habits.

To know when they made their habits.

Large pigeons in small trees.

Large pigeons in small trees.

Come panic come.

Come close.

Acts three acts.

Come close to croquet.

Four saints.

Rejoice saints rejoin saints recommence some reinvite.

Four saints have been sometime in that way that way all hall.

Four saints were not born at one time although they knew

each other. One of them had a birthday before the mother of the other one the father. Four saints later to be if to be one to be to be one to be. Might tingle.

Tangle wood tanglewood.

Four saints born in separate places.

Saint saint saint saint.

Four saints an opera in three acts.

My country tis of thee sweet land of liberty of thee I sing.

Saint Therese something like that.

Saint Therese something like that.

Saint Therese would and would and would.

Saint Therese something like that.

Saint Therese.

Saint Therese half in doors and half out out of doors.

Saint Therese not knowing of other saints.

Saint Therese used to go not to to tell them so but to around so that Saint Therese did find that that that and there. If any came.

This is to say that four saints may may never have seen the day, like. Any day like.

Saint Ignatius. Meant and met.

This is to say that four saints many never have. Any day like. Gradually wait.

Any one can see that any saint to be.

Saint Therese	Saint Ignatius
Saint Matyr	Saint Paul
Saint Settlement	Saint William
Saint Thomasine	Saint Gilbert
Saint Electra	Saint Settle
Saint Wilhelmina	Saint Arthur
Saint Evelyn	Saint Selmer
Saint Pilar	Saint Paul Seize
Saint Hillaire	Saint Cardinal
Saint Bernadine	Saint Plan
	Saint Giuseppe

Any one to tease a saint seriously.

Act I

Saint Therese in a storm at Avila there can be rain and warm snow and warm that is the water is warm the river is not warm the sun is not warm and if to stay to cry. If to stay to if to stay if having to stay to if having to stay if to cry to stay if to cry stay to cry to stay.

Saint Therese half in and half out of doors.

Saint Ignatius not there. Saint Ignatius staying where. Never heard them speak speak of it.

Saint Ignatius silent motive not hidden.

Saint Therese silent. They were never beset.

Come one come one.

No saint to remember to remember. No saint to remember. Saint Therese knowing young and told.

If it were possible to kill five thousand chinamen by pressing a button would it be done.

Saint Therese not interested.

Repeat First Act

A pleasure April fool's day a pleasure.

Saint Therese seated.

Not April fool's day a pleasure.

Saint Therese seated.

Not April fool's day a pleasure.

Saint Therese seated.

April fool's day April fool's day as not as pleasure as April fool's day not a pleasure.

Saint Therese seated and not surrounded. There are a great many persons and places near together. Saint Therese not seated there are a great many persons and places near together.

Saint Therese not seated.

There are a great many persons and places near together.

Saint Therese not seated at once. There are a great many places and persons near together.

Saint Therese once seated. There are a great many places and persons near together. Saint Therese seated and not surrounded. There are a great many places and persons near together.

Saint Therese visited by very many as well as the others really visited before she was seated. There are a great many persons and places close together.

Saint Therese not young and younger but visited like the others by some, who are frequently going there.

Saint Therese very nearly half inside and half outside outside the house and not surrounded.

How do you do. Very well I thank you. And when do you go. I am staying on quite continuously. When is it planned. Not more than as often.

The garden inside and outside of the wall.

Saint Therese about to be.

The garden inside and outside outside and inside of the wall. Nobody visits more than they do visits them.

Saint Therese. Nobody visits more than they do visits them Saint Therese.

As loud as that as allowed as that.

Saint Therese. Nobody visits more than they do visits them.

Who settles a private life.

Saint Therese.   Who settles a private life.

Saint Therese.   Who settles a private life.

Saint Therese.   Who settles a private life.

Saint Therese.   Who settles a private life.

Enact end of an act

All of it to be not to be not to be left to be to him and standing.

Saint Therese seated.

Left to be not to be not to be left to be left to be and left to be not to be.

Saint Therese seated and if he could be standing and standing and saying and saying left to be.

Introducing Saint Ignatius.

Left to be.

Saint Therese seated seated and left to be if to be if left to be if left if to be Saint Ignatius standing.

She has no one to say so.

He said so actually.

She can have no one no one can have any one any one can have not any one can have not any one can have can have to say so.

Saint Therese seated and not standing half and half of it and not half and half of it seated and not standing surrounded and not seated and not seated and not standing and not surrounded and not surrounded and not not not seated not seated not seated not surrounded not seated and Saint Ignatius standing standing not seated Saint Therese not standing not standing and Saint Ignatius not standing standing surrounded as if in once yesterday. In place of situations. Saint Therese could be very much interested not only in settlement Saint Settlement and this not with with this wither wither they must be additional. Saint Therese having not commenced.

Did she want him dead if now.

Saint Therese could be photographed having been dressed like a lady and then they taking out her head changed it to a nun and a nun a saint and a saint so. Saint Therese seated and not surrounded might be very well inclined to be settled. Saint Therese actively.

Made to be coming to be here.

How many saints can sit around. A great many saints can sit around with one standing.

Saint Therese a great many saints seated.

They move through the country in winter in winter entirely. Saint Therese in moving. Now three can be seated in front.

A saint is easily resisted. Saint Therese. Let it as land Saint Therese. As land beside a house. Saint Therese. As land beside a house and at one time Saint Therese. Saint Therese. As land beside a house to be to this this which theirs beneath Saint Therese.

Saint Therese saints make sugar with a flavor. In different ways when it is practicable. Saint Therese in invitation.

Saint Therese. Could she know that that he was not not to be to be very to be dead not dead.

Saint Therese so much to be with it withheld with that.

Saint Therese. Nobody can do so.

Saint Therese Saint Therese must be must be chain left chain right chain chain is it. No one chain is it not chain is it, chained to not to life chained to not to snow chained to chained to go and and gone. Saint Therese might be come to be in this not indifferently.

Saint Therese. Not this not in this not with this.

Saint Therese must be theirs first.

Saint Therese as a young girl being widowed.

Saint Therese. Can she sing.

Saint Therese. Leave later gaily the troubadour plays his guitar.

Saint Therese might it be Martha.

Saint Louise and Saint Celestine and Saint Louis Paul and Saint Settlement Fernande and Ignatius.

Saint Therese. Can women have wishes.

Scene Two

Many saints seen and in between many saints seen.

Saint Therese and Saint Therese and Saint Therese.

Many saints as seen and in between as many saints as seen.

Seen as seen.

Many saints as seen.

Saint Therese and sound.

She is to meet her.

Can two saints be one.

Saint Therese and fastening.

Very many go out as they they do.

Saint Therese. And make him prominent.

Saint Therese. Could a negro be be with a beard to see and to be.

Saint Therese. Never have to have seen a negro there and with it so.

Saint Therese. To differ between go and so.

Saint Therese and three saints all one. Saint Settlement Saint Fernande Saint John Seize Saint Paul Six. Saint Therese with these saints.

Who separated saints at one time.

Saint Therese. In follow and saints.

Saint Therese. To be somewhere with or without saints.

Saint Therese can never mention the others.

Saint Therese to them. Saints not found. All four saints not more than all four saints.

Saint Therese come again to be absent.

Scene III

Saint Therese. To an occasion louder.

Saint Therese coming to be selfish.

Saint Therese allow.

All four saints remembering not to be with them. Could all four saints not only be in brief.

Saint Therese.   Contumely.

Saint Therese advancing. Who can be shortly in their way.

Saint Therese having heard.

In this way as movement.

In having been in.

Does she want to be neglectful of hyacinths and find violets. Saint Therese should never change herbs for pansies and dry them.

They think there that it is their share.

And please.

Saint Therese makes as in this to be as stems.

And while.

Saint Therese settled and some come. Some come to be near not near her but the same.

Surround them with the thirds and that.

Saint Therese might be illustrated. Come to be in between.

Beginning earlier.

And anything.

Around.

Saint Therese seated with the name and choosing.

How many are there halving.

Scene III

Therese in Saint Ignatius and Saint Settlement to be sure.

Saint Therese having known that no snow in vain as snow is not vain. Saint Therese needed it as she was. Saint Therese made it be third. Snow third high third there third. Saint Therese in allowance.

How many saints can remember a house which was built before they can remember.

Ten saints can.

How many saints can be and land be and sand be and on a high plateau there is no sand there is snow and there is made to be so and very much can be what there is to see when there is a wind to have it dry and be what they can understand to undertake to let it be to send it well as much as none to be to be behind. None to be behind. Enclosure.

Saint Therese.   None to be behind. Enclosure.

Saint Ignatius could be in porcelain actually.

Saint Ignatius could be in porcelain actually while he was young and standing.

Saint Therese could not be young and standing she could be sitting.

Saint Ignatius could be in porcelain actually actually in porcelain standing.

Saint Therese could be admittedly could be in moving seating. Saint Therese could be in moving sitting.

Saint Therese could be.

Saint Ignatius could be.

Saint Ignatius could be in porcelain actually in porcelain standing.

They might in at most not leave out an egg. An egg and add some. Some and sum. Add sum. Add some.

Let it in around.

With seas.

With knees.

With keys.

With pleases.

Go and know.

In clouded.

Included.

Saint Therese and attachment. With any one please.

No one to be behind and enclosure. Suddenly two see.

Two and ten.

Saint Two and Saint Ten.

Scene IV

Did wish did want did at most agree that it was not when they had met that they were separated longitudinally.

While it escapes it adds to it just as it did when it has and does with it in that to intend to intensity and sound. Is there a difference between a sound a hiss a kiss a as well.

Could they grow and tell it so if it was left to be to go to go to see to see to saw to saw to build to place to come to rest to hand to beam to couple to name to rectify to do.

Saint Ignatius Saint Settlement Saint Paul Seze Saint Anselmo made it be not only obligatory but very much as they did in little patches.

Saint Therese and Saint Therese and Saint Therese Seze and Saint Therese might be very much as she would if she very much as she would if she were to be wary.

They might be that much that far that with that widen never having seen and press, it was a land in one when altitude by this to which endowed.

Might it be in claim.

Saint Therese and conversation. In one.

Saint Therese in conversation. And one.

Saint Therese in and in and one and in and one.

Saint Therese left in complete.

Saint Therese and better bowed.

Saint Therese did she and leave bright.

Snow in snow sun in sun one in one out.

What is the difference between a picture of a volcano and that.

Watered and allowed makes a crown.

Oysters ham and rose tree rose he arose and he arose.

Saint Therese not questioned for this with this and because.

They can remain latin latin there and Virgil Virgil Virgil virgin virgin latin there. Saint Ignatius to twenty.

A scene and withers.

Scene three and scene two.

How can a sister see Saint Therese suitably.

Pear trees cherry blossoms pink blossoms and late apples and surrounded by Spain and lain.

Why when in lean fairly rejoin place dismiss calls.

Whether weather soil.

Saint Therese refuses to bestow.

Saint Therese with account. Saint Therese having felt it with it.

There can be no peace on earth with calm with calm. There can be no peace on earth with calm with calm. There can be no peace on earth with calm with calm and with whom whose with calm and with whom whose when they well they well they call it there made message especial and come.

This amounts to Saint Therese. Saint Therese has been and has been.

What is the difference between a picture and pictured.

All Saints make Sunday Monday Sunday Monday Sunday
Monday set.

One two three Saints.

Scene III

Saint Therese has been prepared for there being summer.
Saint Therese has been prepared for there being summer.

Scene IV

To prepare.

One a window.

Two a shutter.

Three a palace.

Four a widow.

Five an adopted son.

Six a parlor.

Seven a shawl.

Eight an arbor.

Nine a seat.

Ten a retirement.

Saint Therese has been with him.

Saint Therese has been with him they show they show that
summer summer makes a child happening at all to throw a ball too
often to please.

Saint Therese in pain.

Saint Therese with blame.

Saint Therese having been following with them here.

In this way to begin to thin.

Those used to winter like winter and summer.

Those used to summer like winter and summer.

Those used to summer like winter and summer.

Those used to summer like winter and summer like winter and
summer.

Those used to summer like winter and summer.

They make this an act One.

Act Two

All to you.

Scene One

Some and some.

Scene One

This is a scene where this is seen. Saint Therese has been a queen not as you might say royalty not as you might say worn not as you might say.

Saint Therese preparing in as you might say.

Act One.

Saint Therese.   Preparing in as you might say.

Saint Therese was pleasing. In as you might say.

Saint Therese Act One.

Saint Therese has begun to be in act one.

Saint Therese and begun.

Saint Therese as sung.

Saint Therese act one.

Saint Therese and begun.

Saint Therese and sing and sung.

Saint Therese in an act one. Saint Therese questions.

How many have been told twenty have been here as well. Saint Therese and with if it is as in a rest and well.

Saint Therese does not live around she is very well understood to have been with them then.

She is very intently with might have been seen rested and with it all. It never snows in Easter.

Saint Therese as if it were as they say they say so.

Saint Ignatius might not have been born.

Saint Therese can know the difference between singing and women. Saint Therese can know the difference between snow and thirds. Saint Therese can know the difference between when there is a day to-day to-day. To-day.

Saint Therese with the land and laid. Not observing.

Saint Therese coming to go.

Saint Therese coming and lots of which it is not as soon as if when it can left to change change theirs in glass and yellowish at most most of this can be when is it that it is very necessary not to plant it green. Planting it green means that it is protected from the wind and they never knew about it. They never knew about it green and they never knew about it she never knew about it they never knew about it they never knew about it she never knew about it. Planting it green it is necessary to protect it from the sun and from the wind and the sun and they never knew about it and she never knew about it and she never knew about it and they never knew about.

Scene once seen once seen once seen.

Scene V

Saint Therese unsurrounded by reason of it being so cold that they stayed away.

Scene VI

Saint Therese using a cart with oxen to go about and as well as if she were there.

Scene VII

One two three four five six seven all good children go to heaven some are good and some are bad one two three four five six seven. Saint Therese in a cart drawn by oxen moving around.

Scene VIII

Saint Therese in time.

Scene IX

Saint Therese meant to be complete completely.

Saint Therese and their having been it always was what they liked likened because it was moved.

Saint Therese in advance advances advantage advance advantages. Saint Therese when she had been let to come was left to come was left to right was right to left and there. There and not

there by left and right. Saint Therese once and once. No one surrounded trees as there were none.

This meant Saint Ignatius Act II.

Act II

Saint Ignatius was very well known.

Scene II

Would it do if there was a Scene II.

Scene III and IV

Saint Ignatius and more.
Saint Ignatius with as well.
Saint Ignatius needs not be feared.
Saint Ignatius might be very well adapted to plans and a dis-
tance.

Barcelona in the distance. Was Saint Ignatius able to tell the
difference between palms and Eucalyptus trees.

Saint Ignatius finally.
Saint Ignatius well bound.
Saint Ignatius with it just.
Saint Ignatius might be read.
Saint Ignatius with it Tuesday.
Saint Therese has very well added it.

Scene IV

Usefully.

Scene IV

How many nails are there in it.
Hard shoe nails and silver nails and silver does not sound
valuable.
To be interested in Saint Therese fortunately.
Saint Therese. To be interested in Saint Therese fortunately.
Saint Ignatius to be interested fortunately.
Fortunately to be interested in Saint Therese.

To be interested fortunately in Saint Therese.

Interested fortunately in Saint Therese fortunately interested in Saint Therese Saint Ignatius and Saints who have been changed from the evening to the morning.

In the morning to be changed from the morning to the morning in the morning. A scene of changing from the morning to the morning.

Scene V

There are many saints.

Scene V

They can be left to many saints.

Scene V

Many Saints.

Scene V

Many many saints can be left to many many saints scene five left to many many saints.

Scene V

Scene five left to many saints.

Scene V

They are left to many saints and those saints these saints these saints. Saints four saints. They are left to many saints.

Scene V

Saint Therese does disgrace her by leaving it alone and shone. Saint Ignatius might be five.

When three were together one woman sitting and seeing one man lending and choosing one young man saying and selling. This is just as if it was a tribe.

Scene V

Closely.

Scene V

Scene five Saint Therese had a father photographically. Not a sister.

Saint Therese had no mother and no other appointed to be left at hand.

Saint Therese famously and mind. To mind. To have to have to have have Helen. Saint Therese have to have Helen have to have Helen. Saint Therese have to have to have to have Saint Therese to have to have Helen. An excuse.

Saint Therese as well as that.

Saint Therese robin.

Saint Therese not attached to robin.

Saint Therese.   Robin not attached to Robin.

Saint Therese.   Attached not attached to Robin.

Saint Therese.   Why they could.

Saint Therese.   Why they could why they could.

Saint Therese Saint Therese Saint Therese Saint Therese Ignatius why they could Saint Therese.

Saint Ignatius why they could.

Scene VI

Away away away away a day it took three days and that day. Saint Therese was very well parted and apart apart from that. Harry marry saints in place saints and sainted distributed grace.

Saint Therese in place.

Saint Therese in place of Saint Therese in place.

Saint Therese.   Can any one feel any one moving and in moving can any one feel any one and in moving.

Saint Therese.   To be belied.

Saint Therese.   Having happily married.

Saint Therese.   Having happily beside.

Saint Therese.   Having happily had with it a spoon.

Saint Therese.   Having happily relied upon noon.

Saint Therese with Saint Therese.

Saint Therese.   In place.

Saint Therese and Saint Therese Saint Therese to trace.
Saint Therese and place.
Saint Therese beside.
Saint Therese added ride.
Saint Therese with tied.
Saint Therese and might.
Saint Therese.   Might with widow.
Saint Therese.   Might.
Saint Therese very made her in.
Saint Therese.   Settled settlement some so.
Saint Therese Saint Therese.
Saint Therese in in in Lynn.

Scene VII

One two three four five six seven scene seven.
Saint Therese scene seven.
Saint Therese scene scene seven.
Saint Therese could never be mistaken.
Saint Therese could never be mistaken.
Saint Therese scene seven.
Saint Therese.   Scene seven.
Saint Settlement Saint Therese Saint Ignatius Saint Severine
Saint William Saint John Saint Ignatius Saint Alexander Saint Law-
rence Saint Pilar Saint Celestine Saint Parmenter Saint Lys Saint
Eustace and Saint Plan.
Saint Therese.   How many saints are there in it.
Saint Therese.   There are very many many saints in it.
Saint Therese.   There are as many saints as there are in it.
Saint Therese.   How many saints are there in it.
Saint Therese.   There are there are there are saints saints in it.
Saint Therese Saint Settlement Saint Ignatius Saint Lawrence
Saint Pilar Saint Plan and Saint Cecilia.
Saint Therese.   How many saints are there in it.
Saint Cecilia.   How many saints are there in it.
Saint Therese.   There are as many saints as there are in it.
Saint Cecilia.   There are as many saints as there are saints in
it.
Saint Cecilia.   How many saints are there in it.

Saint Therese.   There are many saints in it.

Saint Lawrence Saint Celestine. There are saints in it Saint Celestine Saint Lawrence there are as many saints there are as many saints as there are as many saints as there are in it.

Saint Therese.   There are many saints there are many saints many saints in it.

Saint Therese.   Thank you very much.

Saint Therese.   There are as many saints there are many saints in it.

A very long time but not while waiting.

Saint Ignatius.   More needily of which more anon.

Saint Ignatius.   Of more which more which more.

Saint Ignatius Loyola.   A saint to be met by and by by and by continue reading reading read read readily.

Never to be lost again to-day.

To-day to stay.

Saint Ignatius Saint Ignatius Saint Ignatius temporarily.

Saint Jan.   Who makes whose be his. I do.

Saint Therese scene seven one two three four five six seven.

Saint Therese.   Let it have a place.

Saint Therese Saint Ignatius and Saint Genevieve and Saint Thomas and Saint Chavez.

All four saints have settled it to be what they must know makes it be what it is when they are defended by attacks.

Saint Genevieve can be welcomed any day.

Saint Chavez can be with them then.

Saint Ignatius can be might it be with them and furl.

Saint Therese with them in with them alone.

Saint Plan.   Can be seen to be any day any day from here to there.

Saint Settlement aroused by the recall of Amsterdam.

Saint Therese.   Judging it as a place to be used negligently.

Saint Ignatius by the time that rain has come.

Saint Genevieve meant with it all.

Saint Plan.   Might meant with it all.

Saint Paul.   Might meant might with it all.

Saint Chavez.   Select.

Saints. All Saints.

Scene Eight

All Saints.   All Saints At All Saints.

All Saints.   Any and all Saints. All Saints. All and all Saints.
All Saints. All in all Saints. All Saints. All Saints. All Saints. Saints
all in all Saints. All Saints. Settled in all Saints. All Saints. Settled
all in all saints. Saints. Saints settled saints settled all in all saints.
All saints. Saints in all saints. Saint Settlement. Saints all saints all
saints. Saint Chavez. In all saints Saint Plan in saint in saint in all
saints saints in all saints. Saint Ignatius. Settled passing this in having given in which is not two days when everything being ready
it is no doubt not at all the following morning that it is very much
later very much earlier with them to find it acceptable as about
about which which as a river river helping it to be in doubt. Who
do who does and does it about about to be as a river and the order
of their advance. It is to-morrow on arriving at a place to pass
before the last.

Scene eight.   To Wait.

Scene one.   And begun.

Scene two.   To and to.

Scene three.   Happily be.

Scene Four.   Attached or.

Scene Five.   Sent to derive.

Scene Six.   Let it mix.

Scene Seven.   Attached eleven.

Scene Eight.   To wait.

Saint Therese.   Might be there.

Saint Therese.   To be sure.

Saint Therese.   With them and.

Saint Therese.   And hand.

Saint Therese.   And alight.

Saint Therese.   With them then. Saint Therese Saint Therese.
Nestle. Saint Therese. With them and a measure. It is easy to measure a settlement.

Scene IX

Saint Therese.   To be asked how much of it is finished.

Saint Therese.   To be asked how much of it is finished.

Saint Therese.   To ask Saint Therese Saint Therese to be asked how much of it is finished.

Saint Therese.   Ask Saint Therese how much of it is finished.

Saint Therese.   To be asked Saint Therese to be asked Saint Therese to be asked ask Saint Therese ask Saint Therese how much of it is finished.

Saint Chavez.   Ask how much of it is finished.

Saint Plan.   Ask Saint Therese how much of it is finished.

Saint Therese.   Ask asking asking Saint Therese how much of it is finished.

Saint Settlement

Saint Chavez   How much of it is finished.

Saint Plan

Saint Therese.

Saint Therese.   Ask how much of it is finished.

Saint Chavez.   Ask how much of it is finished.

Saint Therese.   Ask how much of it is finished.

Saint Settlement

Saint Therese

Saint Paul

Saint Plan   Ask how much of it is finished.

Saint Anne

Saint Cecile

Saint Plan.

Once in a while.

Saint Therese.   Once in a while.

Saint Plan.   Once in a while.

Saint Chavez.   Once in a while.

Saint Settlement.   Once in a while.

Saint Therese.   Once in a while.

Saint Chavez.   Once in a while.

Saint Cecile.   Once in a while.

Saint Genevieve.   Once in a while.

Saint Anne.   Once in a while.

Saint Settlement.   Once in a while.

Saint Therese.   Once in a while.

Saint Therese.   Once in a while.

Saint Ignatius.   Once in a while.

Saint Ignatius.   Once in a while.

Saint Ignatius.   Once in a while.
Saint Settlement.   Once in a while.
Saint Therese Once in a while.
Saint Therese.
Saint Therese.   Once in a while.
Saint Ignatius.   Once in a while.
Saint Ignatius Once in a while.
Saint Therese.
Saint Therese.   Once in a while.
Saint Therese.   Once in a while.
Saint Therese.   Once in a while.
Saint Plan.   Once in a while.
Saint Ignatius Once in a while.
Saint Therese.

Scene X

Could Four Acts be Three.

Saint Therese.   Could Four Acts be three.
Saint Therese Saint Therese Saint Therese Could Four Acts be three Saint Therese.

Scene X

When.

Saint Therese.   Could Four Acts be when four acts could be ten Saint Therese. Saint Therese Saint Therese Four Acts could be four acts could be when when four acts could be ten.
Saint Therese.   When.
Saint Settlement.   Then.
Saint Genevieve.   When.
Saint Cecile.   Then.
Saint Ignatius.   Then.
Saint Ignatius.   Men.
Saint Ignatius.   When.
Saint Ignatius.   Ten.
Saint Ignatius.   Then.
Saint Therese.   When.
Saint Chavez.   Ten.
Saint Plan.   When then.

Saint Settlement.   Then.
Saint Anne.   Then.
Saint Genevieve.   Ten.
Saint Cecile.   Then.
Saint Answers.   Ten.
Saint Cecile When then.
Saint Anne.
Saint Answers.   Saints when.
Saint Chavez.   Saints when ten.
Saint Cecile.   Ten.
Saint Answers.   Ten.
Saint Chavez.   Ten.
Saint Settlement.   Ten.
Saint Plan.   Ten.
Saint Anne.   Ten.
Saint Plan.   Ten.
Saint Plan.   Ten.
Saint Plan.   Ten.

Scene XI

Saint Therese.   With William.
Saint Therese.   With Plan.
Saint Therese.   With William willing and with Plan willing
and with Plan and with William willing and with William and with
Plan.
Saint Therese.   They might be staring.
Saint Therese.   And with William.
Saint Therese.   And with Plan.
Saint Therese.   With William.
Saint Therese.   And with. Plan.
Saint Therese
Saint Plan
Saint Placide   How many windows are there in it.
Saint Chavez
      and
Saint Settlement.
Saint Therese.   How many windows and doors and floors are
there in it.

Saint Therese.   How many doors how many floors and how many windows are there in it.

Saint Plan.   How many windows are there in it how many doors are there in it.

Saint Chavez.   How many doors are there in it how many floors are there in it how many doors are there in it how many windows are there in it how many floors are there in it how many windows are there in it how many doors are there in it.

Changing in between.

Saint Therese.   In this and in this and in this and clarity.

Saint Therese.   How many are there in this.

Saint Chavez.   How many are there in this.

Saint Chavez.   How many are there in this.

Saint Settlement.   Singularly to be sure and with a Wednesday at noon.

Saint Chavez.   In time and mine.

Saint Therese.   Settlement and in in and in and all. All to come and go to stand up to kneel and to be around. Around and around and around and as round and as around and as around and as around.

One two three.

There is a distance in between.

There is a distance in between in between others others meet meet meet met wet yet. It is very tearful to be through. Through and through.

Saint Therese.   Might be third.

Saint Therese.   Might be heard.

Saint Therese.   Might be invaded.

Saint Therese and three saints and there.

Commencing again yesterday.

Saint Therese.   And principally, Saint Therese.

Scene X

Saint Ignatius.   Withdrew with with withdrew.

Saint Ignatius.   Occurred.

Saint Ignatius.   Occurred withdrew.

Saint Ignatius.   Withdrew Occurred.

Saint Ignatius.   Withdrew occurred.

Saint Ignatius occurred Saint Ignatius withdrew occurred withdrew.

Saint Sarah. Having heard that they had gone she said how many eggs are there in it.

Saint Absalom. Having heard that they are gone he said how many had said how many had been where they had never been with them or with it.

Saint Absalom. Might be annointed.

Saint Therese. With responsibility.

Saint Therese. And an allowance.

Saint Settlement. In might have a change from this.

Saint Chavez. A winning.

Saint Cecile. In plenty.

Saint Eustace. Might it be mountains if it were not Barcelona.

Saint Plan. With wisdom.

Saint Chavez. In a minute.

Saint Therese. And circumstances.

Saint Therese. And as much.

Saint Chavez. With them.

An interval.

Abundance.

An interval.

Saint Chavez. Abundance.

Saint Chavez. And an interval.

Saint Sarah. With them near one.

Saint Michael. With them near one with them.

Saint Chavez. Tire.

Saint Cecile

Saint Chavez

Saint Therese One two and alike like liked.
    and   Considerable.
  themselves.

Saint Chavez. Windows and windows and ones.

Saint Cecile. Obligation.

Saint Sarah. Their wonder.

Saint Michael. And their wonder.

Saint Chavez. And whether.

Saint Michael. With windows as much as.

Saint Cecile. More to be considered.

Saint Michael
　　and
Saint Sarah.

Saint Chavez.　In consideration of everything and that it is done by them as it must be left to them with this as an arrangement. Night and day cannot be different.

Saint Therese.　Completely forgetting.

Saint Therese.　I will try.

Saint Therese.　Theirs and by and by.

Saint Chavez.　With noon.

Act III

With withdrawn.

There is very much announcement and by the time they leave they leave altogether one at a time they do not leave it left and right and in the middle they withdraw what they need when they might meet with what after all is why they are not only with them but in the midst of them and withdrawn and left meaning to be with this as their belonging to it and as it is what is it when they are in the middle of theirs around they might be very nearly alike as if it is understood. Once and one at a time.

Barcelona can be told.

How do you do.

Very well I thank you.

This is how young men and matter. How many nails are there in it.

Who can try.

They can be a little left behind.

Not at all.

As if they liked it very well to live alone.

With withdrawn.

What can they mean by well very well.

Scene One

And seen one. Very likely.

Saint Therese.　It is not what is apprehended what is apprehended what is apprehended what is apprehended intended.

Scene One

Saint Chavez.   It is very likely that there are many of them.

Saint Ignatius.   Instantly and subsistently.

Saint Stephen.   And leading at night.

Saint Plan.   Within with went in.

Saint Stephen.   In a little time gradually.

Saint Manuel.   Would they refuse to sanction it if they were asked and there was no way to have them carry out anything.

Saint Stephen.   With them instantly.

Saint Eustace.   In place of lurking.

Saint Chavez.   By means of it all.

Saint Plan.   Within a season of deliberation.

Saint Stephen.   And reasonably insisting.

Saint Chavez.   At that time.

Saint Ignatius.   And all. Then and not. Might it do. Do and doubling with it at once left and right.

Saint Chavez.   Left left left right left with what is known.

Saint Chavez.   In time.

Scene II

It is easy to resemble it at most.

Most and best.

It is easy to resemble it most and leave it to them with individuality.

Saint Ignatius.   In seems.

Saint Ignatius.   In seems.

Saint Ignatius.   Within it within it within it as a wedding for them in half of the time.

Saint Ignatius.   Particularly.

Saint Ignatius.   Call it a day.

Saint Ignatius.   With a wide water with within with drawn.

Saint Ignatius.   As if a fourth class.

Scene II

Pigeons on the grass alas.

Pigeons on the grass alas.

Short longer grass short longer longer shorter yellow grass

Pigeons large pigeons on the shorter longer yellow grass alas
pigeons on the grass.

If they were not pigeons what were they.

If they were not pigeons on the grass alas what were they. He
had heard of a third and he asked about it it was a magpie in the
sky. If a magpie in the sky on the sky can not cry if the pigeon on
the grass alas can alas and to pass the pigeon on the grass alas and
the magpie in the sky on the sky and to try and to try alas on the
grass alas the pigeon on the grass the pigeon on the grass and alas.
They might be very well very well very well they might be they
might be very well they might be very well very well they might be.

Let Lucy Lily Lily Lucy Lucy let Lucy Lucy Lily Lily
Lily Lily Lily let Lily Lucy Lucy let Lily. Let Lucy Lily.

Scene One

Saint Ignatius prepared to have examples of windows of curtains of hanging of shawls of windows of curtains of windows of
curtains of windows of curtains of hangings of shawls of windows
of hangings of curtains of windows of hangings of curtains of
shawls.

Saint Ignatius and please please please please.

Scene One

One and one.

Scene One

Might they be with they be with them might they be with
them. Never to return to distinctions.

Might they be with them with they be with they be with them.
Never to return to distinctions.

Saint Ignatius.   In line and in in line please say it first in line
and in line and please say it first please say it first say it with first
in line and in line in line.

Saint Ignatius.   Met to be to be to leave me be with him in
partly left to find find with it call call with to them to them that
have to be with it as when letting letting it announce announced

complacently in change change having fallen two to one in restitution in their inability to leave. Leave left as lost. Might white. From the stand-point of white.

Saint Sulpice.   A masterpiece.

Saint Ignatius   When it is ordinarily thought-
        and   ful and making it be when they
      friends.   were wishing at one time insatiably and with renounced where where ware and wear wear with them with them and where where will it be as long as long as they might with it with it individually removing left to it when it very well way well and crossed crossed in articulately minding what you do.

The friends at once. What is it when it is perilously left to it where there are more than there were.

And all and as if there is a mound.

He asked for a distant magpie as if they made a difference.

He asked for a distant magpie as if he asked for a distant magpie as if that made a difference.

He asked as if that made a difference.

He asked for a distant magpie.

He asked for a distant magpie.

As if that made a difference he asked for a distant magpie as if that made a difference. He asked as if that made a difference. A distant magpie. He asked for a distant magpie. He asked for a distant magpie.

Saint Ignatius.   Might be admired for himself alone.

Saint Chavez.   Saint Ignatius might be admired for himself alone and because of that it might be as much as any one could desire.

Saint Chavez.   Because of that it might be as much as any one could desire.

Saint Chavez.   Because of that because it might be as much as any one could desire it might be that it could be done as easily as because it might very much as if precisely why they were carried.

Saint Ignatius.   Left when there was precious little to be asked by the ones who were overwhelmingly particular about what they were adding to themselves by means of their arrangements which might be why they went away and came again.

It is every once in a while very much what they pleased.

Saint Ignatius.   With them and with them and uniformly.

Saint Chavez.   To make it and why they were with them just as soon.

Saint Chavez.   And roses very well. Very well and roses very well roses smell roses smell and very well and very well as roses smell roses smell very well. If hedge roses are moss roses larger. If moss roses are larger are there questions of how very well there are strangers who have to be known by their walk.

In a minute.

Saint Ignatius.   In a minute by the time that it is graciously gratification and might it be with them to be with them to be with them to be to be windowed.

Saint Ignatius.   As seen as seen.

Saint Ignatius surrounded by them.

Saint Ignatius and one of two.

Saint Ignatius.   And one of two.

Saint Ignatius.   And one of two literally.

Saint Ignatius.   And one of two and one of two.

Saint Ignatius.   And one of two literally.

Saint Ignatius.   And one of two and one of two. One of two.

Saint Ignatius.   Might when when is exchangeable.

Saint Ignatius.   Might when.

Saint Chavez.   In change.

Saint Chavez might be with them at that time. All of them. Might be with them at that time.

All of them might be with them all of them at that time.

Might be with them at that time all of them might be with them at that time.

Scene II

It is very easy to love alone. Too much too much. There are very sweetly very sweetly Henry very sweetly Rene very sweetly many very sweetly. They are very sweetly many very sweetly Rene very sweetly there are many very sweetly.

Scene III

There is a difference between Barcelona and Avila. What difference.

Scene

There is a difference between Barcelona and Avila.

There is a difference between Barcelona. There is a difference between Barcelona and Avila. There is a difference between Barcelona and Avila.

Scene IV

And no more.

Scene V

Saint Ignatius. Left to left left to left left to left. Left right left left right left left to left.

Saint Pellen. There is every reason why industriously there should be resolution and intermittence and furnishing of their delight.

By this time with them in intermingling and objection with them and with them and intermediately and allowance and left and more and benignly and acceptably accepting in their and by mischance with them indeterminately finally as change.

When they do change to.

Saint Vincent. Authority for it.

Saint Gallo. By this clock o'clock. By this clock by this clock by this clock o'clock.

Saint Pilar. In the middle of their pleasurable resolution resolving in their adequate announcing left to it by this by this means. And out.

Saint Chavez. With a plan.

Saint Pellen. In sound.

Saint Gallo. Around.

Saint Pellen. In particular.

Saint Chavez. Innumerably.

Saint Ignatius might be what is underestimately theirs in plain and plan and for which is left to because in this with it as much as is in connecting undividedly theirs at that time. In this. Coming to be thrown.

They might use having it as high.

Left it to right.

Having used might it be with it as with it as mentioning when.

Having it as having it used usually to actually to additionally to integrally to to the owned to the owning owning out.

Might it be two at one time time and mine mine and time.

Saint Ignatius returns to come when.

Saint Plan. Without it with them.

Saint Chavez
  and   Without it with them with them without it.
Saint Pilar.

Saint Chavez.   Without it with them without it.

With them with out it.

Saint Ignatius.   Might be memorized.

Saint Chavez

Saint Pilar   With them with it.

and with them.

Saint Pilar.   With them with with with with out with them.

Saint Chavez.   Uniting it one at a time individually.

Saint Pilar.   Need it in liking what is a choice between floating and adding. Floating and adding makes smiles.

Saint Hilyar.   With them and to to to add to add to it.

Might having it we do.

Saint Ignatius.   Foundationally marvellously aboundingly illimitably with it as a circumstance. Fundamentally and saints fundamentally and saints and fundamentally and saints.

Saint Chavez.   Found round about.

Saint Pilar
  and   Additionally in currents.
Saint Chavez.

Saint Chavez.   Found round about without.

Saint Chavez.

Saint Pilar   With what and when it is universally leaving
  and   it additionally to them as windowed win-
Saint Fernande.   dowed windowed windowed where.

Answerably.

Scene VI

They might have heard about them altogether.

Scene VII

Saint Chavez.   It is very well known that that which has been noticed as needing violence and veils may be what they meant when they said it.

Saint Chavez.   By that time.

Saint Chavez.   What they meant by it when they said it. By that time.

Saint Chavez.   There has been an incredible reason for their planning what is not by any manner of means their allowance in having let it be theirs by negligence.

Saint Andrew
            and   Letting it be third at all.
Saint John Seize.

Saint Sarah
            and   By it a chance.
Saint Leonard.

Saint Ferdinand
            and   With this one at at time.
Saint Plan.

Saint Plan
            and   With them and must.
Saint Arthur.

Saint Agnes.   Letting it alone.

Saint Henry.   With me by and by.

Saint Sylvester.   Leaning and letting it be what to wish.

Saint Plan.   Leaning and letting it be what to wish.

One Saint.   Whose has whose has whose has ordered needing white and green as much as orange and with grey and how much and as much and as much and as a circumstance.

Saint Ignatius.   Windowing shortly which makes what have they joined to parks and palaces. Undoubtedly.

One and two might be through.

Through certainly.

Saint Therese.   With them and for instance.

Saint Therese.   Like and it might be as likely it might be very likely that it would be amounting to once in a while as in a way it could be what was meant by that at once. There is a difference between at most at once.

In at the time.

Saint Therese.   Intending to be intending to intending to to to to. To do it for me.

Saint Ignatius.   Went to.

Saint Ignatius.   Two and two.

Saint Chevez.   Might be what was when after all a petal two and water three.

Scene V

Alive.

Scene VI

With Seven.

Scene VII

With eight.

Scene VIII

Ordinary pigeons and trees.

If a generation all the same between forty and fifty as as. As they were and met. Was it tenderness and seem. Might it be as well as mean with in.

Ordinary pigeons and trees. This is a setting which is as soon which is as soon which is as soon ordinary setting which is as soon which is as soon and noon.

Ordinary pigeons and trees.

Scene IX

Saint Therese.   Face and face face about. Face to face face and face face out.

Saint Therese.   Add to additional.

Saint Chavez.   Might make milk sung.

Saint Chavez.   Might make. In place. Saint Therese.

Saint Therese.   In face of in face of might make milk sung

sung face to face face in face place in place in place of face to face.
Milk sung.

Saint Ignatius.   Once in a while and where and where around
around is a sound and around is a sound and around is a sound and
around. Around is a sound around is a sound around is a sound and
around. Around differing from annointed now. Now differing from
annointed now. Now differing differing. Now differing from annointed now. Now when there is left and with it integrally with it
integrally withstood within without with out with drawn and in
as much as if it could be withstanding what in might might be so.

Saint Chavez.   In in time.

Many might be comfortabler. This is very well known now.
When this you see remember me. It was very well known to every
one. They were very careful of everything. They were whatever it
was necessary to have to alter. They might be as thankful as they
were that they were not perfectly predispossessed to deny when
they were able to be very soon there. There one at a time. Having
arranged magpies so only one showed and also having arranged
magpies so that more than one showed. If magpies are so arranged
that only one shows it is not more noticeable than if they are so
arranged that more than one is showing against the horizon in such
a way that they are placed directly not only where they were but
where they are. Adding coming forward again.

A great deal of the afternoon is used by this as an advantage.
It is meritorious that we do not care to share. It is meritorious by
them with them able and ably.

Saint Ignatius.   Forty to fifty with fifty and all and a wall and
as all and as called called rather.

Saint Therese.   A widow weeded way laid way laying and as
spelled.

Saint Chavez.   Might and right very well to do. It is all colored
by a straw straw laden.

Saint Ignatius.   Very nearly with it with it soon soon as said.

Saint Ignatius.   Windowing clearly.

Stant Chavez. Having asked additionally theirs instead.

Saint Therese.   Once in a minute.

Saint Therese.   In a minute.

Saint Ignatius.   One two three as are are and are are are to be
are with them are with them are with them with are with are with
with it.

Scene IX

Letting pin in letting let in let in in in in in let in let in wet in wed in dead in dead wed led in led wed dead in dead in led in wed in said in said led wed dead wed dead said led led said wed dead wed dead led in led in wed in wed in said in wed in led in said in dead in dead wed said led led said wed dead in. That makes they have might kind find fined when this arbitrarily makes it be what is it might they can it fairly well to be added to in this at the time that they can candied leaving as with with it by the left of it with with in in the funniest in union.

Across across across coupled across crept a cross crept crept crept crept across. They crept across.

If they are between thirty and thirty five and alive who made them see Saturday.

If they are between thirty-five and forty and they are thought to be who made them see Saturday with having it come in and out in and three thirty.

Between thirty-five and forty-five between forty five and three five as then when when they were forty-five and thirty five when then they were forty five and thirty five when they were then forty five and thirty five and thirty two and to achieve leave relieve and receive their astonishment. Were they to be left to do to do as well as they do mean I mean I mean. Next best to having heading him.

Might it be left after all where they left left right left. Might it be left where they might have having it left after all left right left after all.

When they have heard it mine.

Left to their in their to their to be their to be there all their to be there all their all their time to be there to be there all their to be all their time there.

With wed led said with led dead said with dead led said with said dead led wed said wed dead led dead led said wed.

With be there all their all their time there be there vine there be vine time there be there time there all their time there.

Needed indented.

Can they and chest, choice, choice of a chest.

It is better and best and just as good as if they needed to have and wanted to have and did want to have and did want to have to have had it had it with them when they might just as easily endeavor in every way to have paraphernalia leave it as their habitual reference to when they are not by the time that they have been very likely to needlessly believe that they went to come to come handily as a desperately arranged charm. Might it be why they were not only but also went as well.

Let it be why if they were adding adding comes cunningly to be additionally cunningly in the sense of attracting attracting in the sense of adding adding in the sense of windowing and windowing and frames and pigeons and ordinary trees and while while away.

ACT III

Did he did we did we and did he did he did he did did he did did did he did did he did be categorically and did he did he did he did he did he did he in interruption interruption interruptedly leave letting let it be be all to me to me out and outer and this and this with in indeed deed and drawn and drawn work.

Saint Ferdinand singing soulfully.

Saint Chavez. Singing singing is singing is singing is singing is singing between between singing is singing is between singing is.

Saint Plan. Theirs and sign. Saint Cecile. Singing theirs and signing mine.

Saint Philip. Will it be less at first that they are there and be left by the time that it is carried as far as further.

Saint Philip. Let it be gone as it has to be gone in plenty of time.

Saint Sarah. She might be coming to have to have infancy.

Saint Michael. With a stand and would it be the same as yet awhile and glance a glance of be very nearly left to be alone.

Saint Therese. One at at time makes two at a time makes one at a time and be there where where there there where where there. Very well as if to say.

Saint Cecile. With it and as if as if it were a left to them and feel. I feel very well.

Saint Chavez. By the time that they were left perfect.

Saint Ignatius. Might be why they were after all after all who came. One hundred and fifty one and a half and a half and after and after and after and all. With it all.

Saint Chavez.   A ball might be less than one.
All together one and one.

ACT IV

How many acts are there in it. Acts are there in it.

Supposing a wheel had been added to three wheels how many acts how many how many acts are there in it.

Any Saint at all.

How many acts are there in it.

How many saints in all.

How many acts are there in it.

Ring around a rosey.

How many acts are there in it.

Wedded and weeded.

Please be coming to see me.

When this you see you are all to me.

Me which is you you who are true true to be you.

How many how many saints are there in it.

One two three all out but me.

One two three four all out but four.

One two all about but you.

How many saints are there in it.

How many saints are there in it.

How many acts are there in it.

One two three four and there is no door. Or more. Or nor. Or door. Or floor or door. One two three all out but me. How many saints are there in it.

Saints and see all out but me.

How many saints are there in it.

How many saints are there in it. One two three four all out but four one two three four four four or four or more.

More or four.

How many Acts are there in it.

Four Acts.

Act four.

Saint Therese deliberately. Encouraged by this then when they might be by thirds words eglantine and by this to mean feeling it as most when they do too to be nearly lost to sight in time in time and mind mind it for them. Let us come to this brink.

The sisters and saints assembling and reenacting why they went away to stay.

One at a time regularly regularly by the time that they are in and and in one at at time regularly very fairly better than they came as they came there and where where will they be wishing to stay here here where they are they are here here where they are they are they are here.

Saint Therese.   It is very necessary to have arithmetic inestimably and left by this in the manner in which they are not at all as patient as they were patiently were. One at a time in rhyme.

Saint Chavez.   The envelopes are on all the fruit of the fruit trees.

Scene II

Saint Chavez.   Remembered as knew.

Saint Ignatius.   Meant to send, and meant to send and meant meant to differ between send and went and end and mend and very nearly one to two.

Saint Cecile.   With this and now.

Saint Plan.   Made it with with in with withdrawn.

Scene III

Let all act as if they went away.

Scene IV

Saint Therese.   Who mentioned that one followed another laterally.

All Saints.   One at a time.

Saint Chavez.   One at a time.

Saint Settlement
          and   There can be two Saint Annes if you like.

Saint Anne.

Saint Philip.   With them and still.

Saint Cecile.   They will they will.

Saint Therese.   Begin to trace begin to race begin to place begin and in in that that is why this is what is left as may may follows June and June follows moon and moon follows soon and it is very nearly ended with bread.

Saint Chavez.　Who can think that they can leave it here to me.
When this you see remember me.
They have to be.
They have to be.
They have to be to see.
To see to say.
Laterally they may.

Scene V

Who makes who makes it do.
Saint Therese and Saint Therese too.
Who does and who does care.
Saint Chavez to care.
Saint Chavez to care.
Who may be what is it when it is instead.
Saint Plan Saint Plan to may to say to say two may and inclined.
Who makes it be what they had as porcelain.
Saint Ignatius and left and right laterally be lined.
All Saints.
　　To Saints.
Four Saints.
　　And Saints.
Five Saints.
　　To Saints.
Last Act.
Which is a fact.

GERTRUDE STEIN was born in Pennsylvania in 1874. At Radcliffe she was an outstanding student of William James in psychology, and conducted laboratory experiments with Hugo Munsterberg, which led her to study the anatomy of the brain at Johns Hopkins. In 1902 she joined her brother Leo in Paris, and lived abroad until her death in 1946. Her salon in the rue de Fleurus, over which she presided with Alice B. Toklas, became the gathering place for prominent writers and painters, among them Sherwood Anderson and Hemingway, Matisse and Picasso.

VINTAGE BIOGRAPHY AND AUTOBIOGRAPHY

V-428   ABDEL-MALEK, ANOUAR   *Egypt: Military Society*
V-625   ACKLAND, LEN AND SAM BROWN   *Why Are We Still in Vietnam?*
V-340   ADAMS, RUTH (ed.)   *Contemporary China*
V-196   ADAMS, RICHARD N.   *Social Change in Latin America Today*
V-568   ALINSKY, SAUL D.   *Reveille for Radicals*
V-365   ALPEROVITZ, GAR   *Atomic Diplomacy*
V-503   ALTHUSSER, LOUIS   *For Marx*
V-286   ARIES, PHILIPPE   *Centuries of Childhood*
V-511   BAILEY, STEPHEN K.   *Congress Makes a Law*
V-604   BAILYN, BERNARD   *Origins of American Politics*
V-334   BALTZELL, E. DIGBY   *The Protestant Establishment*
V-335   BANFIELD, E. G. AND J. Q. WILSON   *City Politics*
V-674   BARBIANA, SCHOOL OF   *Letter to a Teacher*
V-198   BARDOLPH, RICHARD   *The Negro Vanguard*
V-185   BARNETT, A. DOAK   *Communist China and Asia*
V-270   BAZELON, DAVID   *The Paper Economy*
V-60   BECKER, CARL L.   *The Declaration of Independence*
V-563   BEER, SAMUEL H.   *British Politics in the Collectivist Age*
V-199   BERMAN, H. J. (ed.)   *Talks on American Law*
V-211   BINKLEY, WILFRED E.   *President and Congress*
V-81   BLAUSTEIN, ARTHUR I. AND ROGER R. WOOCK (eds.)   *Man Against Poverty*
V-508   BODE, BOYD H.   *Modern Educational Theories*
V-513   BOORSTIN, DANIEL J.   *The Americans: The Colonial Experience*
V-358   BOORSTIN, DANIEL J.   *The Americans: The National Experience*
V-621   BOORSTIN, DANIEL J.   *The Decline of Radicalism: Reflections on America Today*
V-414   BOTTOMORE, T. B.   *Classes in Modern Society*
V-44   BRINTON, CRANE   *The Anatomy of Revolution*
V-625   BROWN, SAM AND LEN ACKLAND   *Why Are We Still in Vietnam*
V-234   BRUNER, JEROME   *The Process of Education*
V-590   BULLETIN OF ATOMIC SCIENTISTS   *China after the Cultural Revolution*
V-578   BUNZEL, JOHN H.   *Anti-Politics in America*
V-549   BURNIER, MICHEL-ANTOINE   *Choice of Action*
V-684   CALVERT, GREG AND CAROL   *The New Left and the New Capitalism*
V-30   CAMUS, ALBERT   *The Rebel*
V-33   CARMICHAEL, STOKELY AND CHARLES HAMILTON   *Black Power*
V-664   CARMICHAEL, STOKELY   *Stokely Speaks*
V-98   CASH, W. J.   *The Mind of the South*
V-556   CASTRO, JOSUE DE   *Death in the Northeast*
V-272   CATER, DOUGLASS   *The Fourth Branch of Government*
V-290   CATER, DOUGLASS   *Power in Washington*
V-551   CHEVIGNY, PAUL   *Police Power*
V-555   CHOMSKY, NOAM   *American Power and the New Mandarins*
V-640   CHOMSKY, NOAM   *At War With Asia*
V-554   CONNERY, ROBERT H. (ed.)   *Urban Riots: Violence and Social Change*